INFORMAT[...]
AND WO[...]
PROCESS[...]

An Introduction

Margaret King Senior Lecturer, Harlow College; Chief Examiner, LCCI Word Processing
Antony Bone Business Information Systems Consultant

Stanley Thornes (Publishers) Ltd

First published in 1985 by
Stanley Thornes (Publishers) Ltd
Old Station Drive
Leckhampton
CHELTENHAM GL53 0DN

Reprinted 1986
Reprinted 1987

British Library Cataloguing in Publication Data

King, M.R.
Information processing.
1. Information storage and retrieval systems
I. Title   II. Bone, A.R.
001.5   T.58.6

ISBN 0-85950-211-2

Typeset in 10½/12½ Souvenir Light
by Blackpool Typesetting Services Limited
Printed and bound in Great Britain at The Bath Press, Avon

CONTENTS

DEDICATION

To Paul John and Roger Charles.

The former patiently suffered many 'baked bean' Sundays with little more than the occasional groan.

The latter's insistence over the years that once committed you must honour your 'obligations and commitments' provided one of us (who needed motivating) with the impetus to complete his share of the task.

PREFACE

The primary objective of this book is to provide an easy-to-read, simple-to-understand and yet comprehensive introduction to information and word processing.

Originally the material for this book was devised for students undertaking courses leading to the London Chamber of Commerce and Industry Information and Word Processing examinations. However, in its current much-extended form it provides coverage of syllabuses for the Royal Society of Arts, Pitman, City and Guilds and BTEC.

While having a bias towards the educational market, the book will fail in its main aim if it does not appeal to wider audiences, be they industrial or commercial trainers, company board members or anyone with an interest in this technology.

The book is intended to be an introductory text and does not assume any prior knowledge. It builds from the simple to the complex. It divides roughly into three sections. The first deals with information processing and encompasses micro, mini and mainframe computing to which most modern information processing is allied. It should appeal to anyone with an interest in this area. The second section looks, in some detail, at word processing. It covers the topic theoretically and does not relate to any one type of system, which makes it useful to operators and authors (that is, those people who will operate word processors and those people who will make use of word processing services). The final portion of the book covers the use and implementation of information processing systems and should prove helpful both to students and companies installing new systems.

Finally, a note about 'information processing'. There are numerous definitions for this 'label' – indeed, this book provides one. Most authors agree however, that the core of information processing lies in the collection and assembly of facts or data into a form that will prove meaningful to the recipient of this material. An alternative label 'information systems' – was not used for the book title. This book concentrates on the technological advances whose processing capabilities have greatly enhanced the potential of information systems, and does not encompass the people, clerical procedures, business cycles, governmental or social needs, constraints etc. which the authors believe are integral components of any human system – including, therefore, information systems.

Overall, we hope that you enjoy reading it and find it informative and easy to understand.

Margaret King
Antony Bone
1985

INTRODUCTION

Consider this statement:

'30 000 plus 10%.'

Clearly it could mean anything and therefore it does not inform. However, 'Your salary will be £30 000 plus 10% bonus.' is a meaningful statement – it is information. If then, at an interview, you had asked what your salary would be and, after some thought, the interviewer had said £30 000 plus 10% bonus, you would have experienced INFORMATION PROCESSING.

So, what is information processing? It is, put simply, the processing of facts into a form that will be of value to the receiver of the processed material.

Surely, therefore, information processing is not new or exciting. As described in the example above, information processing is clearly neither new nor exciting (unless, of course, that really was the salary being offered!). However, look at what was involved:

- Your query communicated to the interviewer.

- The interviewer's ability to 'take in' or 'accept' the input of your query.

- The interviewer's processing of your query. This would involve recalling many factors from his or her memory, and using other facts from, say, your application.

- The interviewer's ability to 'output' or communicate to you the information you required.

Now this is where, by using modern technology, information processing really does become exciting. At the core of this technology lies the computer. It has abilities to:

- process many types of information

- work at speeds far higher than humans can

- 'remember' enormous volumes of facts

- take in and output information at ever increasing speeds

- communicate with other computers over thousands of miles in seconds.

As a result, much of the information that we used to have to 'remember', the computers of today and tomorrow will remember for us. Clearly, technological information processing will have an impact on virtually every aspect of life. Today we are at the beginning of this exciting new era.

As information processing and computer technology are so interwoven it is necessary to appreciate how rapid the developments in both areas have been.

Computers as we think of them have been around for about 30 years but their historical development stretches much further back in time. People have always striven to make machines that help them, and since earliest pre-history they have used aids for counting. One of the earliest aids was the abacus – a collection of beads on a series of rods, the position of the beads indicating the number.

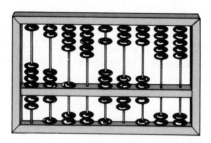

An abacus

As time progressed, various improved computational aids were developed. Among the most successful was the slide rule which appeared in the seventeenth century and was a great aid in the multiplication and division of numbers.

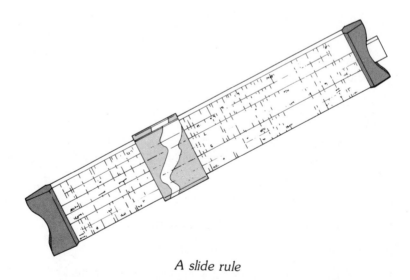

A slide rule

However, it was the development of a calculating machine by Blaise Pascal which truly heralded the computer. This machine, which worked by turning wheels and cogs, could add, subtract, multiply and divide (with some effort!). It was, however, not successful commercially because in those days machines were expensive and clerks were cheap.

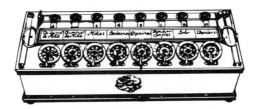

Pascal's calculator

An improved version was developed shortly afterwards by Gottfried Wilhelm Leibniz. It is interesting that the principles of operation he used were still widely used in calculating machines in the 1960s.

It was a brilliant Englishman – Charles Babbage – who finally laid out the structure of a computing system. His first machine – the Differential Engine – cost a fortune to build and was so far ahead of its time that the technology of the 1830s simply could not develop it.

However, undaunted, Babbage realized that all the machines that had been developed up until his time could only do one job – the one they were built to do. He began to design a new machine which could do a whole variety of tasks as and when the owner wanted. This device, which he called the Analytical Engine, was the first 'true' programmable computer.

It had:

- a set of input devices – methods of feeding numbers or instructions into its interior

- a processor – the part of the machine that calculated the numbers

- a control unit – which made sure that the computer performed the right tasks in the correct sequence

- a store or memory – where numbers were held to await their turn to be processed

- an output mechanism.

These five essential components form the essence of any computer, ancient or modern.

To program the machine, Babbage envisaged using cards with holes in – the pattern of holes indicating the tasks to be performed. Only recently have punched cards become uncommon as a method of input to computers.

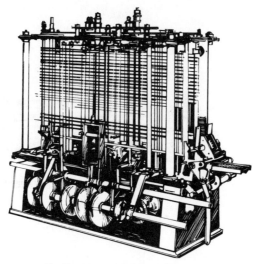

Babbage's Analytical Engine

Unfortunately, Babbage was decades ahead of his time and his machines were never built.

Forty years passed before the next real advance occurred. In 1887 Herman Hollerith developed an electrically powered tabulating machine which used:

- punched cards for input
- electrical charges to operate its processing
- dials for output.

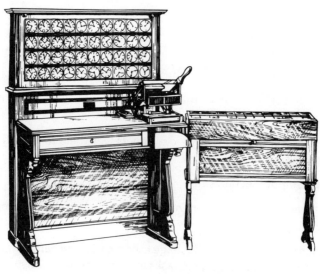

Hollerith's tabulating machine

This machine managed to complete the huge task of counting involved in the 1890 US census in just six weeks – compared with eight years for the 1880 census!

This machine also marked the first real commercial success for mechanical data processors. It formed the foundation for the company Hollerith started, which has grown into the International Business Machine Corporation – or IBM.

In the 1930s the first computers as we now recognize them were developed.

It is strange to note that totally independently in the United Kingdom, Germany and the United States people began to design and build machines very similar in principle. So what marks these machines as computers?

Well, until this period all the machines had 'computed' in tens. Hollerith's tabulating machine, for example, had a units dial which turned nine times before, on the tenth turn, it caused the tens dial to move once. Ten turns of the tens dial would cause the hundreds dial to turn once and so on. The new machines, however, used telegraphic switches or valves and these could be only on or off. They could therefore only have two possible states. As a result these machines counted in twos – or BINARY NUMBERS as counting in twos is called.

Although this idea of counting in twos seems strange to us, it is extremely efficient for machines and therefore even the very earliest binary (or digital) computers were much faster than anything that had been used before.

Now the pace of development really hots up with a mix of individual genius, government and large corporation backing and finance. Briefly the major milestones from 1940 to 1983 have been:

- 1940–45: Colossus – a valve-operated computer developed by a highly secret team of British scientists. This machine used punched paper tape for input and was used to crack German codes. Many people think that Colossus won the war for the Allies.

- 1943: Harvard Mark I – relay (mechanical switches) – operated computer. This was significant because it was developed by IBM and was therefore the first commercially built computer. However, relay technology was already obsolete by the time the Mark I was finished.

- 1947: ENIAC (Electronic Numerical Integrator and Calculator) – the first general-purpose computer which could (with great difficulty) be made to do different tasks.

- Late 1940s: EDVAC – the first computer that could store programs within itself. This concept – of a computer 'remembering' how to do a particular task once instructed – was developed by J. Von Neumann. It marks the point at which the true power of computers moved from the finite to the potentially infinite.

- 1950: LEO – the first computer to be used commercially (by the giant British food corporation, Lyons).

- 1955: The transistor – developed by Bell Laboratories, this tiny switching device opened the door to the huge expansion in computers. Valve computers were huge, costly to operate and generated a great deal of heat which needed to be removed, resulting in complex and expensive cooling systems. The transistor computer was much smaller, cheap to operate and cool.

- 1965: The chip – this device, which is in effect hundreds of thousands of switches (like transistors) on a single minute slice of silicon, has heralded the era of information processing. On one chip a computer capable of switching millions of times per second can be constructed. (We shall look at chips in more detail – but it is worth remembering that the chips in calculators you can buy for a few pounds now have more computing power than room-size machines of 20 years ago which cost millions of pounds!)

So why the sudden growth of interest in information processing? The answer lies in the computer itself. As we have seen, computers developed to help people with calculations; they grew into machines that could 'remember' various tasks; they became faster and faster, smaller and smaller and cheaper and cheaper until, with the chip, computers have reached a point where they are capable of doing millions of tasks or instructions per second and cost very little to make and operate. The rate of development has been enormous and so suddenly we are in a situation where it is possible to put computers virtually anywhere.

This means that where it used to be difficult and time consuming to process information or pass information between people, offices or countries, it is suddenly much easier. How we deal with this ability to process information is the basis of this book.

THE COMPUTER

Chapter Objectives

After studying this chapter you should be able to:

1. Discuss what it is about computers that makes them so useful in information processing.
2. Identify the four functional parts of any computer system and explain their respective functions.
3. Explain the differences between a mainframe computer, a minicomputer and a microcomputer.
4. Discuss why networks are so important to information processing.

END OF OBJECTIVES END OF OBJECTIVES END OF OBJECTIVES END OF OBJECTIVES

INTRODUCTION

As was stated in pages 1–6, information processing has evolved with computer technology. It is therefore necessary that we understand more about the computer and how it works. Essentially, the computer is no more than a tool which may be used for a variety of jobs ranging from the control of machinery to word processing.

There are three types of computer in use at present:

- The ANALOGUE computer – is typically used for industrial and scientific applications and does not really concern us. However, a brief description of an analogue computer is given in the Glossary.
- The DIGITAL computer – forms the core of information processing.
- The HYBRID computer – is both analogue and digital.

There is nothing peculiar about using machines to do work for us – human history is littered with examples of people's ingenuity in this field. You may well ask then, what makes a computer so special? The answer lies in the computer's ability to:

- store information
- make decisions about the information with which it is provided

7

- carry out tasks at a great speed

- communicate huge amounts of information across great distances at high speeds.

How can we easily appreciate a computer's functions? Consider how a letter is produced in an office:

- The secretary will need to be told what the letter is to contain. This will be done via dictation or manuscript and this raw information forms the INPUT for the job of producing a letter.

- The secretary will then have to PROCESS this raw information to produce a well-formatted, attractively presented letter. A notepad may be used to jot down the margins and work out tab settings, centred headings, etc. Additionally, a dictionary may be needed to check spellings.

- From the secretary's typewriter come the results of the processing – a finished letter. This letter represents the OUTPUT. When the letter is finished, the paper on which the notes were made will be thrown away – it is only a temporary work area.

- Finally, a copy of the letter is filed away, probably in a filing cabinet. The filing cabinet is a BACKING STORE.

A computer does much the same. It is provided with DATA as some form of input, it processes the data, and then some kind of output is provided as the finished product. In order to perform these tasks, the computer needs to have four main functional parts:

- input devices
- CENTRAL PROCESSING UNIT (CPU)
- output devices
- backing stores.

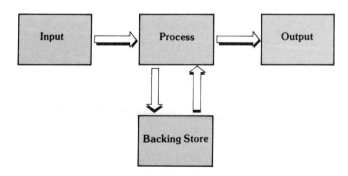

A standard information processing configuration

Input Devices

We shall consider several different kinds of input device, for example, bar codes, graphic pads, voice, etc. However, the one with which you all are probably familiar is, of course, the QWERTY keyboard. With a computer keyboard, as you press each key on the keyboard electrical pulses representing the characters are input to the central processing unit.

Graphics pad

Bar codes

Voice

Keyboard

Input devices

The Central Processing Unit (CPU)

This is where all the work is done. It is, if you like, the 'brain' of the computer. The CPU consists of four sections:

- A MEMORY UNIT, which is just what it says – the place where the computer holds the information until it is needed. It is also the temporary work area (like the one our secretary used when doing all the rough calculations).

- An ARITHMETIC LOGIC UNIT (ALU), where the computer does all its calculations and compares and sorts bits of data. For example, it will add, subtract, divide and multiply and make comparisons (greater than, less than, equal to, etc.).

- A CONTROL UNIT, which is the 'nerve centre' of the machine. It reads, interprets and obeys instructions. It controls the movement of data within the computer. It has to keep track of the sequence of operations and send the data to the correct places at the correct times.

- A CLOCK, which controls, with great accuracy, the speed at which the CPU does all its operations and keeps all the computer's functioning in step with its beat.

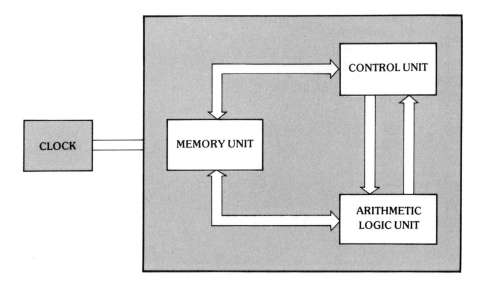

A central processing unit

We have input our data – it went to the CPU for processing and now we want to see the results of the processing – so we move on to consider output devices.

Output Devices

There are several types of output device, for example, the VDU (VISUAL DISPLAY UNIT), graph plotters and printers. We shall be looking at each of these in more detail later in the book. The output devices change the electrical pulses into a form which we can understand.

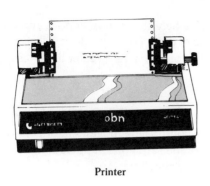

Printer

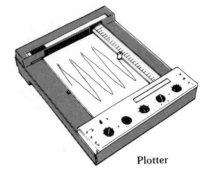

Plotter

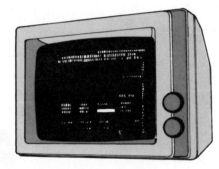

VDU

Output devices

Backing Store

Like the typist who filed the copy of the typed letter in the filing cabinet, the computer needs somewhere to file information. The computer's 'filing cabinet' is called a backing store.

Although the CPU has its own memory, this is limited in the amount of data it can hold. Further, when most computers are switched off, the information in the memory is lost (this is called a VOLATILE MEMORY). So there has to be somewhere outside the main memory to store the data in a permanent form. The most common ways of storing data are on MAGNETIC TAPE and MAGNETIC DISK and many word processors store information on FLOPPY DISK. Once permanently stored on disk, the information can be accessed at any time by reloading it into the computer's memory. Similarly, most home computers record their information on normal CASSETTE TAPES or floppy disks. This information can be 'replayed' or 'reloaded' into the memory.

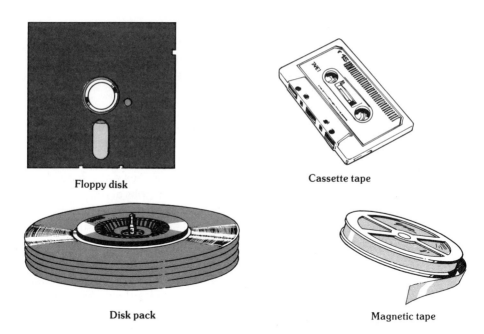

Floppy disk

Cassette tape

Disk pack

Magnetic tape

Backing storage media

So the four functional parts of any computer, whatever its size, are input devices, CPU, output devices and backing store. The way in which these parts are connected and the number of devices used is called the CONFIGURATION for the computer system.

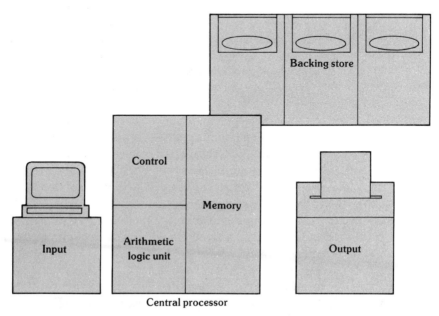

Backing store

Control

Memory

Input

Arithmetic logic unit

Output

Central processor

Elements of a computer configuration

In the 1950s all computers were big, expensive and used a lot of power. They were called 'MAINFRAMES' because the parts were mounted on frames in large metal cabinets. Large powerful computers are still called mainframes, but now there are also smaller machines called MINICOMPUTERS and even smaller desk-top ones called MICROCOMPUTERS:

- Mainframe computers – the equipment for a large modern mainframe computer configuration may fill several rooms even though modern main-frame computers are much smaller than mainframes of even five years ago. These machines can carry out millions of instructions every second and work so fast that they seem to do many different jobs at once. They often have backing storage which allows billions of characters to be stored, yet be almost instantly available when needed. Mainframes can usually support large numbers of input and output (I/O) devices.

- Minicomputers – these computers are smaller than the giant mainframes and are unable to handle as much data or to work as fast as them. A modern minicomputer, however, is many times more powerful than the vast main-frames of the early days of computers. These machines also do different jobs apparently simultaneously and can use backing stores which hold hundreds of millions of characters. It is usual for a minicomputer to support fewer input and output devices than a mainframe.

- Microcomputers – although microcomputers are not as powerful as the larger machines, their relative cheapness has meant that many more people can afford to have a computer. These machines can be connected to backing stores and so are able to store data. Their relative slowness has meant that in most cases they can only do one job at a time. However, advances in technology now mean that microcomputers which use very fast 'CHIPS' (see Chapter 2) are capable of doing more than one job at a time. Indeed, several manufacturers have recently produced microcom-puters using chips which are as powerful as their minicomputers.

Referring back to the letter our secretary produced earlier, we must ask why a letter was needed. The answer lies in the need to communicate information from a source to a destination. A significant part of everything we do involves communicating the results of our processes from one place to another. Com-puters, therefore, to be of most value must be able to communicate. Being electronic machines they can easily be connected together – just as your tele-phone can be connected to another telephone either next door or in the United States. When computers are linked together and are able to communicate freely they are said to form a NETWORK.

Networks are not uncommon in other areas too such as road networks, airline networks, telephone networks, etc. They are all ways in which different areas can communicate with each other.

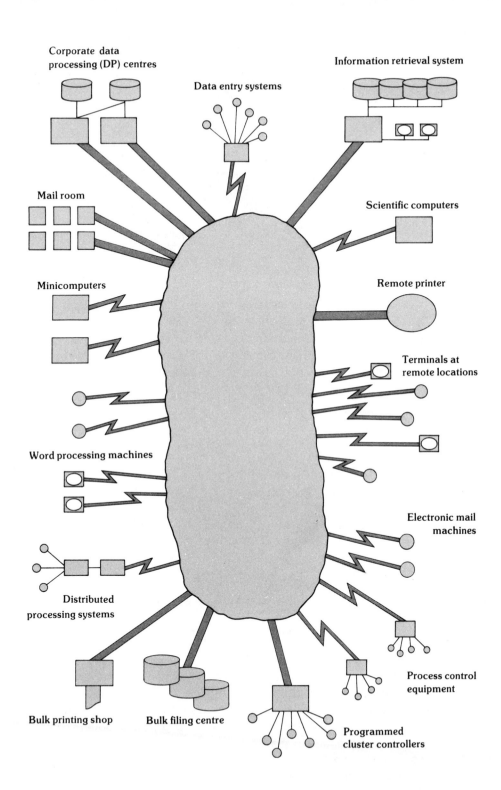

Corporate data processing (DP) centres

Data entry systems

Information retrieval system

Mail room

Scientific computers

Minicomputers

Remote printer

Terminals at remote locations

Word processing machines

Electronic mail machines

Distributed processing systems

Bulk printing shop

Bulk filing centre

Programmed cluster controllers

Process control equipment

A computer network

Two secretaries sharing a dictionary

Again, considering the production of a letter, a secretary may use a typewriter shared with another secretary. Similarly a dictionary may be shared by two secretaries in an office. In both cases, two processors are sharing resources.

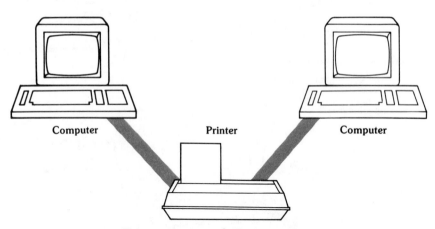

Computer   Printer   Computer

Two computers sharing a printer

In the same way, some computer networks allow computers to share resources. Clearly, it makes sense to have only one filing cabinet if it can satisfy the filing needs of both secretaries. So, too, it often makes sense for computers near each other to use a network which allows them to share backing stores, printers, etc. These networks usually allow computers in close proximity both to communicate with each other and to share resources and are referred to as local area networks (LANs). Particularly since microcomputers have become very common, interest in and development of LANs and wide area networks (WANs) has been growing rapidly. These networks and the communications they encompass will form one of the keys to information processing in future.

SUMMARY

Most computers used for information processing are digital.

They have input devices and output devices which allow the machine to communicate with the outside world. They usually have a backing store where they can store information until it is needed. The part of a computer that does the information processing is called the Central Processing Unit (CPU).

The CPU consists of a control unit, which manages all the functions of the CPU; a memory which temporarily holds data the computer is using; a clock the beat of which keeps all the computer's functions in step; and an arithmetic/logic unit (ALU) which performs calculations and comparisons.

As the information in the CPU memory can be changed easily and is 'forgotten' when the computer is turned off, this memory is called volatile.

Backing storage is often magnetic.

The way the input devices, output devices, backing stores and processor are linked together is called a computer configuration.

Large, powerful computers are termed mainframes. They can carry out millions of instructions per second. Smaller machines are called minicomputers, while very small computers, whose CPU usually comes as one 'chip' containing all the necessary electronic circuitry, are termed microcomputers. It is the advent of the chip that has led to the enormous growth in information processing. Chips can be found in every computer today.

Networks are links between different computers which allow them to communicate information at high speeds, often over great distances. Frequently, networks allow different computers to share input, output and backing store devices (or peripherals).

SELF-CHECK QUESTIONS

1. Name the two types of computer in use at present.

2. Draw a diagram of the four main functional parts of any computer system.

3. **a** What does CPU stand for?

   b What are the four sections of the CPU? Draw a diagram to illustrate your answer.

   c What function does each section of the CPU perform?

4. Give two examples of each of the following:

   a input devices

   b output devices

   c backing stores.

5. The way in which the parts of a computer system are connected and the number of devices used is called a _____.

6. What are the three sizes of computer?

7. When computers are linked together and able to communicate freely they are said to form a _____.

8. When two or more computers share the same backing stores, printers, etc. they are said to be sharing _____.

9. What is the function of the CPU clock?

10. Why is a filing cabinet similar to a backing store?

11. What happens when you press a key on the computer keyboard?

12. What is the function of an output device?

13. What are the most common ways of storing data in permanent form?

14. Why are large room-sized computers called mainframes?

15. Manufacturers often make microcomputers that are as powerful as minicomputers. How do they achieve this?

16. The functions that a computer undertakes have been said to resemble those of a secretary producing a letter. Describe another example that could have been used.

17. It is stated that a large part of everything we do involves communication. List as many forms of communication as you can and discuss whether you think a computer could help make the process more efficient.

18. It has been said that computers on a network can communicate. Why do you think that this is useful?

19. Word search. 16 words that have been mentioned in the book so far are hidden below. See whether you can find them all.

```
K S C A Q T E P G R I S V I M
C P R B A C K I N G S T O R E
L O Q K N V A U C I M A L U M
O U C R A E B F T L P L A P O
F U D L L S A O O M E S T K R
J M T C O M P U T E R K I R Y
D Y S P G C S D O A I R L J I
M I K U U E K M Y D P S E U W
C A S S E T T E S F H E J I D
I F T K C N L M X A E T A S K
N V B B Y M A I N F R A M E A
D A U G R U N N I S A H S N I
U N A B D I G I T A L U M S L
```

2

HOW DOES THE COMPUTER WORK?

Chapter Objectives

After studying this chapter you should be able to:

1. Describe how a computer processes information.

2. Explain how 'word length' gives some indication of the power of a computer.

3. Explain how the amount of storage available to a computer is measured.

4. Discuss the importance of using standard codes to represent data characters.

END OF OBJECTIVES END OF OBJECTIVES END OF OBJECTIVES END OF OBJECTIVES

CHIPS WITH EVERYTHING

All computers, whatever their shape or size, are electronic. That is, all their work is done by pulses of electricity. The pulses of electricity which do all the work inside a computer are controlled by electronic components. The components in the first electronic computers were called valves. Then in the 1950s transistors were invented and, as these were much smaller and used much less power than valves, it was possible to build smaller, more reliable computers. However, the greatest advance in computer evolution came with the development of the 'chip'. A chip is usually made from a thin wafer of a substance called silicon on which it is now possible to produce hundreds of thousands of 'components' packed closely together.

Some chips are so tiny that they can fit through the eye of a needle and yet each chip contains more electronic components than the room-sized computers of years ago. There are many different kinds of chip and each kind has circuits specially designed to do a certain job. There are special chips for:

● the control unit

● the memory store

19

- the arithmetic unit
- the clock.

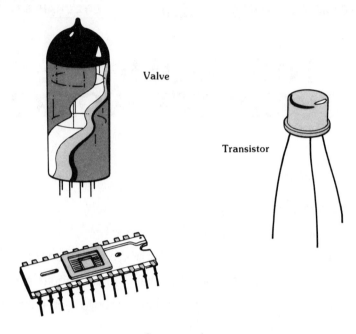

Valve

Transistor

Integrated circuit

Some chips have circuits that can do the work of most of the parts of a computer. These are called MICROPROCESSORS and are the basis for all microcomputers and much of the new information technology. The very latest form of chip – called a TRANSPUTER – is literally a whole CPU on a single chip.

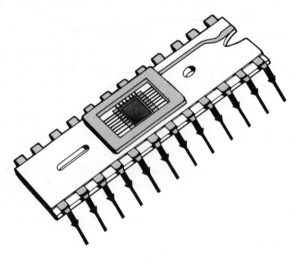

A transputer

When a computer is built, the chips for each part of the computer are mounted on a board and are connected by narrow bands of metal printed on the board which carry the electricity to and from the chips. These boards are called PRINTED CIRCUIT BOARDS or CARDS. On some designs of computer there is a main circuit board on to which various other special function boards can be easily plugged. These main boards are referred to as MOTHER BOARDS and the special connectors into which other boards are plugged are called SLOTS.

BITS AND BYTES

How can a computer which contains only a mass of silicon chips process numbers, words or even pictures? The answer (at least for digital computers) lies with the electric current which passes through the chips in a series of pulses. These pulses form a code which the computer can understand. There are only two types of signal that form the code used by digital computers: 'pulse' and 'no pulse', or 'on' and 'off'. This code is called BINARY CODE (from the Latin *bi* meaning two) and another way of expressing it, which makes it easier to write down, is by using the digits 1 and 0 – '1' for pulse and '0' for no pulse.

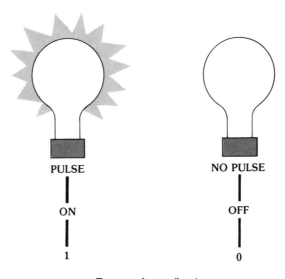

Binary digits (bits)

These electrical pulses are usually referred to as BINARY DIGITS or, in short form, BITS. How are these bits used to form a code useful to a computer? Let us try to build a code out of bits – remember that one bit can only be a 1 or a 0. If we used just one bit this could only be 'on' or 'off' and let us say we used:

● 'off' to represent A and

● 'on' to represent B.

Obviously, we have a problem because we would have no way of representing all the letters of the alphabet and the numbers 0 to 9, etc.

If we used two bits to represent characters, then we could have:

- off/off (00)
- off/on (01)
- on/off (10)
- on/on (11).

This still only gives us four patterns which we could use. Three bits gives us eight patterns (000, 001, 010, 100, 011, 101, 110, 111). It is interesting to notice the way in which the number of patterns or combinations increases. Each 'bit' can be either '0' or '1', that is, it can be one of two things. So:

- one bit can have two patterns
- two bits have $2 \times 2 = 4$ patterns
- three bits have $2 \times 2 \times 2 = 8$ patterns.

How many patterns can you get with 5 bits? Did you get 32? If not, try re-reading this section.

One 'bit' is either 'on' or 'off'
Thus using one bit:
$0 = A$
$1 = B$
Only 2 patterns (2×1) are possible

Two bits $= 2 \times 2 = 4$ patterns
$00 = A$
$01 = B$
$10 = C$
$11 = D$

Three bits $= 2 \times 2 \times 2 = 8$ patterns
$000 = A$
$001 = B$
$010 = C$
$011 = D$
$100 = E$
$101 = F$
$110 = G$
$111 = H$

Five bits?
$= 2 \times 2 \times 2 \times 2 \times 2 = 32$ patterns

If you consider the QWERTY keyboard and think how many different characters there are on it you will see that we have:

● upper case A – Z

● lower case a – z

● numbers 0 – 9

● the special punctuation characters such as full stop, comma, question mark, etc.

A QWERTY keyboard

Although the number does tend to vary, there are about 80 different characters on most keyboards. For a computer to be able to tell the difference between characters, each character must have its own special pattern of 0s and 1s or bits. You will see that putting 8 bits together as a pattern will allow the computer to have 256 unique patterns ($2 \times 2 \times 2 \times 2 \times 2 \times 2 \times 2 \times 2$) each one of which can be used to represent a character or a special COMMAND. What is a special command? Well, the computer needs to recognise not only letters and numbers but also a space, a tab, a carriage return, etc. That is why, for example, with word processing you can move the CURSOR to a position on the screen, press the space bar and it will change whatever character is being displayed to a space. This happens because all you are really doing is telling the computer to change the pattern of 8 bits from one character pattern to the space character pattern. The 256 different combinations available by using 8 bits are enough to cater for almost every requirement that a normal computer will demand. Thus, 8-bit codes have become very common. A parcel of 8 bits is called a BYTE. Thus 8 bits represent one byte.

8 bits $= 2 \times 2 \times 2 \times 2 \times 2 \times 2 \times 2 \times 2 = 256$

For example: 00010100
00011100

8 bits = 1 byte = 1 character

Bytes are very important when talking about computers and many forms of information processing. For example, the standard way of judging the amount of backing store available to a computer is in bytes. Usually quoted capacities are KILOBYTES and MEGABYTES.

- a kilobyte (K for short) is 1024 bytes (or about one thousand bytes)

- a megabyte (Mb for short) is about one million bytes.

Therefore, when you read about a microcomputer having 64 K RAM (Random Access Memory) this means that it can store in its volatile memory 65 536 bytes or characters (that is, 64×1024). Similarly, if you read about a mainframe with a 288 Mb disk drive, this means that it can store on its magnetic disk backing store about 288 million characters! Very large configurations have a series of magnetic disk backing stores which provide storage for thousands of millions of characters. One thousand million characters is called a GIGABYTE.

1 kilobyte (K) = 1024 bytes

1 megabyte (Mb) = 1 million bytes

64 K = 65 536 characters
288 Mb = 288 million characters

So now we know that digital computers use bits, or combinations of bits. Most home microcomputers use 8 bits or 1 byte at a time. That means their CPUs can only handle single bytes. The newer business microcomputers and most mini-computers can handle 16 bits or 32 bits at a time. Mainframe computers can deal with up to 128 bits at a time.

Although measured in thousandths or millionths of a second, the time taken to fetch or return information to the volatile memory is considerably greater than the time taken for the CPU to carry out its processes in the arithmetic/logic unit (ALU). Clearly, therefore, the more information the CPU can deal with at one moment, the more powerful the computer. The number of bits the CPU can deal with at one time is defined as the WORD LENGTH of the computer. Thus a 16-bit computer is said to have a word length of 16 bits. Often the memory of the machine is organized into words as well.

So how does the computer use these bits? Let us use a new example (after all, our letter from Chapter 1 has probably been posted already). Consider baking a cake – this takes three things:

- the recipe

- the ingredients

- the processor (you).

You will produce the cake by:

- following the recipe

- collecting and processing the ingredients as you move through the recipe instructions.

The recipe represents the PROGRAM you are using. This program controls what you do to the ingredients, when you do it and how you do it. The ingredients represent the data you are using during your processing.

The computer will also always need a program to tell it what to do plus data that it will use during the processing. However, as was said earlier, the CPU will only recognise bits, or more correctly, combinations of bits. Thus, with an 8-bit microcomputer, for example, both its recipe and its data will be in patterns of 8 bits. As 8 bits only allow 256 possible patterns, the same pattern may be used for instructions or data. So how does the CPU 'know' whether the byte that it is currently handling represents data or instructions?

Well, going back to the cake example you will always:

- read the first instruction

- handle any ingredients

- read the next instruction

- handle the next batch of ingredients

- repeat this cycle until the cake is complete.

A cake-making process

Once you have read the instruction you will carry it out using the ingredients mentioned. You will then read the next instruction. It is up to you to remember which stage in the recipe you had reached so that you can carry on from there. This cycle of:

- reading an instruction

- handling ingredients

- reading the next instruction, etc.

is carried out until the process is finished.

The computer works in exactly the same way. The control unit 'knows' that the first pattern or patterns of bits will mean an instruction. It will keep processing these as instructions until the instructions 'tell' it to handle data. It then handles the bit patterns as the data but will remember where in the program it had reached. After processing the data as instructed, it goes back to reading the bit patterns as instructions until told to change. This cycle continues until the process or program is finished.

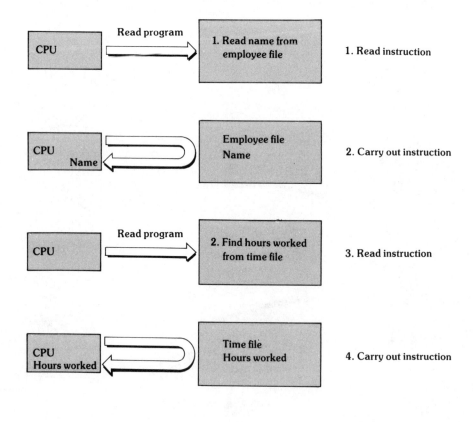

A computer process

ASCII and EBCDIC

It would be quite possible for every type of computer to use its own codes for both instructions and data. For example, one machine might use the pattern 10000001 to represent the instruction ADD, while another machine may use the combination 11111110 to represent ADD. While this may not at first appear to be important, just consider what would happen if the instructions for one machine were given to another, different, machine. The second machine would be totally 'baffled' and would not be able to carry out the instructions, much as you would struggle to understand a Japanese recipe. This lack of understanding does in fact exist and therefore it is not at all easy to transfer programs from computer to computer.

Although not being able to transfer programs is irritating, it does not cause anything like the problems that arise if data could not be transferred from machine to machine. Consider a computer trying to send a letter to a printer for printing. The printer will be receiving a series of bits and it must be able to recognize the coding being used by the computer so that, when the computer sends a pattern of bits which it understands as the letter A the printer recognizes the pattern and prints A.

If every computer manufacturer made both the computer and the printer, they could ensure that the printer and the computer recognized the same code. However, it is essential for many reasons which we shall discuss in this book that computers use the same code for data. Luckily, two main codes exist and one or other of these is used on virtually every commercial computer:

- ASCII – the most common code – is found on every microcomputer and most minicomputers (ASCII stands for American Standard Code for Information Interchange)

- EBCDIC – the other common code – (EBCDIC stands for Extended Binary Coded Decimal Interchange Code).

SUMMARY

Most modern computers are built using silicon chips which contain thousands of electronic components. The chips are fitted on to boards which have narrow metal bands printed on them to conduct the electricity that computers use. These boards are called printed circuit boards. A mother board is one into which special function boards can be slotted.

Digital computers work using pulses of electricity, which are either 'on' or 'off'. As they can be only one of two states, these pulses are called binary digits or, in short form, bits.

Bits are combined together in patterns to form a code. 8 bits give 256 different combinations. 8 bits are referred to as a byte. 1024 bytes are a kilobyte (K for short), about one million bytes are called a megabyte (Mb for short) and one thousand million bytes are called a gigabyte. Characters (or data) are considered as bytes.

The number of bits that a CPU can deal with is referred to as word length. Most home microcomputers are 8-bit machines which means that they can handle 8 bits at one time. They are 8-bit word machines. The newer business microcomputers use 16 bits and are 16-bit word machines.

The computer uses bits both for programs (its instructions) and data. There are two widely used codes that allow data to be transferred easily from one machine to another – ASCII and EBCDIC.

SELF-CHECK QUESTIONS

1. The very latest form of chip is a whole CPU on a single chip:

    a   What is it called?

    b   What elements would be contained in this chip?

2. Explain the following terms:

    a   bit

    b   byte

    c   kilobyte

    d   megabyte

    e   gigabyte

3. Which of the following microcomputers is likely to be the most powerful? Give reasons for your answer.

    a   an 8-bit microcomputer

    b   a 16-bit microcomputer

    c   a 32-bit microcomputer

4. The number of bits that the CPU can deal with at one time is defined as the _____ _____ of the computer.

5. What do you understand by:

    a   a microcomputer with a 64 K RAM

    b   a 288 Mb disk drive?

6. What is the name given to the set of instructions that a computer needs to tell it what to do?

7. When computers are built, chips are mounted on boards and are connected by narrow bands of metal which carry the electricity. What are these boards called?

8. What do ASCII and EBCDIC stand for and why is it important to have such codes?

9. How does a computer know whether it is dealing with program instructions or data?

10. You are word processing. You go to the middle of a sentence and press the space bar a few times and it appears that you are erasing the sentence. Why?

11. What is a chip usually made from?

12. Explain the terms 'mother board' and 'slot'.

13. Why is it essential that each character has a unique bit pattern?

14. How many different combinations can be achieved by putting 8 bits together?

15. How many bytes would be used for the words:

   a configuration

   b disk drive?

3

HARDWARE AND SOFTWARE

Chapter Objectives

After studying this chapter you should be able to:

1. Describe the relationship between hardware and software.

2. Identify the three basic types of computer program and explain the function of each.

3. Explain the difference between high-level and low-level programming languages.

4. Compare the different methods by which high-level languages are translated into a machine-readable format.

END OF OBJECTIVES END OF OBJECTIVES END OF OBJECTIVES END OF OBJECTIVES

HARDWARE

We have already mentioned that a computer has four functional parts:

- input devices
- CPU
- output devices
- backing store.

These separate units are called HARDWARE and are linked together by electric cables so that the pulses of electric current can travel from device to device. When they are linked together they form the computer system. So hardware is the physical units – the parts we can see and touch.

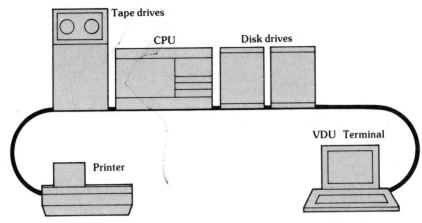

A computer configuration

SOFTWARE

At present, computers cannot do anything unless told exactly what to do. However, they do not understand human languages, except in a limited way, and so we have to instruct them in languages which they can understand. These special languages are called PROGRAMMING LANGUAGES. A COMPUTER PROGRAMMER is someone whose job it is to write down the series of instructions that the computer must do to complete a task. As the computer acts on only one piece of information at a time, the program has to be worked out very precisely to make sure that the instructions are written in the correct order. Computer programs are called SOFTWARE.

```
** CIS COBOL V4.5                    STOCK1.CBL                  PAGE: 0001
**
** OPTIONS SELECTED :
**      ANIM RESEQ
**
000010 IDENTIFICATION DIVISION.                                    0118
000020 PROGRAM-ID. STOCK-FILE-SET-UP.                              0118
000030 AUTHOR. MICRO FOCUS LTD.                                    0118
000040 ENVIRONMENT DIVISION.                                       0118
000050 CONFIGURATION SECTION.                                      0118
000060 SOURCE-COMPUTER.                                            0118
000070 OBJECT-COMPUTER.                                            0118
000080 SPECIAL-NAMES. CONSOLE IS CRT.                              0118
000090 INPUT-OUTPUT SECTION.                                       0118
000100 FILE-CONTROL.                                               0118
000110     SELECT STOCK-FILE ASSIGN "STOCK.IT"                     0184
000120     ORGANIZATION INDEXED                                    0186
000130     ACCESS DYNAMIC                                          0186
000140     RECORD KEY STOCK-CODE.                                  0186
000150 DATA DIVISION.                                              01BE
000160 FILE SECTION.                                               01BE
000170 FD  STOCK-FILE: RECORD 32.                                  01BE
000180 01  STOCK-ITEM.                                             01BE
000190     02  STOCK-CODE PIC X(4).                                01BE
000200     02  PRODUCT-DESC PIC X(20).                             01C2
000210     02  UNIT-SIZE PIC 9(4).                                 01D6
000220 WORKING-STORAGE SECTION.                                    01DC
000230 01  SCREEN-HEADINGS.                                        01DC 00
000240     02  ASK-CODE PIC X(21) VALUE "STOCK CODE   <    >".     01DC 00
```

A computer program

There are basically three types of program:

- computer operating systems
- utility programs
- applications programs.

Computer Operating Systems

These specialized programs are needed to tell the computer how to manage the various hardware units. For example, these programs:

- fetch data from the keyboards
- control the operation of the CPU
- send data to VDUs and printers
- file and retrieve data from backing store, etc.

With many microcomputers, the operating system program is written into the computer's memory – usually at the time of manufacture. This program is stored in a special form of memory called ROM (Read Only Memory). The computer can only read the information in ROM and cannot erase it or store new information in it.

However, to aid with the programming of ROMs, newer chips have been developed which allow the ROM to be programmed after it has been manufactured. These chips are called PROMs (Programmable Read Only Memory). Once programmed, they cannot be changed. Still newer types can have their programs erased using ultraviolet light – these are called EPROMs (Erasable Programmable Read Only Memory). Just to make things fun, there are now ROMs that can be electrically changed – these are called EEPROMs (Electrically Erasable Programmable Read Only Memory).

With all mini and mainframe computers and some microcomputers, their operating programs are stored on backing store (usually magnetic disk) and must be loaded into the volatile memory every time the machine is turned on. This process involves reading into RAM a small program which 'tells' the computer how to load other programs which then control the loading of still further programs. This process is called BOOT-STRAPPING – the computer 'pulls' itself up by its bootstraps!

These programs are referred to as the OPERATING SYSTEM SOFTWARE without which, as you can appreciate, the computer could not function. The operating system software is important, because it operates all devices, controls all the memory of the CPU and manages all the computer's activities.

Every company manufacturing mini and mainframe computers tends to have developed its own operating systems. However, this is not so with microcomputers where there are some common operating systems used by many manufacturers. For 8-bit microcomputers an operating system called C/PM (Control Program for Microcomputers) is very common. With the newer 16-bit machines, several operating systems are being used, for example, MS-DOS and UNIX. UNIX and other similar operating systems allow more than one user to share a single CPU. These are MULTI-USER OPERATING SYSTEMS. All minicomputers and mainframes use multi-user operating systems.

Utility Programs

These are special programs which act as 'tools' for users of computers: they make many functions much easier by providing software specially designed to assist in the task. They may be compared to a spade which 'assists' in the digging of a field. It is these programs that:

- sort information

- reorganize files stored on backing store

- copy files

- change one type of file to another

- allow information stored in the memory or on backing store to be examined byte by byte, etc.

Applications Programs

These programs tell the computer how to perform different tasks that are useful to the computer's users. Examples are payroll, stock control, personnel records, word processing or even calculating weather forecasts. Usually these instructions are stored on backing store and loaded into the volatile memory called RAM (Random Access Memory) although some programs are stored in ROM. It is this type of APPLICATIONS SOFTWARE that the vast majority of commercial programmers produce and maintain.

It is also common to buy application software from businesses specializing in writing computer programs. These businesses are often termed SOFTWARE HOUSES. If the applications software has been written in such a way that any business requiring this type of computer system can use the software produced, the software is termed a PACKAGE. Packages for most commercial applications – accounting, stock control, payroll, word processing, etc. – are now common and these packages contain both the software and the DOCUMENTATION needed to describe how to operate this software. Other forms of package – such as word processing, spreadsheets or databases – are designed to assist in the production of commercial information rather than to perform one specific task. Often, purchase of the package will include a charge for the maintenance of the software and for other support provided to the purchaser.

With most computers, applications programs must be loaded from backing store into RAM before the machine 'runs' the program. However, it is increasingly common to store applications programs on ROM for microcomputers (or personal computers as they are sometimes called).

There are some computers designed for specialist jobs. When you turn them on they automatically load specialist programs. These programs allow the machine to do only one job. These machines are called DEDICATED MACHINES. The most common example of these is WORD PROCESSORS.

Programming Languages

Computers, as we have said, work on electronic impulses – either 'ons' or 'offs' – 0s or 1s. Programmers working with the earliest computers had to work out what they wanted the machine to do by using the binary code for each particular instruction. This highly specialized and extremely tedious type of programming is called MACHINE CODE PROGRAMMING.

Obviously, this type of programming is slow and therefore later machines had special programs written for them which allowed programmers to program using abbreviations (MNEMONICS) for the instructions which they wanted the machine to carry out. These programs would then translate the input mnemonics into machine code and there was almost always one mnemonic for one CPU instruction. This type of programming, which is still used because it is efficient, is called ASSEMBLY LANGUAGE PROGRAMMING. However, as each type of CPU has its own set of machine code instructions, it is difficult to transfer programs from one type of CPU to another. Programming in this language is still a specialized task. Machine code and assembler are called LOW-LEVEL LANGUAGES.

For computers to become really commercially useful it is clear that they should be able to understand languages such as English. While this stage of development has still not been reached, HIGH-LEVEL LANGUAGES have been developed which are much easier to understand and are much closer to English than low-level languages. Programs written in these languages can be transferred from machine to machine relatively easily and, unlike assembler languages, one high-level instruction usually equates to many machine instructions. Examples of these high-level languages are:

- BASIC (Beginner's All-Purpose Symbolic Instruction Code)
- COBOL (Common Business Orientated Language)
- FORTRAN (FORmula TRANslation)
- PASCAL (after Blaise Pascal – remember him from the Introduction?).

These high-level languages are also described as being 3rd-generation languages. Machine code programming was the 1st generation, Assembler was the 2nd and high-level languages are the 3rd. Each successive generation has resulted in programs being produced much faster than previously. Over the past few years a new generation of languages – the 4th generation – has arrived. These are often tools which allow applications to be generated by the computer rather than by being laboriously written out by programmers or are very high-level languages which allow complex programs to be written using only a few lines of instructions. As a result, applications are developed much more rapidly and cheaply. Examples of these languages are FOCUS, QUERY-BY-EXAMPLE, SQL and NATURAL.

1st generation — machine code.
Written in hexadecimal and binary

```
01C2        0000000111000010
01D6        0000000111010110
01DC        0000000111011100
0001        0000000000000001
DC00        1101110000000000
01DC        0000000111011100
```

2nd generation — Assembler

```
LDA # 65
JSR & FFE3
LDX # & 10
STX & 0400
JMP & # 1000
```

3rd generation — high level languages. Written in BASIC and COBOL

BASIC

```
10    INPUT ANSWERS
20    IF ANSWERS = "NO" OR
      ANSWERS = "N" THEN
      PROC_FINISHED
30    IF ANSWERS = "MAYBE"
      THEN PROC_ARE_YOU_
      SURE ELSE  PROC_YOU_
      MUST_MEAN_YES
```

COBOL

```
PROCEDURE DIVISION
LA_START.
      DISPLAY SPACE.
      MOVE SPACE TO SCREEN.
LOOP.
      MOVE N TO N2.
      SUBTRACT 2 FROM N2.
      MULTIPLY N2 BY N2.
      DIVIDE N2 BY 4.
      IF TERM < 0.00001 THEN
      GO TO HALT.
```

4th generation — very high
level language — SQL

```
Select DOC_CODE, DOC_DATE,
      SUM (GLE_VALUE)
from GENERAL_LEDGER_
      ENTRIES. DOCUMENTS
where DOC_CODE = GLE_
      SOURCE_DOC_CODE
and GLE_ACCOUNT =
      "EXPENSES"
order by DOC_DATE
```

Examples of codings in 1st, 2nd, 3rd and 4th generation languages

Currently there are huge research projects into 'intelligent computers'. These machines will be able to 'work out' answers without needing a programmer to instruct them how to reach the answer. However, the task facing builders of these 5th-generation computers is how to teach them to think. In order to communicate with these CPUs, special 5th-generation languages – the languages of artificial intelligence – are being used. These languages – LOGO, PROLOG and LISP – could be as common in 20 years' time as the third-generation languages are now.

Most commercial programming is still done using 3rd-generation languages because these are well known and established. However, the high cost of software is gradually forcing a much wider awareness of the benefits of 4th-generation techniques.

Compilers and Interpreters

It should be remembered that for a machine to be able to understand these high-level languages it must have a program that will translate them into machine code. This translator program may work in one of two ways.

The first way involves the translation program taking each line of your application program and turning that line of instructions into machine code which the CPU then carries out. This may be compared with a language translator at a meeting who translates each sentence from, say, English into Russian as the sentence is spoken. These translator programs in a computer are called INTERPRETERS.

The second way involves the translation of all the application program from the high-level language into machine code. Only after all the translation has been done can the CPU carry out the application as it uses the translated version of the program. This form of translation may be compared to the translation of a book from English into Russian. The whole book is translated before it is available to be read. These translators are called COMPILERS. The high-level language program is termed the SOURCE PROGRAM while the program which results from the translation is called the OBJECT PROGRAM. The object program is in machine code and is the program that the CPU actually uses.

So, there are two ways of translating programs which we can understand into the machine code which a computer can understand:

- Interpreters, which have to translate the program line by line every time the program is used.

- Compilers, which translate the whole source program, that is, the program as we understand it into an exact copy but in machine code (the language that the CPU understands). The machine code copy is called the object program.

An interpreter (translating immediately from one language into another)

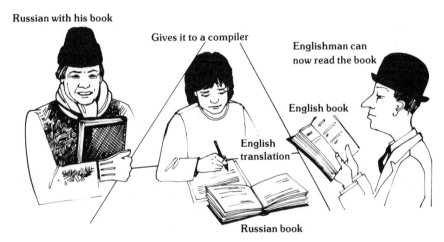

A compiler (translating from one language into another)

It is much easier to develop programs using interpreters: they can be tried out and changed easily but do not run, that is, carry out their instructions as fast as a compiled program.

To sum up, computer hardware units by themselves do nothing but with software they can be made to function as a unit and to perform useful tasks.

It is in the area of software development that the growth of information processing is occurring.

SUMMARY

Hardware is the term used to describe the physical parts of the computer configuration. Software is the term used to describe the instructions the computer follows when carrying out tasks. Special programming languages are used to instruct computers. A set of instructions is called a program.

Operating system programs manage the computer by providing the instructions necessary to control all the hardware and software being used. In microcomputers these programs are often stored in Read Only Memory (ROM). This is non-volatile memory. It is possible to use different forms of ROM. Programmable ROM (PROM) may have any program stored but, once stored, it cannot be changed. EPROMs (erasable PROMs) can have their programs erased by exposing the chip to ultraviolet light. Once erased, a new program can be stored.

Minicomputers and mainframes read their operating programs into RAM (Random Access Memory) every time the computer is started. This process is called boot-strapping.

There are many different operating systems for computers. For microcomputers C/PM, MSDOS and UNIX are common examples. Some microcomputers can now share the CPU between several terminals as they have 'multi-user' operating systems.

Utility programs help people to perform tasks involved in managing the computer.

Application programs instruct the computer to perform specific useful tasks such as payroll or accounting. A package is a set of programs designed to fulfil a function for any business. When buying a package, documentation describing how to use the programs is provided. Often a charge is made for maintenance and support.

Early computers were programmed in bits. This form of programming, called machine code programming, is very slow and highly specialized. Later computers used special programs which allowed the use of an abbreviation for each CPU instruction. Programming using these abbreviations is called assembler programming. Machine code and assembler are low-level languages.

High-level languages are now widely used to program computers. These languages are much more like English and programs may be relatively easily transferred from one type of computer to another.

The newest languages, called 4th-generation languages, allow the computer to generate many of the program instructions or else to use few commands to perform complex programs.

A translator program that translates a high-level language into machine code line by line each time the application is used is called an interpreter. A translator program which translates the entire application program from a high-level language into a machine code program is called a compiler.

When a compiler is used, the high-level program it translates is called the source program while the machine code version it produces is called an object program. The computer will only use the object program.

SELF-CHECK QUESTIONS

1. Explain what is meant by:

   a computer hardware

   b computer software.

2. What are the three 'types' of computer program?

3. What is the function of the operating system?

4. Why are utility programs useful?

5. What do the following terms stand for:

   a CP/M

   b RAM

   c ROM

   d PROM

   e EPROM

   f EEPROM?

6. Mainframes, minicomputers and some microcomputers load their operating programs from backing store into RAM. This process of loading is called

   _____ _____ .

7. Give examples of:

   a 1st-generation programming languages

   b 2nd-generation programming languages

   c 3rd-generation programming languages

   d 4th-generation programming languages.

8. Why is machine code programming a specialized and tedious task?

9. Compilers and interpreters translate high-level languages into machine code. Which of the two

   a translates the program line by line

   b translates the whole program before the CPU processes it?

10. Payroll, stock control and word processing are all examples of _____ programs.

11. What does a computer programmer do?

12. How is the program on an EPROM erased?

13. Without s_____ s_____ a computer could not function.

14. Give examples of operating systems used in 16-bit machines.

15. Application programs are usually stored and loaded into _____ memory called R_____ A_____ M_____.

16. What is the function of a software house?

17. If you bought a software package what should you get in addition to the program?

18. Explain what is meant by a dedicated machine.

19. Explain the difference between machine code programming and assembler language programming.

20. Explain the following:

    a   source program

    b   object program.

Which one does the computer use to carry out its processing?

21. Explain what is meant by low-level and high-level programming languages.

22. What do you feel are the benefits to be gained by using 4th-generation programming languages?

4

SYSTEMS

Chapter Objectives

After studying this chapter you should be able to:

1. Identify the four common elements of any system.

2. Compare a traditional and a modern information processing system.

3. Apply the principles of a computer system to other systems.

4. Distinguish between open and closed systems.

END OF OBJECTIVES END OF OBJECTIVES END OF OBJECTIVES END OF OBJECTIVES

INTRODUCTION

So far we have described computers. We have talked about their having:

● an input

● an output

● a processor

● an information store

and we have said that these form the elements of the computer. We have looked at software and how it is the software that 'tells' the computer how to operate and how to do those tasks we want the machine to do. The hardware and software together are often talked about as being a COMPUTER SYSTEM.

COMPUTER SYSTEMS

People often hear or read about systems, for example, a solar system, a biological system. So what is it about these apparently very different functions that allows each to be called a system? Consider the following characteristics:

● They all have more than one part: they are built up of many different building blocks. The blocks may be the same (such as two planets) or different (such as a VDU and a printer).

41

- They all react or work together to achieve common goals. Often this is diffi-cult to appreciate. The solar system, for example, would appear to have no common goals and the planets have no control over what they do. How-ever, the planets do influence each other through their gravitational pull and, in addition to other goals, have the common one of remaining in con-stant and stable orbits around the sun.

- Each has a boundary or limiting edge. Since the system interacts so closely with other systems, it is often hard to decide just where the limit lies. For example, if we consider ourselves as a system we may say that our boun-dary is our skin yet each one of us reacts together to form another system – the society or social system in which we live.

- Finally, and perhaps most significantly, systems tend to remain stable. If any element in the system becomes unstable the change is corrected by other system elements. This sounds complicated but is actually simple.

Again, look at ourselves as examples of a system. Our bodies work most effici-ently at a temperature of about 98.4 degrees F. If we exercise, our temperature starts to rise, our system senses the rise and causes changes to take place which are designed to lower the body temperature and return the system to a stable level. This process of checking and changing is called feedback.

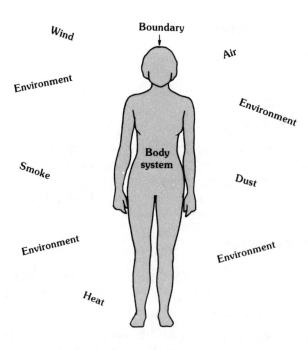

The human being as a system

Now let us look at a simple example – a computer system that does accounting for a business.

- The computer is provided with information about each customer including the customer's credit limit.

- Each time the customer orders something, the information is entered into the computer which adds to this the outstanding balance and checks the result against the credit limit. If the balance is greater than the credit limit, the computer system will reject the customer's order and will only allow the customer to order the goods after some money has been paid off the outstanding balance.

Obviously, what we have described is different from a calculator which would simply keep adding the customer orders together without any form of checking or control. The calculator is unable to make a decision and incapable of signalling to us that something is wrong. The calculator is therefore not a system but the computer and its software is a system.

If we think about the computer system we can see that we, the users, are outside, or external to, the computer. We form part of the environment in which the machine works. It takes information from us, does things with it and then gives a result. So we can see with this system that it has a boundary between itself and its environment. Every system will have a boundary.

Most systems interact with their environment, that is, they receive information or materials from their environment and they distribute information or materials to the environment. These are called OPEN SYSTEMS. CLOSED SYSTEMS are isolated and have no interaction with their environments.

The computer system has a boundary but so does the calculator. However, we also said that the computer:

- takes the information we give it

- processes it

- then checks the results of its process to make sure that everything is in order.

If there is a mistake or if the result is outside the limits allowed for the system, it will 'realise' this and will then 'tell' its external environment that an error has occurred. For example, when the credit limit is exceeded, the computer system:

- 'tells' itself that the credit limit is exceeded

- refuses to accept the new order

- then tells us that it will not take the new order.

If it did not have some mechanism to keep itself 'in balance' it would add the order to the balance.

This feature of 'telling' or 'regulating' is the FEEDBACK mechanism.

When a system keeps itself in check or in balance, it is using NEGATIVE FEED-BACK. That is, it is saying to itself: 'You have gone far enough, don't go any further'. The opposite of this, POSITIVE FEEDBACK, happens when the system is designed to be continuously increasing or reinforcing. For example, the education system should operate on positive feedback. Every time you do well, you should receive positive feedback through encouragement, praise, compliments, etc. from your teachers and this should encourage you to try to do even better. Most business systems, however, rely on negative feedback, that is, they are trying to keep some form of stability and control.

So we now have two unique and distinguishing features of any system:

- A system must have a boundary by which you can talk about the outside world and the system.

- It must have some form of feedback whereby it tells itself how it is doing. An open system is one that interacts with the environment outside its boundaries.

Most of the business and commercial world can be thought of in terms of business systems. A manufacturing system, for example:

- takes raw materials from its environment into a factory; the walls of the factory may be considered the system boundary

- puts the raw material through a number of processes and continuously checks each process; any faulty pieces are rejected and new ones made to replace them

- finally, puts all the pieces together and the finished product leaves the factory.

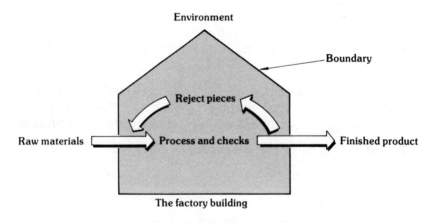

A factory system

Note that when it leaves the factory system it goes into a selling system, a transport system or a distribution system. There are therefore systems within systems within systems (which is why it is important to decide what are the limits of the system you are considering).

We should perhaps realise that the whole new technology of information processing is only system designers extending the boundaries of systems or allowing one system to interact more efficiently with another.

For example, we used to have a letter:

- drafted by an author

- passed to a typist for typing and checking

- returned to the author who also checked it

- put into an envelope, put into an out-tray and taken to the mail room.

- franked

- taken to the post office

- sorted, distributed, sorted and delivered to another mailroom

- delivered to the department to which it had been addressed

- received by the person to whom it had been sent.

This is actually a traditional information processing system.

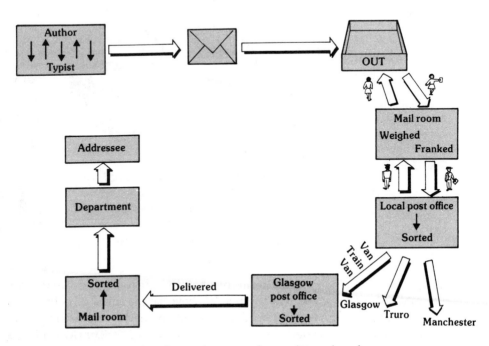

Sending a letter — the traditional cycle

Computer manufacturers and designers first developed word processors to improve the letter-production system – part of the information processing systems we have just talked about. Now, however, it is possible for the letter to be:

- dictated by the author into the computer via the VDU

- typed by the typist, using the dictated transcript kept in the backing store

- checked by the machine for spelling and grammar mistakes

- checked by the author at a screen and perhaps changes made

- sent electronically from word processor to word processor

- received by the addressee in a form displayed on his or her own screen.

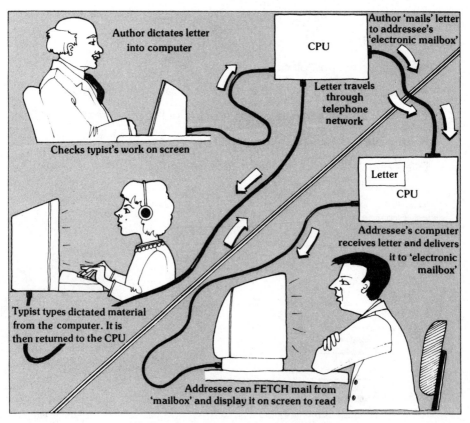

Sending a letter — the modern cycle

Nothing has actually changed in terms of what we were trying to do, that is, get information from one person to another. We have simply linked all of this together in one integrated (that is, all connected together) mechanical system. Manufacturers and designers talk about this as being an INFORMATION PROCESSING SYSTEM.

Is what we have described so far all that comprises a system? The answer to this must be 'no', because every system we have talked about and every system you can think of will have a 'reason for being' or a common aim. All the elements of the system process together, or work together, to meet this 'reason for being'. Consider again the 'letter' example. The objective of this system, or the goal for which it was working, was to get the information from the author to the recipient. To do this, numerous elements joined together, each interacting and collectively working towards this common goal.

To sum up then, a system will have:

- a boundary
- elements that interact together
- some form of self-regulation through feedback
- a goal.

SUMMARY

There are many different types of system but they all have four common features, namely:

- an edge or boundary
- elements or parts that work or interact together
- a mechanism by which information about the performance of the system is 'fed back' into the system causing it to modify or change the way it acts
- an objective, goal, or reason for being.

Systems that interact with their environment are termed open systems. Closed systems (which have no effect or are unaffected by their environment) are very rare.

Negative feedback acts to keep systems in balance.

SELF-CHECK QUESTIONS

1. When a system interacts with its environment it is called an _____ _____.

2. What do you understand by a system 'interacting' with its environment?

3. Explain what is meant by 'feedback' mechanism.

4. What is the difference between positive feedback and negative feedback?

5. Why do most business systems rely on negative feedback?

6. Identify the four elements of any system.

7. Is a calculator a system? Give reasons for your answer.

8. Taking the 'letter' example mentioned in this chapter, compare the traditional information processing system and the modern information processing system.

9. Using one of the following examples, explain and identify the four elements of the system:

   a library system
   a hospital system
   a manufacturing system
   an accounting system.

5

INPUT DEVICES

Chapter Objectives

After studying this chapter you should be able to:

1. Explain the purpose of any input device.

2. List the most common input devices currently in use.

3. Choose the most appropriate form of input for a given application.

END OF OBJECTIVES END OF OBJECTIVES END OF OBJECTIVES END OF OBJECTIVES

INTRODUCTION

The next three chapters will discuss input, output and secondary storage devices (backing stores). All devices that are peripheral (external) to the CPU are termed PERIPHERAL DEVICES – this chapter will concentrate on input peripherals.

Input devices provide a way by which communication between the people who are concerned with the computer's operation and the computer itself may be made: this is why we concentrate on them first. As was stated earlier, there are several types of input device and we shall look at each one in turn.

PUNCHED CARDS AND PUNCHED PAPER TAPE READERS

PUNCHED CARDS and PUNCHED PAPER TAPE used to be the traditional methods of input to computers. Basically, holes were punched in the card or tape using a KEYPUNCH MACHINE. Each character was represented by a pattern of holes: each hole represented a binary '1' and each 'no hole' represented a binary '0'.

Since the computer could not check the information as it was punched, often a second operator would type the same data but on a machine called a VERIFIER. This machine did not actually punch holes but checked to see whether what the first operator had typed agreed with what the second operator entered! Faulty cards were rejected.

A punched card

Special machines called READERS were used to input the information into the computer. The most modern types of reader would shine a beam of light across the card or tape and the device would generate a '1' each time the light shone through a hole.

Often with older-style computers, information from the computer was punched out on to cards and tapes by a keypunch machine, meaning that they could be both input and output devices. However, as this method of input is rapidly becoming obsolete it will not be discussed in detail.

The big advantage with cards and paper tape was that large amounts of information could be prepared away from the computer (OFF-LINE) and then input in large batches. Because the computer is so fast, this is a very efficient way of processing large quantities of data for applications such as a payroll. The process of preparing large amounts of data and then giving these large batches to the computer for processing is called BATCH PROCESSING and is an efficient use of computer time.

(The opposite of batch processing is REAL-TIME PROCESSING by which data is input directly into the computer and causes all the files to be changed immediately, rather than some time after input as happens with batch processing.)

KEY-TO-DISK/TAPE MACHINES

Both card readers and paper tape readers are relatively slow methods of input. So, although batching is an efficient way of using computer time, the slowness of paper readers is a limiting factor. Therefore a new form of batch input has been developed in which information is keyed directly on to a magnetic disk or tape. The information is then read by the computer from the magnetic medium at speeds hundreds of times faster than from cards or paper tape. This idea of storing data on a magnetic medium and then the computer reading this data is widely used in many aspects of new technology. Almost any of the forms of input that we shall go on to discuss in this book can employ this idea of storing information before processing.

These input devices have not traditionally been connected to office processing systems, although the idea of KEY-TO-DISK is becoming more widely used. It is possible, at little cost, to connect a normal electric typewriter to a key-to-disk system, and thus to store draft text before putting it into the word processor for final editing. This makes sense because a word processing workstation is an expensive way of inputting first-draft manuscript, and it allows a company to make use of normal electric typewriters it already owns.

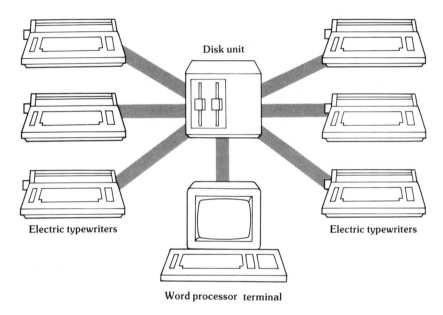

Disk unit

Electric typewriters

Electric typewriters

Word processor terminal

A key-to-disk configuration in the office

OPTICAL CHARACTER READERS (OCRs)

The OPTICAL CHARACTER READER (OCR) is a device capable of reading typewritten text and converting it to a means suitable for computer input. OCRs:

● scan each character photoelectrically

● then convert its shape into a pattern of electronic signals.

When first introduced, OCRs could only distinguish the characters of specially designed typefaces and although this is still the case with many machines, the more advanced readers can recognize over 300 different FONTS (type styles).

51

With some OCRs, an unrecognizable character or a crossing-out on the type-script will cause the machine to stop to allow the operator to confirm the character's identity.

The current OCRs:

● read up to 200 pages per hour

● have an error rate as low as one in 100 000 characters.

The great advantage of OCRs is that duplicate keying of documents which have already been typed is avoided and keyboarding bottlenecks are avoided, thus freeing word processors for their proper function.

OPTICAL MARK READERS (OMRs)

Another device for entering data into the computer's memory is the OPTICAL MARK READER (OMR). This device uses preprinted forms on which marks are made in pencil and each position on the form represents a specific predefined value or character. The machine is capable of converting pencil marks into computer input by recognizing the values or characters from their position on the form.

Example:

1. The speed of a daisy-wheel printer is measured in:

    a Lines per minute   b Bits per second

    c Words per minute   d Megabytes

    e Characters per second

1. a	2. a	3. a
b	b	b
c	c	c
d	d	d
e	e	e

An OMR mark sheet

OMRs are used a great deal for marking multiple-choice examinations and handling questionnaires for market research. They are also used to process meter readings for some gas and electricity boards. The meter reader marks boxes on cards indicating the amount shown on the meter. Each card will already have the customer's name and account reference on it. These cards can then be processed, in batches, through an OMR.

MAGNETIC INK CHARACTER READER (MICR)

Yet another input device currently in use is the MAGNETIC INK CHARACTER READER (MICR). This device reads specially produced characters which are printed with magnetic ink. The character set is limited to 14 characters (numbers 0 – 9 and 4 special characters).

The MICR character set

At present, MICRs are used almost exclusively by banks for sorting cheques which can be read at the rate of approximately 2500 per minute. This system is an interesting example of the use of information processing. When the information is entered (using an MICR) into the central clearing facility's computer, a series of transactions happen. Expressed simply the central computer:

- informs your bank's computer of your account number and how much to take off your account

- at the same time informs the payee's bank's computer of his or her account and how much to add to it.

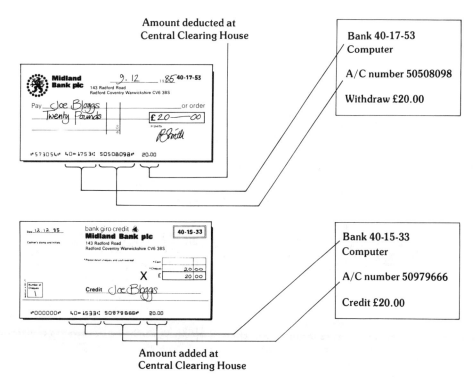

A cheque transaction

BADGE/CARD READERS

These devices are becoming widely used. They:

- accept a special plastic card containing a magnetic strip
- read information encoded on the strip
- process this information.

Badge or card readers are now found in many factories where they have replaced the old clock-card machines. When you 'clock in' or 'clock out' with your badge, the reader automatically notes your employment number and your clocking-in and clocking-out times. This information is fed directly into the payroll and manufacturing systems.

Other common uses for these readers are in money-dispensing machines at banks. The reader:

- reads your personal identity number (PIN) from the card
- you then key your number into the machine
- the machine compares the numbers, and if they are the same, allows you to withdraw money.

There is a growing move towards the introduction of readers in stores linked to bank computers. Then, instead of drawing money out, we shall be able to pay for goods simply by:

- entering our PIN
- entering the amount
- confirming the transaction.

Money (in the form of electronic 'bits') will be removed automatically from our account and credited to the store's account.

A special form of these devices uses 'intelligent cards'. These are cards with a microchip built into them, which allows the reader not only to read information from the card, but to store information as well.

 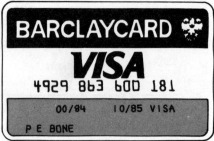

Examples of cards

BAR CODE READERS

BAR CODE READERS are devices used only for fixed items of data and are there-fore not in use with many information processing systems.

Bar codes are:

- produced by special printers

- read by an OPTICAL WAND or a LIGHT PEN which scans the bars (a series of thick and thin lines) and converts them into computer-readable form.

An example of a bar code

Bar code readers are currently in use at POINT-OF-SALE TERMINALS in some supermarkets and discount stores. Most prepacked goods now have bar codes on the wrappers. They operate as follows:

- the bar code is scanned by the reader

- the computer adds the price to the total bill

- the computer automatically adjusts the stock records.

Such devices are also used in some library loan systems and in the identification of blood samples in hospitals. You can see a bar code on the back cover of this book.

VOICE INPUT (MICROPHONES)

VOICE INPUT is regarded as the ultimate in computer input. Its use in word pro-cessing could revolutionize the modern office but it is still largely at the experi-mental stage.

While systems using voice input have been demonstrated, there remain many problems. One problem is created by homophones (that is, words that have identical pronunciation but different meanings and spellings, for example, there/their). This problem has been tackled by the use of software which can recognize homophones and highlight them on a screen. The text can then be corrected by the operator if necessary.

KIMBALL TAG READERS

These readers process Kimball tags that are small cards (approximately 2 in ×
1 in) containing a number of circular holes to represent data. They are used
very like small punched cards and are mostly associated with retail goods.
Often, when you buy clothes they will have Kimball tags on them. Each tag
holds about 12 digits representing the code and price and usually the tag is
attached during manufacture and removed when the garment is sold. The tag is
fed into a tag reader which converts the data into a medium the computer
understands. The information from the cards is fed into stock control computer
programs which automatically update stock levels and reorder when stocks fall
below the required level.

An example of a Kimball tag

THE KEYBOARD

The most widely used form of input in the office is the QWERTY keyboard. It is
interesting to note that the QWERTY keyboard was invented in about 1873 and
the layout of the keys was designed to slow down the typist in order to prevent
the typebars from jamming together.

Attempts have been made over the years to introduce more efficient keyboards.
These have been based on scientific principles such as the frequency of use of
letters and groups of letters and in an attempt to balance the work of the two
hands. The most frequently quoted of these revised keyboards includes:

- the Dvorak, patented in 1932

- the Maltron, designed with the keyboard shaped and the height of the keys
  varied in relation to the shape of the hand.

The Maltron keyboard

These efforts were, however, doomed to failure as it would be commercially impracticable to change from the established layout. Over the years more and more keyboards have come into use and more and more people have been trained to use them. Thus, to introduce a new keyboard would involve the retraining of millions of typists and the scrapping of similar numbers of machines.

A recent, and quite successful design is the Microwriter keyboard. This is designed to be used with one hand with the keys being pressed in combinations meant to mimic the letter being typed.

The Microwriter

Often the keyboard of a word processor or terminal differs from an ordinary typewriter in that it will have a number of additional keys. These are known as FUNCTION KEYS or sometimes COMMAND KEYS. Each of these keys will be responsible for a different function, for example, centring, paging, deleting. Some word processors use mnemonics for the different functions, for example, 'D' for delete, 'O' for output. The number and layout of the function keys will vary according to the make of the machine. Further, all the keys on a word processor are electronic in operation, that is, unlike manual typewriters that work by moving levers, etc, word processor keys generate a byte pattern equal to the character or command.

An amusing story occurred as a result of electronic keyboards being introduced for use by typists trained on manual or electric typewriters. Manufacturers thought that typists would enjoy typing on these keyboards as they were virtually silent. However, they found that speeds actually dropped because the typists were stopping to check the screen to see whether what they had typed had been registered. Since then manufacturers have introduced electronic 'clicks' which sound when keys are depressed.

TOUCH-SENSITIVE SCREENS

These are special screens which have the ability to sense when and where the screen is touched. They are therefore very useful for non-typists. Choices can be displayed on the screen by providing options. Touching the screen next to the option wanted is a simple method of input.

Covering the screen is a fine wire grid or a grid produced by infrared beams of light. When the screen is touched, only those wires or beams under your finger will be affected. The computer can work out which part of the grid is being affected and therefore where the screen is being touched.

LIGHT PENS

Light pens (or wands) are devices which can sense variations in colour and will generate an input signal which the computer can understand. They may be used either to:

- 'draw' on a screen or

- 'wipe' over bar codes as they do when acting as bar code readers.

Because they feel very like a pen or pencil, they are most frequently used when it is necessary to provide drawing-type facilities, such as design, on a computer. Design using a computer is called COMPUTER-AIDED DESIGN (CAD).

DIGITIZING TABLETS

Another input device used as a drawing aid is a digitizing tablet. This is a flat pad often with a special stylus or pen attached. Lines drawn across the pad are translated into a signal, which the computer can process, allowing a drawing to be made.

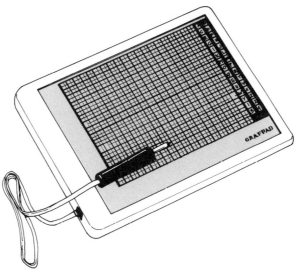

A digitizing tablet

MOUSE DEVICES

These are small boxes which can be moved around any work surface causing the cursor on the screen to move. They were first made widely available on a microcomputer called the Apple Lisa and are probably called mouse devices because they vaguely resemble a small animal scurrying around. As they make using a computer terminal easy, especially for people not trained in keyboard skills, they are becoming fairly standard input devices for office automation terminals designed for managers and non-typists.

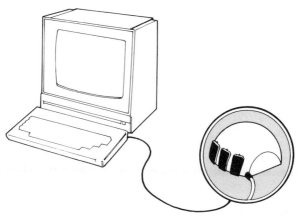

A mouse

The number of devices allowing input to an information processing system is continuously growing. In this chapter we have covered only the more common input peripherals but you should remember that virtually any device which can be made to generate an electrical signal could be an input device to an information processing system.

SUMMARY

All the parts of a computer system, other than the processing unit, are called peripheral devices. Input peripherals allow information to be fed into a computer.

Punched cards and punched paper tape used to be the traditional methods of input to a computer. The main advantage of this was that large amounts of data could be prepared off-line. Batch processing involves preparing large amounts of data and then giving these batches to the computer to be processed.

Key-to-disk/tape is the more modern method of batch processing. Information is keyed directly on to disk or tape and the information is read by the computer from this magnetic medium. This process is faster than the traditional methods. This method of input can now be employed in offices. Normal electric type-writers can be connected to a key-to-disk system. The draft text stored on the disks can subsequently be loaded into the word processor.

Optical character readers (OCRs) are devices capable of reading typewritten text. Text to be fed into the OCR must normally have been prepared using a special typeface (font). This method of input avoids the necessity of duplicate keying-in of documents.

Optical mark readers (OMRs) are input devices which use preprinted forms on which pencil marks are made. The OMR will convert the pencil marks into a form suitable for computer input. It is commonly used for:

- marking multiple-choice examinations
- handling market-research questionnaires
- processing meter readings.

Magnetic ink character readers (MICRs) are devices which read specially produced characters printed with magnetic ink. MICRs are used almost exclusively by banks for sorting cheques.

Badge/card readers accept a special plastic card containing a magnetic strip and read and process the information encoded on the strip. They are commonly used for:

- clocking in and out at factories
- dispensing money at banks' cash points.

Bar code readers are devices used for fixed items of data. The bar code (a series of thick and thin lines) is produced by a special printer and is read by an optical wand or light pen. Bar codes are currently used:

- at point-of-sale terminals in supermarkets and discount stores

- in some library loan systems

- in the identification of blood samples in hospitals.

Voice input (microphone) although currently at the experimental stage is re-garded as the ultimate form of input to a computer.

Kimball tag readers process small cards (Kimball tags) which contain a number of holes. They are used rather like punched cards and are mostly associated with retail goods.

The most common form of input in the office is the QWERTY keyboard. The keyboard of a word processor or terminal usually has additional keys called function or command keys. The keyboard is electronic and every time a key is depressed a byte pattern is generated.

Touch-sensitive screens have the ability to sense where the screen is touched. The screen is covered by a fine wire grid or a grid produced by infrared beams of light.

Light pens or wands are very like a pen or pencil. They can sense variations in colour and will generate an input signal that the computer can understand. They are used to draw on the screen as well as being used as bar code readers.

A digitizing tablet is a flat pad on which lines can be drawn and is used for draw-ing and design. Computer-aided design (CAD) is the name given to design using a computer.

Mouse devices are small boxes which can be moved around any work surface. The cursor moves around the screen correspondingly.

Although only the common input devices have been discussed, it should be remembered that virtually any device that can be made to generate an electrical signal could be an input device to an information processing system.

SELF-CHECK QUESTIONS

1. What is the name given to all devices which are external to the CPU?

2. What is the purpose of an input device?

3. What used to be the traditional method of input to computers?

4. _____ _____ is the term used when information is prepared away from the computer.

5. Explain the term 'batch processing'.

6. a How is the key-to-disk form of input being implemented in office processing systems?

   b What is the advantage of using this form of input?

7. What does OCR stand for?

8. a What is the purpose of an OCR?

   b How does an OCR work?

9. At what speed does an OCR operate?

10. When might an OCR be useful?

11. What does OMR stand for?

12. Why is an OMR useful for marking examination questions?

13. What is the name given to the input device that is used by banks for sorting cheques?

14. Give three examples of where bar code readers are currently in use.

15. Bar codes are produced by special printers. What reads the bar codes?

16. _____ _____ using a microphone can be regarded as the ultimate in computer input.

17. When you buy clothes they sometimes have small tags on them. These tags measure approximately 2 in × 1 in and have a number of circular holes in them. They are used rather like punched cards. What are they called?

18. What is the most widely used form of input in the office?

19. Name three types of keyboard.

20. Give two examples of how the keyboard of a word processor differs from an ordinary typewriter.

21. What is the purpose of a function (or command) key?

22. What is a useful form of input for a non-typist?

23. a What is the name given to design using a computer?

   b What form of input is frequently used when it is necessary to provide the facilities to 'draw' directly on the screen?

   c What is the name given to the flat pad which is also used for drawing and may have a special pen attached?

24. Explain a mouse device.

25. What form of input has replaced the old-fashioned clock card?

26. Which input device do you consider would be most suitable for the following:

    a   recording examination marks

    b   a page of typewritten text – produced with a special typeface

    c   drawing a diagram

    d   keeping a check on all the clothes sold in a chain of shops

    e   keeping a check on a library lending scheme

    f   keeping a check on groceries sold in a supermarket

    g   someone who has no keyboard skills but needs to spend a lot of time retrieving information

    h   analysing the results of a market-research survey

    i   clearing cheques in a bank's clearing house

    j   keeping a check on the times that employees work and using these hours for calculating wages?

6

OUTPUT DEVICES

Chapter Objectives

After studying this chapter you should be able to:

1. Explain the purpose of any output device.
2. List and describe the most common output devices.
3. Compare impact and non-impact printers.
4. Describe the paper-feed mechanisms associated with printers.
5. Explain the methods adopted for producing COM.

END OF OBJECTIVES END OF OBJECTIVES END OF OBJECTIVES END OF OBJECTIVES

INTRODUCTION

Virtually all the information stored, processed or transmitted within an information processing system will be coded into binary digits or bits. It is possible for us to decode these binary digits but the task is extremely slow and tedious. Therefore, just as we have devices to translate or code information for input, there are also many devices to convert binary information into a form we readily understand. These devices are called output devices and this chapter looks at the more common types associated with information processing systems.

PRINTERS

As the results from computer processing are frequently required in printed form, the printer is an output device of considerable significance. Printers cover a much wider range of capabilities than most other peripherals, and this is reflected in their range of costs.

Early printers were mechanical devices, that is, they had lots of moving parts. These were:

- expensive
- relatively slow
- prone to breakdowns.

Basically, the higher the mechanical content of a machine, the more likely it is to break down because it is the moving mechanical parts which suffer wear and tear. Today, printers rely more on electronics than mechanics and are consequently faster, cheaper and more reliable.

There are several types of printer currently available and they can be separated into two main categories:

- IMPACT PRINTERS. These work by applying pressure against a ribbon on to the paper – just like a typewriter. The contact made transfers ink from the ribbon to the paper to form the required image.

- NON-IMPACT PRINTERS. These produce images without any physical impact being made on the paper.

Impact Printers

Type Bars

The earliest automatic typewriters used ordinary TYPE-BAR mechanisms in which the type was arranged in the familiar semi-circular baskets. They both looked and worked very like manual typewriters with a series of levers connected to each letter. The high number of moving parts tended to make them unreliable. They were painfully slow and are not used in modern word/information processing equipment.

Golf-ball Heads

An improvement over the type-bar mechanism was the GOLF BALL which:

- raised the printer's speed

- improved reliability

- reduced the number of moving parts.

The golf ball moves along a fixed platen and swivels and turns to match the keys tapped. Golf-ball heads can be changed to produce many different typestyles and different pitches. The typical speed of a golf-ball printer is approximately 15-20 characters per second (cps) and, although still used by some typewriter manufacturers, these printers are not common with modern systems as they cannot reach the desired speeds.

A golf-ball head

Daisy-wheel Printers

The DAISY-WHEEL printer is very common in the word processing market. The printing element, as the name suggests, consists of flexible arms extending from the centre like petals on a daisy flower. The type-heads (or letters) are at the tip of the petals – one character to each. Like the golf ball, the daisy wheel moves across a fixed platen.

A daisy-wheel

A variation on the daisy-wheel printer is the THIMBLE. It uses the same principle as the daisy wheel except that it looks rather like an upturned cup.

A thimble

Many daisy-wheel printers are:

● bi-directional, that is, they print both ways from left to right and from right to left

● logic-seeking, that is, they can be spun in either direction with the printer choosing the quickest direction to the character required for printing.

The daisy wheels are easily changed and many different type-styles are available. Variable pitch, ten, twelve or fifteen characters to the inch or proportional spacing are all possible.

Daisy-wheel printers operate at speeds ranging from about 12 cps to 55 cps. Assuming the British standard of five characters to the word, the fastest machines operate at 540 wpm!

These printers produce high-quality printing and thus are most suitable for word processing applications. They are sometimes referred to as LETTER-QUALITY PRINTERS.

Dot-matrix Printers

In this type of printer, characters are formed by a number of dots. The print head consists of a number of needles, the number and spacing of which affect the print quality. Generally speaking, the closer the packing of the needles and the greater their number, the better will be the quality of the final print.

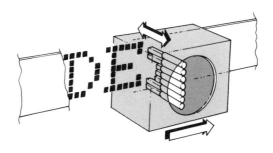

A dot-matrix print head

A typical 'matrix' of dots per character is 5×7, but this size is insufficient for the production of descenders (g,j,p,q,y) below the print line and for the printing of superscripts and subscripts. A matrix of 7×9, however, does allow for these features although even with these, because the characters are made up of a series of dots, the output has not normally been considered to be of 'letter quality'. The great advantage of dot-matrix printers is their speed of operation ranging from 30 cps on the cheaper models to 200 or more cps on the faster, more expensive models.

Current print quality available on dot-matrix printers rules out most models for use in word processing systems. However, developments are taking place which could make them the printers of the future, especially in the 'electronic office'.

The latest types do produce near-letter quality (NLQ) by double printing, that is, the printer prints a line of text then moves the head down fractionally before printing the same line. This overtyping produces a very good quality print. These printers are slightly faster than daisy-wheel printers and can interchange fonts on the same line. Additionally, with many of them, it is possible to print normal high-speed (120 cps) matrix or letter quality (55 cps).

Furthermore, dot-matrix printers have the ability to reproduce high-resolution graphics, pictures and even signatures and this flexibility may make them the most relevant for the purpose of printing 'electronic mail'.

Dot Matrix Letters

Line Printers

This type of printer is most common with computer systems which require high-speed rather than quality printing. It is a complex and relatively expensive device which operates at high speeds, ranging from 200 to 2000 lines per minute, with up to 136 characters per line. At these speeds it gives the appearance of printing an entire line in one action, hence the term 'line printer'. These are INTELLIGENT PRINTERS, that is, they have some built-in computing power of their own. This capability allows the printer to print each letter as soon as it arrives at the correct position on the line. Thus it might print:

- an 'A' at position 40
- then a 'Z' at position 70
- then a 'P' at position 41 and an 'O' at position 71 (at the same time).

In effect, the line is printed randomly with letters appearing anywhere on it. The printer 'knows' what should be printed where and what has been printed and once all the required characters for a complete line have been printed, the printer will move on to the next line and the process is repeated. Although line-matrix printers, with a large number of matrix heads, are appearing, line printers are of two main types:

- drum printers
- chain printers.

A DRUM PRINTER comprises a drum (barrel) with characters embossed around the circumference. The drum rotates continuously at high speeds and a set of hammers (one per print position) strike the required characters.

In a CHAIN PRINTER the characters are embossed on a chain and the chain rotates continuously in a horizontal plane. Like the drum printer there is a hammer for each print position. This strikes at the exact instant when the appropriate character is opposite the print position.

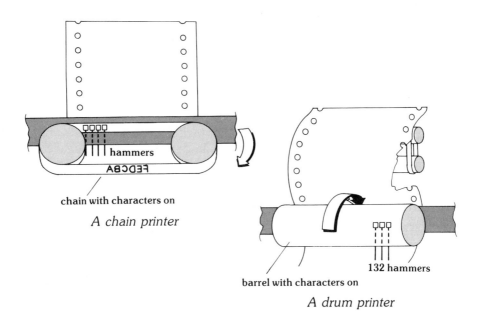

chain with characters on

A chain printer

barrel with characters on

132 hammers

A drum printer

Non-impact Printers

Thermal Printers/Spark-jet Printers

A thermal printer is a non-impact dot-matrix printer. The image is created by the reaction of specially treated paper with heat generated by the print-head as it passes over the surface. The heat is often produced by an electric spark from the print-head passing through the paper on to the platen. The special thermal paper is produced by coating an ordinary base paper with a very thin layer of heat-sensitive chemicals. The main advantages of thermal printers and all non-impact printers are their:

● silent operation

● speed

● reliability.

However, one of the disadvantages of thermal printers is that the special paper is often expensive.

Ink-jet Printers

The ink-jet printer mechanism was developed by A.B. Dick for use in the computer industry and was refined by IBM to allow printing speeds of approximately 90 cps (which is about 1100 words per minute).

The characters are formed on paper by electrostatically spraying it with a stream of ink drops in the shape of the character(s) required. These drops are dried by being absorbed into the paper.

ink-jet print

Letters being printed by an ink-jet printer

The characters are not produced singly in their entirety, but by the print-head making several passes along the line, producing part of each letter at each pass.

Since no typewriter face bars, elements or petals hit the surface of the paper, this technique is almost soundless. Despite having a high output speed, the quality of the print is excellent making this equipment much in demand in busy offices. Unlike thermal printers, ink-jet printers use ordinary paper and some can produce multi-coloured print by using different coloured inks. These will have as many jets as there are colours of ink.

Laser-Xerographic Printers

These printers operate like a normal photocopier except that a laser beam is used to produce characters on the photocopier-type drum rather than by transferring the image from a sheet of paper. They operate as follows:

- the laser beam shines on to the drum causing the electrical surface of the drum to change

- the toner then sticks to those parts of the drum on which the laser has shone

- the paper is passed over the drum

- the toner is transferred on to the paper

- the paper is heated causing the toner to become fixed.

INTELLIGENT COPIERS have now been developed from laser printers. Some of these act as both input and output devices. They will change a document into digital form so that they can be stored on disk (an OCR) and will allow digital information to be printed off as a document by using the techniques described. They contain their own microprocessor which controls the laser scanner and printer and information sent by the computer will be stored and used by this microprocessor to control the printing or digitizing process.

As these printers are microprocessor-controlled and the laser beam can be moved in any direction, they:

- produce very high-quality print

- allow numerous types of type-styles to be used on the same page

- allow the size of characters to be changed

- can intersperse text with diagrams and graphs

- can be used as a normal photocopier
- will often allow multiple copies and collating of output.

The major advantage with this type of printer is the high quality and speed with output ranging from about 10 pages per minute to 100 per minute (equivalent to between 600 and 6000 lines per minute).

The price of laser printers has fallen steeply over the past few years. Until recently, the cheapest cost tens of thousands of pounds. Today it is possible to buy a small desk-top laser printer for around £2000.

PLOTTERS

Another class of output-on-paper devices are plotters. These devices consist of a flat surface over which a pen passes. The computer will control the pen to draw out a pattern or diagram. They are most often used to produce large engineering-type diagrams or graphs up to A0 size and many now have various coloured pens which allow different colours to be used in the same diagram.

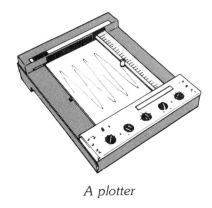

A plotter

PAPER FEEDERS

All printers required to do large volumes of printing need some mechanism to feed the paper into the printer as it is inefficient to hand-feed them. Three types of paper feeder are used.

Hopper, Bin or Sheet Feeders

These are mounted on top of the printer and allow one sheet of paper at a time into the print area. A bin at the front collects the printed output. Some of these have two paper-feed bins and take the first sheet from the front bin and the continuation sheets from the rear bin – a particularly useful feature when using letter-headed paper. They are loaded with loose-leaf paper and are common with lower-speed printers.

A hopper feeder

Tractor Feeders/Pin Feeders

These mechanisms are most common with high-speed impact printers. The mechanism consists of toothed cogs at each end of the platen or a special cogged mechanism which fits on top of the printer. The continuous paper used has a series of holes on each edge which fit over the cogs and as the cogs are turned they draw the paper over the platen. With most tractor feeders it is possible to change the distance between the cogs, thus allowing the use of different widths of paper.

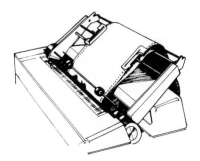

A tractor feeder

Cartridge Feeders

These are found on the laser or intelligent copiers and are just like those found on normal photocopiers. The paper is loaded into a cartridge tray which is placed into the machine. The feed mechanism then draws out one page at a time for printing.

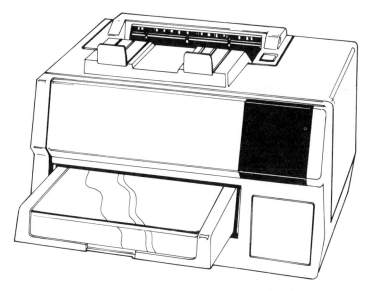

A laser printer with a cartridge feed

COMPUTER OUTPUT ON MICROFILM (COM) RECORDERS

The storage of large volumes of printed material on paper may pose the problem of inadequate storage space. Early attempts to alleviate this problem involved the photographing of printed documents on 16 mm film, thereby reducing its bulk; the stored documents could be read using a viewer which projected the information on to a small screen.

Today, documents can be photographed directly from the computer on to microfilm and this technique is known as Computer Output on Microfilm (COM). Microfilm is now used extensively in:

● libraries

● building societies

● finance houses, etc.

For the fast retrieval of information, two methods are used for producing COM documents. The first involves the use of lasers to print directly on to the film while in the other method the information is projected on to a screen (which is inside the COM recorder) and a camera is used to photograph the images.

The most common forms of microfilm in use are 16 mm roll film and micro-fiche. Microfiche is becoming more popular. It is sheet film usually measuring 105 mm × 148 mm and is more flexible than roll film especially for distribution purposes. Microfiche can be produced directly by a COM recorder and the special software available can produce an index on the microfiche itself. Information is then accessed by means of a special viewer.

Although still very expensive, there are available COM readers that are fully integrated into information processing systems. These devices are, in reality, more a form of storage in that they store output which can be readily retrieved for reprocessing when necessary. They store information on microfiche under the control of a computer, which also physically files the sheets, and stores an index on disk. If information so stored is subsequently required, the inquirer can:

● look through the index

● select the topic or sheet reference.

The computer will then:

● retrieve the sheet

● redigitize the information

● display the digital image on the VDU screen.

A COM reader

THE VISUAL DISPLAY UNIT (VDU)

These are generally similar to a television screen, and may sometimes be referred to as:

● a cathode ray tube (CRT)

● a monitor

● a visual display terminal (VDT).

Results and messages are displayed on a screen rather than printed on paper. There are different types of VDU including those that display alphanumeric characters and those that display graphical symbols as well. Most VDUs produce images using a series of dots – much as a dot-matrix printer does. The more dots that can be displayed, the better the images produced. The dots are termed PIXELS and the more pixels there are to the screen, the higher the RESOLUTION the VDU is said to have.

VDUs vary in size, shape and colour according to the design of the manufacturer. At the bottom end of the market we have the 'thin window' single display line, which is only capable of showing the last 30 or so characters typed. The most common size displays 80 characters across and 24 lines down, while some screens are full A4 size.

Normally VDUs use cathode ray tubes. These are, however, both bulky and heavy which limits their suitability for light, portable computers. This has resulted in a trend towards liquid-crystal or gas-plasma displays. These are similar to the type of display found on many digital watches or calculators. These display units are thin and light and are therefore ideal for lightweight portable microcomputers which will become a key feature in information processing systems especially as a new generation of people, familiar with using screens rather than paper hard copy, become the users of systems.

VOICE OUTPUT

Two forms of voice output (via loudspeaker) are under development and although experimental are likely to become more commonly used in information processing. To produce voice output, either prerecorded words must be stored on disk or the computer must be programmed to know how to produce voice-like sounds.

Information systems that can acoustically read out text typed in via word processors already exist.

A much simpler use of voice output is, however, already being used. It is possible to input a voice message which is linked to a particular document then, whenever the document is displayed on the VDU, the voice message will be replayed. These are often referred to as VOICEGRAMS.

SUMMARY

Output devices translate binary digits into a form readily recognized by humans.

There is a wide variety of printers that create output on paper. They fall into two categories: impact and non-impact.

Impact printers create an image by having a print element which actually strikes the paper through a ribbon.

Non-impact printers produce images without any physical impact being made on the paper.

Early printers used type bars just as in typewriters. Later, letter-quality printers used a golf-ball print element while the latest use a print wheel that resembles a daisy flower and are therefore called daisy-wheel printers. They print at speeds of between 12 and 55 cps. Many of these printers are bi-directional and logic-seeking.

Dot-matrix printers produce characters by a matrix of dots. These printers work at speeds of 30 to 200 cps. By printing a line and then moving the print element slightly and reprinting the line it is possible for these printers to produce near letter-quality print.

Dot-matrix printers can produce graphs, pictures and signatures.

Drum printers and chain printers are the most common forms of line printer. The former uses a rotating barrel or drum with characters on, while the latter uses a chain with characters on which rotates continuously in front of the paper. Both have a number of print hammers, often one for each print position. Line printers operate at high speeds of between 200 and 2000 lpm.

Non-impact printers are quiet, reliable and fast.

Thermal or spark-jet printers produce images via a series of dots. They use a special paper which is coated with heat-sensitive chemicals. A spark from the print head to the platen produces the dot.

Ink-jet printers work at about 90 cps. They produce high-quality print by spraying a fine jet of ink on to the paper.

Laser-Xerographic printers use a technique like that found in photocopiers except that the image formed on the copier drum is produced by a laser beam under computer control. They operate at high speeds producing pages at a time. Speeds range from about 10 pages per minute to 100 pages per minute. As they work like a photocopier it is possible for these printers to produce almost any form of output including printing that looks like handwriting.

Intelligent copiers have developed from these printers. These devices can be used as OCRs or as printers and can collate, staple and multi-copy.

Plotters use pens to draw images on paper. They are usually flat and produce drawings on paper up to A0 size.

Paper-feed devices are required to supply printers with paper. These are usually bin or cut-sheet feeders which accept normal typing paper and feed in one sheet at a time, tractor or pin feeders which accept continuous paper and cartridge feeders which take normal cut paper.

It is possible to produce output from a computer directly on to microfilm or microfiche (COM). This form of output is produced either by using lasers to produce the image on film or by producing the image on a screen and then photographing the screen.

Visual Display Units (VDUs) are the most common form of computer output device. Most VDUs use cathode ray tubes (CRTs) like those in television sets.

Some displays are single-line displays called 'thin-window displays'. These are used on few machines: the more common size is 80 characters by 24 lines. Increasingly, portable computers are using liquid-crystal or gas-plasma displays as these are light and thin unlike CRTs.

All VDUs can display characters and some with high resolutions can also display graphics.

Two forms of voice output are becoming more common. The first uses pre-recorded words while the other produces words via programs.

It is already possible to find information systems with a voice output that will read information to you or store a recorded message as part of a document. The message is replayed every time someone displays the document on a VDU.

SELF-CHECK QUESTIONS

1. What is the purpose of an output device?

2. Why are printers today faster, cheaper and more reliable than earlier printers?

3. **a** Printers can be separated into two main categories. What are they?

   b Explain the difference between the two.

4. What type of printer is most commonly used for word processing?

5. Most printers are bi-directional. What does this mean?

6. Explain what is meant by the term 'logic-seeking' in connection with printers.

7. What types of printer are most common with computer systems that require high-speed printing?

8. A line printer gives the impression of printing an entire line in one action. What actually happens?

9. What are the two main types of line printer?

10. What kind of printer forms characters by a number of dots?

11. Explain why dot-matrix printers will become of more use in the 'electronic office'.

12. Give two advantages of using a dot matrix printer.

13. Name three non-impact printers.

14. What is the main advantage of non-impact printers?

15. Give one disadvantage of a thermal printer.

16. How does an ink-jet printer work?

17. Give six features of laser-Xerographic printers.

18. What type of output device would be used to produce patterns and diagrams?

19. What is the name given to a paper-feed mechanism that is mounted on top of a printer and is used for feeding single sheets of paper?

20. Some printers use continuous paper with holes down each edge. What is the purpose of the holes?

21. With what type of printer would a cartridge feeder be used?

22. Place the following in order of speed:

    a   ink-jet printer

    b   dot-matrix printer

    c   line printer

    d   daisy-wheel printer

    e   laser printer

23. What does COM stand for?

24. Explain the two methods of producing COM documents.

25. What is the main advantage of microfilm?

26. What do the following stand for:

    a   VDU

    b   CRT

    c   VDT?

27. What is the function of the VDU?

28. What type of display screen is thin and light and thus ideal for portable micro-computers?

7

STORAGE DEVICES

Chapter Objectives

After studying this chapter you should be able to:

1. Explain the purpose of a backing store.

2. List the most common forms of backing store.

3. Identify the features of floppy disks and hard disks.

4. Assess the advantages and disadvantages of the more modern forms of backing store.

END OF OBJECTIVES END OF OBJECTIVES END OF OBJECTIVES END OF OBJECTIVES

INTRODUCTION

As we have already mentioned in this book, the CPU has only a limited amount of memory. Usually most of this memory is random access or volatile memory which loses or 'forgets' everything when the electrical power is switched off. Thus it is necessary to have some form of permanent store for information. Storage outside the CPU is known as secondary storage or backing store and in this chapter we are going to discuss the various types of storage device.

Although early computers used punched cards and punched paper tape as forms of backing store, these are now obsolete and need not concern us although it should be remembered that, for cheapness and ability to resist damage, paper storage is still useful for some applications. We shall concentrate on magnetic storage which is the main way of storing information today. Any form of magnetic storage consists of magnetic impulses being registered for binary digits.

MAGNETIC CARD DEVICES

An early form of magnetic storage device was the MAGNETIC CARD storage machines. These use plastic cards about the size of a punched card and coated with a magnetizable covering similar to that found on cassette tapes.

The cards:

● hold on average about 5000 characters each – one A4 page – and some hold up to 10 000 characters

- were originally developed for the earliest forms of word processor which were really golf-ball typewriters that could store typed information on a magnetic card.

The cards are inserted into a slot in a device called a MAGNETIC CARD READER which is linked to the typewriter.

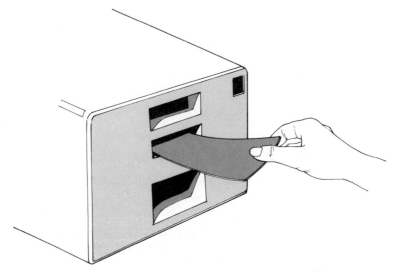

A magnetic card reader

TAPE RECORDERS

Two forms of tape-storage device are common in information processing systems: cassette or cartridge tape recorders and reel-to-reel tape recorders.

CASSETTE recorders are common with home microcomputers. Data is stored by these just as you would store a song on a cassette tape. In fact, if you play one of these tapes through a tape recorder you will hear two sounds: a low tone for a '0' and a high tone for a '1'.

Although easy to use, cassette recorders have one major disadvantage in that they are slow. The speed by which data is recorded on cassette tape is measured in BAUD, which for most cases, is equivalent to bits per second. Thus a tape recorder that operates at 1200 baud will be recording 1200 bits per second on the tape while a 300 baud tape recorder would record 300 bits per second. It should be stressed that it is the computer that controls the speed data is written to or read from a cassette recorder.

Obviously the longer the cassette tape and the faster data is recorded, the more information can be held on it, but the amount of storage ranges between 50 Kb and 250 Kb.

Newer developments with this type of system are called CARTRIDGE or STREAMER tape recorders. Some of these work much like the old-fashioned eight-track tape players in that the tape will go continuously round and round – it does not have a beginning or an end. Others use a cassette or cartridge two or three times larger than a normal audio cassette tape. It is possible to store information on these tapes at high speeds and in large amounts. For example, it is possible to store on one streamer 10 Mb in about two minutes.

Streamer tape recorders are called 'streamers' because of the method used to store data. There are no gaps: it is stored in one continuous stream.

The main advantages of cassette or cartridge tape systems are their:

● ease of use

● storage capacity

● security (information stored is not easily lost through accidental dropping).

A cassette tape

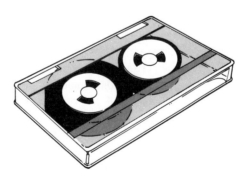

A cartridge tape

Special REEL-TO-REEL tape drives are used for high-speed storage of large amounts of information on tape. For most people they are perhaps the most easily recognized part of computers. If you think of any film you have seen with computers in it, there will always have been big banks of tape drives with tapes spinning around in them.

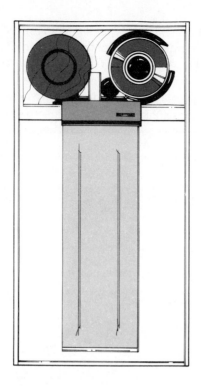

A reel-to-reel drive

The reason why these tape drives are capable of storing much more information than cassette tapes is that the latter put one bit after another on the tape, whereas reel-to-reels use much wider tape and record one byte after another. To do this they have to write at least seven bits across the tape, that is, from top to bottom. Most modern tape systems use nine bits. Bits 1 to 8 inclusive are the eight bits forming a byte. The ninth bit, called the parity bit, is used as a parity check. With an even parity system, if the number of bits added together is odd then the parity bit is set, making sure the total of all bits is always even. Thus if the total of the bits is uneven when the computer reads data from the tape, it knows the tape has been misread. Again, the length of tape affects the amount of information that can be stored and different models vary enormously but 40 Mb to 100 Mb is a reasonable range for storage on this type of tape.

All tape devices store data sequentially, that is, they record data from beginning to end. To find the information you require you must:

- start at the beginning of the tape

- play it through until you arrive at the place at which the information is recorded.

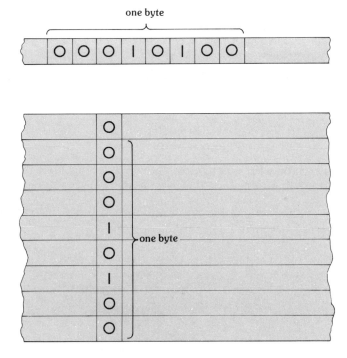

Data stored serially on a cassette tape and in parallel on a reel-to-reel tape

This is just like finding a track on a cassette tape. It is much more useful to have information that is stored on a device which allows 'random access'. What is meant by random access? Consider a record player. If you want a particular track on a record you:

- read the index of the record sleeve to find the number of the track you want

- move the record arm to that track on the record

- lower the arm.

This type of random access storage is common in information processing systems and uses magnetic disk devices to record and retrieve information from magnetic disks. These disk devices fall broadly into two categories:

- floppy/flexible disk devices

- hard disk devices.

DISK DRIVES

There are two types of disk drive: FLOPPY DISK (diskette) drives and HARD DISK drives.

83

Drives for floppy disks use either:

- disks of flexible plastic coated with magnetic material and enclosed in a cardboard sleeve

- disks of flexible plastic coated with magnetic material and enclosed in a rigid plastic case.

The disks:

- look like a 45 gramophone record

- have a window cut in the sleeve through which the heads of the disk drive can touch the magnetic surface and so record information

- come in three standard sizes – 3.5 in, 5.25 in and 8 in (sometimes called micro-floppies, mini-floppies and floppies)

A floppy disk (diskette)

- store between 100 Kb and 1.5 Mb depending on the size of the disks and the way data is stored on the disk.

Drives that allow data to be recorded on only one side of a disk are called single-sided while, naturally enough, drives that access both sides of a disk are called double-sided.

A floppy disk drive

Obviously the more bits that can be stored per square centimetre, the more information that can be stored on a DISKETTE. The number of bits per square centimetre is called the PACKING DENSITY of the disk drive. It is possible with some computers to increase the packing density – to store twice the amount of information on the same area. This facility is called DOUBLE DENSITY.

A third method by which the storage on disks can be increased is to increase the number of 'tracks' on which data is stored. Every disk drive will write data to a disk on concentric 'rings' beginning at the outer edge of the disk and stepping inwards each time a track is filled. Clearly, the narrower the track the more of them there can be on a disk. 35-, 40- and 80-track disk drives are standard.

Thus it can be seen that the lowest storage disk drive will be a single-sided, single-density, 35-track device, while the highest storage will be found on an 80-track, double-sided, double-density device.

The disk drives are cabinets that contain the READ/WRITE mechanisms and the motor that spins the disks. The disks are slotted into the drives. Sometimes a fan, usually at the rear of the cabinet, blows clean filtered air through the drive. This has the dual purpose of preventing over-heating while maintaining an increased atmospheric pressure within the drive to hinder the entrance of any dust particles.

Floppy disks are limited in their storage and spin relatively slowly which limits the rate by which information can be retrieved.

To increase the amount of information that can be stored on disk and to speed up the rate of retrieval, it is necessary to speed up the rate at which the disk turns and to increase the packing density. To increase the packing density means making the recording heads smaller.

However, smaller heads would damage the magnetic coating if they were touching the disk surface – as they do on floppy disks. Thus it is necessary for manufacturers to make disk systems whereby the recording heads do not touch the disk surface. To achieve this they design heads which float or fly very close to, but not touching, the disk surface. This technology has a distinctive advantage in that, to make the heads fly, the disk must also be spinning at very high speeds.

Obviously the disk itself cannot be flexible like the floppy disk or else it would touch the heads and so damage the recording surface. (When this happens on hard disk systems it is called a head crash and results in both the disk and the disk drive heads being ruined.)

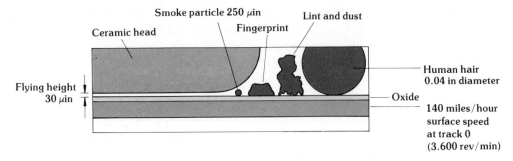

Smoke particle 250 μin

Ceramic head

Fingerprint

Lint and dust

Flying height
30 μin

Human hair
0.04 in diameter

Oxide

140 miles/hour
surface speed
at track 0
(3.600 rev/min)

A disk and read/write heads

Winchester Disk Drives

Hard disk is now the predominant form of information storage on all large-scale information or data processing systems.

For smaller word processing or microcomputer systems, disk drives called WINCHESTER DRIVES are becoming very common. These hard-disk drives are totally sealed from the environment and it is not usual for the disks themselves to be removed. Winchester disks range in their storage capacity from about 1 to 40 Mb, although some newer 5.25-in drives can store 200 Mb. The advantage of Winchester disk systems is that, because they are so well sealed, no dust or dirt can enter into them and so they can be used almost anywhere. The term 'Winchester drives' comes from the name of the town in which IBM first produced this type of disk drive.

A recent development has been ultra-thin Winchester disks which are mounted on an electronics board (see page 21). These HARD CARDS are simple to install as they are slotted into the mother board just as would any other card. Capacities range between 10 and 40 Mb.

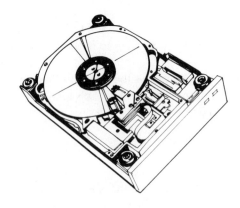

The internal workings of a Winchester

Disk Drives

Larger-scale disk drives may have either removable or fixed disks. Unlike floppy disks, these bigger drives often have a number of disks on a central spindle, thus giving five or perhaps eleven disks all joined together. This is called a DISK PACK. It is possible to store from about 10 Mb to 1 Gb on this type of disk system. The disks themselves actually spin at about 200 kilometres per hour.

A disk pack

As these disk packs and drives are not sealed from the environment it is extremely important to keep them in special air-conditioned and filtered computer rooms.

What makes disks useful is their ability to allow random accessing of information.

This is achieved by having the heads, which either read the information from or write it to the disk, on special arms which can move in and out over the disk surface. These are called read/write heads. Thus if the particular piece of information you want happens to be stored half-way across the disk surface, the computer will instruct the heads to move in towards the centre until they get to the right track on the disk so that the information can be read.

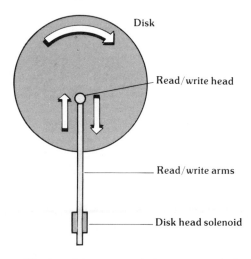

The read/write mechanism on a disk

FUTURE STORAGE

There are other forms of backing store which may well prove to be more common in the future. These are called:

- bubble memory devices
- optical or laser disk.

At the moment they are not widely used, but both have advantages over the traditional disk drive systems and so may well become more commercially accepted in the future. Bubble memory still works with magnetic storage but it can be built into a chip-like device and so can be smaller, faster and store more information than on a floppy disk. It is likely that if it does 'catch on' it could be used in place of RAM as it has the added advantage of not losing the information when the machine is turned off. However, its average ACCESS TIME, that is, the time taken to retrieve information from the storage device is higher than for RAM.

A bubble memory device

Much research is now being conducted into optical disk storage and drives are becoming commercially available. Currently it is not possible to change information stored on optical disks and most optical disk drives only read data pre-stored on a disk. However, as optical disks are very durable and easily transported, there is a growing use of these disks as a form of ROM. Programs (or less frequently data) can be distributed on disk whenever changes are made. These disks are called CD-ROM disks (Compact Disk Read Only Memory).

Some manufacturers now market optical disk drives which allow data to be stored on a disk. Once stored, this data cannot be erased or modified. This is termed a WORM drive – Write only Once, Read Many times.

Laser or optical disks:

- are non-magnetic

- record information on a special shiny disk about the size of a 12-in long-playing record

- store information in binary code in the form of microscopic pits which can be read by a laser beam

- can hold up to 1250 Mb or 1.25 gigabytes. (A gigabyte is 1000 Mb or 1 billion bytes.) When you consider that a major encyclopaedia contains about 250 million characters you can see that the amount of information that can be stored on just one of these disks is enormous.

- are virtually indestructible

- take on average less than a tenth of a second to find any piece of information on them.

A laser disk

SUMMARY

As the CPU has only a limited memory and usually most of this is volatile, it is necessary to have some form of secondary storage (backing store).

Early computers used punched card and punched paper tape but this is now obsolete. The main way to store information today is on a magnetic medium. Magnetic card storage was an early form of storage medium developed for word processors.

Two types of tape storage device are common with information processing systems. Cassette tapes are common with microcomputers but a disadvantage is that they are slow. The speed by which data is recorded on cassette tape is measured in baud which, in most cases, is equivalent to bits per second.

A new development is cartridge or streamer tape recorders. These are of two types:

- the type that works much like an eight-track tape player with the tape going continuously round and round – it has neither beginning nor end

- the type that uses a cassette or cartridge two or three times larger than a normal audio cassette.

Streamers are easy to use, have a large storage capacity and operate at high speeds.

Reel-to-reel tape drives are used for very large amounts of information. All tape devices store information sequentially – they record data from beginning to end. To retrieve data you must start at the beginning of the tape and play it through until you find the required data.

Cassette tapes store data by putting one bit after another on the tape. Reel-to-reel tapes are wider and write at least seven bits across the tape – from top to bottom.

Random access storage is common with information processing systems and uses magnetic disk devices to store data. These devices fall broadly into two categories:

- floppy/flexible-disk drives

- hard-disk devices.

Floppy disks are of flexible plastic coated with magnetic material and enclosed in either a cardboard sleeve or a rigid plastic case. A window cut in the sleeve allows the heads of the disk drive to touch the magnetic surface and to read and write information. Floppy disks come in three sizes: 3.5 in, 5.25 in and 8 in. The amount of data that can be stored depends on whether the disk is:

- single-sided or double-sided

- single-density or double-density

- 35-, 40- or 80-track.

The disk drives are cabinets that contain the read/write heads and a motor which spins the disk.

Hard disks are now the predominant form of storage on large-scale information processing systems. With this form of disk the heads do not touch the disk surface but float very close to it.

Winchester disk drives are becoming common with smaller word processing and microcomputer systems. The disks are totally sealed in a case and it is not usual to remove them. As no dirt or dust can enter into the disks they can be used anywhere.

Larger-scale disk drives use either fixed or removable disks. Some systems have a number of disks on a central spindle. This is called a disk pack. As disk packs and drives are not sealed they need special environmental conditions.

Bubble memory storage devices and optical or laser disks are likely to become more common in the future. Bubble memory is a form of magnetic storage but can be built into a chip-like device.

Laser or optical disks are not magnetic. Information is stored on a shiny disk approximately 12 inches in diameter. Binary code is stored as microscopic pits which can be read by a laser beam.

SELF-CHECK QUESTIONS

1. Why is it necessary to have some form of secondary storage?

2. An early form of magnetic storage was the m_____ c_____.

3. What is a common form of storage with microcomputers?

4. If you played a cassette tape that had data stored on it what would you hear?

5. What is baud equivalent to in most cases?

6. What is the major disadvantage of using a cassette tape?

7. What is the difference between a cassette tape and a cartridge or streamer?

8. We have said in this chapter that a cassette tape works 'sequentially'. Explain what is meant by this.

9. How does a reel-to-reel tape differ from a cassette tape in the way it stores data?

10. Which form of storage provides 'random access'?

11. List four features of a floppy disk.

12. What are the three standard sizes of floppy disk?

13. Explain the following terms when used in relation to floppy disks:
   a   single-sided
   b   double-sided
   c   packing density
   d   double-density.

14. The disk drives contain the read/write heads. They also contain a fan. What is the purpose of the fan?

15. Give two limitations of floppy disks?

16. What are the two main advantages of hard disks?

17. What is the name given to the hard disks that are totally sealed?

18. In large-scale disk drives several disks are joined together on a central spindle. What is this called?

19. Name the two forms of backing storage that may well prove to be common in the future.

20. What is the advantage of bubble memory over RAM?

21. What is the major advantage of laser disks?

22. Word search. Below are 20 words and abbreviations covered in the last three chapters. See whether you can find them.

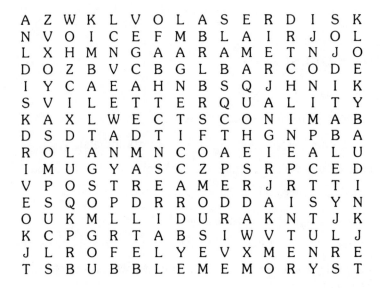

```
A  Z  W  K  L  V  O  L  A  S  E  R  D  I  S  K
N  V  O  I  C  E  F  M  B  L  A  I  R  J  O  L
L  X  H  M  N  G  A  A  R  A  M  E  T  N  J  O
D  O  Z  B  V  C  B  G  L  B  A  R  C  O  D  E
I  Y  C  A  E  A  H  N  B  S  Q  J  H  N  I  K
S  V  I  L  E  T  T  E  R  Q  U  A  L  I  T  Y
K  A  X  L  W  E  C  T  S  C  O  N  I  M  A  B
D  S  D  T  A  D  T  I  F  T  H  G  N  P  B  A
R  O  L  A  N  M  N  C  O  A  E  I  E  A  L  U
I  M  U  G  Y  A  S  C  Z  P  S  R  P  C  E  D
V  P  O  S  T  R  E  A  M  E  R  J  R  T  T  I
E  S  Q  O  P  D  R  R  O  D  D  A  I  S  Y  N
O  U  K  M  L  L  I  D  U  R  A  K  N  T  J  K
K  C  P  G  R  T  A  B  S  I  W  V  T  U  L  J
J  L  R  O  F  E  L  Y  E  V  X  M  E  N  R  E
T  S  B  U  B  B  L  E  M  E  M  O  R  Y  S  T
```

8

USING STORAGE

Chapter Objectives

After studying this chapter you should be able to:

1. Describe how the CPU uses backing storage to increase its power and flexibility.
2. Define the three methods adopted in the use of backing storage.
3. Explain the difference between system drive and work or file drive.
4. Recognize the importance of a DBMS in information processing systems.
5. Describe 'virtual storage' – how it operates and why it is a useful feature.
6. Explain how a disk is formatted.
7. Compare hard-sectored and soft-sectored disks.
8. List the items of information that are contained in a disk index.

END OF OBJECTIVES END OF OBJECTIVES END OF OBJECTIVES END OF OBJECTIVES

INTRODUCTION

We have previously considered the three groupings of peripherals which comprise part of an information processing system plus the central processing unit. In this chapter we shall look at how the CPU uses backing storage to increase the power and flexibility of its operation.

OPERATING SYSTEMS

If you remember, we said that the operating system:

- comprises a number of programs
- controls the operation of the CPU
- manages the use (and operation) of peripheral devices.

To use an analogy, the operating system (OS) is like an office manager. It is the office manager's role to ensure the smooth, efficient operation of the office, thus allowing the other office workers to concentrate on their specific jobs. Thus, in an accounts office the office manager is not usually an accountant but an administrator.

93

Different managers will run the same type of office in different ways and you may well find that when you change jobs it takes quite some time for you to adjust to the new office routines. Operating systems are the same. There are different operating systems for different machines and, in some cases, different operating systems for the same type of machine. Each operating system 'manages' the configuration differently which often makes it awkward to use data from one machine on another and usually impossible to transfer programs directly from one operating system to another.

To return briefly to our analogy, if you are an office worker you can be thought of as a program and the information you handle at work as the data. Now you can send files of data from one organization to another and, with some effort, people in the other organization could use that data. However, if you change jobs it requires much more effort to 'change' or modify the way you work to suit the working practices of the new company. The same is true with computer-based information systems. It is relatively easy to pass data from one type of machine to another but it is much harder to pass programs from machine to machine.

One important role for any office manager is the control and management of the information used by his or her organization or department. The same is true of operating systems. One of the specialist functions of the operating system is the management of files, particularly on disks. Indeed, many systems have special 'sub' operating systems called DISK OPERATING SYSTEMS (DOS).

DISKS

Before we look at the actual process of filing adopted by the disk operating system, we must look in more detail at the disks themselves. You should remember that it is possible to file data on a cassette tape but this is not really recommended as it is:

- slow, and

- unreliable.

Most commercial systems use hard disks (including Winchesters).

However, we shall look at floppy disks as these are very common and the principles of storage used for floppies are similar to those for hard disks.

FORMATTING

With every new disk it is necessary to FORMAT or INITIALIZE the disk. What does this mean? Well, let us consider starting a manual filing system. You would need to organize the system before you actually started to put anything into the files. You may, for example:

- collect a box of files

- place them into the filing cabinet drawer

- label them in the order you decide

- place a label on the front of the drawer, etc.

and all of this would be done *before* you place any documents, etc. into the files.

A similar process is involved when using disks. The computer must 'organize' the disk so that it can file information on the disk and find it subsequently. This process of organizing the disk is called formatting or initializing.

So what actually happens? Well, the disk is divided by the computer into a number of concentric magnetic 'tracks'. The tracks do not spiral in towards the centre of the disk but are rather like a series of rings, each ring being slightly smaller the nearer it is to the centre. Generally there are 40 or 80 tracks to a disk (sometimes referred to as 48 tracks per inch or 96 tpi). The disk drive heads do not actually mark or score the surface but rather place magnetic marks on it.

If we consider the tracks as drawers to a filing cabinet then the system must also have the equivalent of filing pockets within the filing cabinets. To produce these the computer will divide each track into a fixed number of segments or SECTORS. Each sector then represents an area on the disk which can be referred to by its track and sector number.

To divide the tracks into sectors two methods are used. The first method uses disks which have a series of holes at regular intervals concentrically around the disk. A light shone through these holes is used to 'format' the disk. Each time a light shows, the system will put a magnetic mark on the disk to divide it into sectors. This method of formatting, as it relies on physical holes in the disk, is termed HARD-SECTORING.

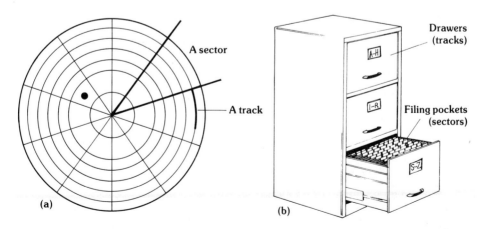

Tracks and sectors of a file (a) on a disk, and (b) in a filing cabinet

95

The second uses disks with only one hole. As the disk rotates, a light will shine through this hole at only one point. This becomes the starting point for each track. The system software will then put magnetic marks on the disk as it rotates, thus dividing it up into sectors. As the sector boundaries are only magnetic marks on the disk, this method of formatting is referred to as SOFT-SECTORING.

Once the disk is formatted, the software can file information on to the disk. Then, as long as it knows:

- what track the information is stored on

- what sector it starts at, and

- how long the file of information is

it can rapidly retrieve the file of information when required.

CATALOGUES OR DISK INDEXES

For the software to be able to find files on a disk rapidly it needs some form of index, just as in a library there is an index giving the location of every book stored. This index is a standard feature of disk operating systems and is referred to by names such as:

- VTOC (volume table of contents)

- index

- catalogue (or American catalog)

- directory.

Different systems will contain different types and amounts of information in this index. However, all will give:

- the file name

- its starting address on the disk (in tracks and sectors)

- its length

- the type of file (a text/document file, a program file, etc.)

Other features commonly found include:

- its load address (the address in RAM where the file must be loaded)

- the 'library' or 'file grouping' to which it belongs

- the date created or changed

- the identity of the person who created the file

- a password.

The remainder of this chapter concentrates on how data is filed on disks and how the operating system manages the disk drives in such a way as to:

- keep the data stored on the disk secure and uncorrupt

- allow easy access to data stored, and

- use the disk drives to increase the performance of the system.

FILES

Almost all information on an information processing system is stored on some form of magnetic medium. This information will be *both* the programs (telling the computer what to do and how to do it) and the data or information that the machine might need during its processes. Thus:

- documents

- data

- programs

- telexes

- voicegrams

- digitized papers, etc.

will all be stored as files. Clearly, each file will be different and the operating system can differentiate between each.

So an application program for word processing will be stored in a file on magnetic storage as will the various documents created during the use of the word processing program. (What is the other common form of storing information – particularly programs – on a computer?) [ROM].

Microcomputers and word processors often have at least two disk drives. They are frequently called:

- the system drive, and

- the work drive or file drive.

With this configuration it is usual to put the programs used by the machine on one disk and the data files on another (although on large-capacity disks this splitting of files becomes less obvious).

Why is this? There are several reasons depending on the system configuration. Firstly, just consider a simple type of microcomputer – such as an Apple or IBM. The word processing software diskette is loaded into drive 0 – the system drive. It is then possible for anyone using the computer to load the word processing programs from this diskette into the machine's RAM. Now, if documents were also filed on to this diskette it would soon become full and a new diskette would need to be loaded. However, because the system disk containing the word processing software had been removed, it is probable that, at some point in your word processing, programs would be needed that were on the disk that had been removed. This would result in:

- taking the document disk out of the disk drive

- loading the software disk into the disk drive

- loading the programs

- taking the software disk out of the disk drive

- loading the document disk into the disk drive.

This would be a tedious exercise, particularly if often necessary.

So, by storing the data files on a diskette separate from the program files and by having two disk drives, it is easy to keep changing data diskettes without affecting the diskette containing the programs.

More sophisticated computers with hard disks will allow different applications to be done at the same time. So one terminal might be using word processing while the next is using a stock control program. If you now think of a disk drive you will remember that it has read/write heads which must be moved in or out depending on where on the disk the particular file of information required is stored.

If all the programs and data files were on the same disk then the heads would be moving in and out much more than is desirable. The speed at which the computer responds to your input would slow down as it would be having to wait for your turn to collect information needed from the disk. This gives another reason for splitting the programs on to a system disk and the data files on to a work or file disk – assuming you have two or more disk drives linked to the computer.

DATABASES

When computers store information in files, it is common to find the same information being stored in several files on the same computer. This is because each application system (for example, wages and personnel) will usually have its own files. Thus:

- name

- address

- department

- salary, etc., etc.

will be duplicated. Then, if one department is notified of a change in a particular detail, it changes *its* files but not those of the other departments. The information on the computer will then be inaccurate – which is clearly not desirable when the computer is part of an information system, as it actually becomes a 'misinformation' system!

This is clearly a significant problem with separate files for each application as data is duplicated and, unless it is all updated at the same time, one file may very well become out of step with another.

Another problem with files arises because every program that uses a file must usually have a full description of every heading or field in the records within that file. Typically, with large systems, there will be many programs that share files. Therefore, if we suddenly need another piece of data (a new field) to be stored on the file and 20 different programs use that file, every program must be changed which is costly and time-consuming.

As a result of these types of problem, special disk operating software has been developed which handles or manages all the data for many different applications or programs. These systems – called DATABASE MANAGEMENT SYSTEMS (DBMS) – operate like a large central filing department. These systems control, organize and maintain the various files of data which together form the DATABASE. If you require information from such a department you go to the department and give the filing clerk your request. He then goes away into the company filing room and extracts from all the information held there only that information you are interested in. Obviously, you are not aware of all the other data stored in the department.

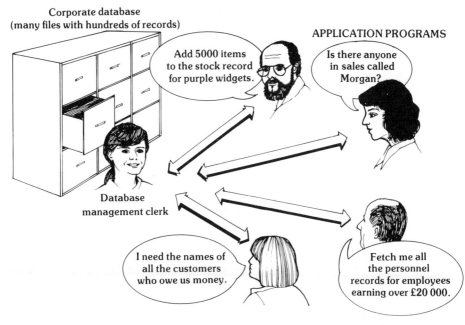

How a database management system operates

Additionally, this type of department will only keep single copies of information and thus when changes occur the information in the whole organization is up to date because it is stored only in one place.

These types of system are becoming more and more powerful and flexible. They will play an enormous role in information processing because, eventually, they will become exactly like giant electronic filing cabinets managed by highly efficient 'secretaries' who will file information away or retrieve information with ease and speed. Indeed there are now being developed DBMS that file and manage not only data files of text and numbers but digitized voices and pictures as well. It will be possible to change the description of information stored very easily without affecting any programs that use the information contained within the database.

VIRTUAL STORAGE

A final use made of backing store by operating systems is to provide what appears to be unlimited volatile memory. Simple computers load all the instructions required for a program into the volatile memory. The remaining memory is then used for the data required during processing. Should this available memory become full the computer 'stops'.

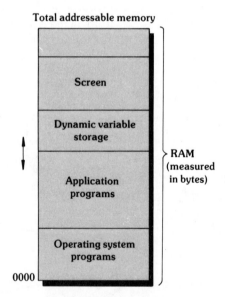

A volatile memory map

Most microcomputers work like this: programs are loaded from the backing store into RAM. The remaining memory is then used to store the data being typed or processed. When this memory becomes full the machine stops and the data has to be stored on to backing store. The memory can then be used again for new data.

Clearly, if several programs were being loaded into the memory, it would soon become so full of program instructions that there would be no memory left for the data required for processing. This used to happen even on large mainframe computers and, as a result, they were not very useful for organizations where many different people were wanting to do different tasks on the computer at the same time. Clearly, with the growth of information processing systems people using the systems would want to carry out many different applications and would thus find the lack of memory a real constraint.

Overcoming this problem would appear to be done easily by just increasing the size of the volatile memory. This solution, however, is not as easy as it appears for two reasons. The first involves the CPU. As we said earlier the CPU contains all the parts that actually carry out the computer's operations. It needs data to carry out its functions and this information is stored in the volatile memory. Each storage location in the memory will have a unique address – just like addresses in a road. The CPU also contains a special device which keeps in the limited memory of the CPU an address of where:

- the next program instruction is, or
- the next items of data required are stored.

It is really keeping an index to the volatile memory – just as a library card index keeps pointers to the addresses of books in the library.

There is a limit to the size of numbers that this device can store. Thus, if the device could only store numbers up to 99, the computer could only use 100 (0–99) places or addresses for information.

So the first reason why it is not possible just to increase the size of volatile memory involves the difficulty in increasing the numbers that can be stored in this special address device or REGISTER.

However, even when it became possible ten years ago to increase the numbers stored in the address register and therefore to increase the number of locations in the volatile memory that could be addressed, volatile memory itself was very expensive. Thus, to have a computer with a large volatile memory was so expensive that most organizations bought computers with less memory and would only operate a few applications such as wages or stock control.

The problem was, then, how to make more efficient use of the limited memory available within the computer.

The eventual solution to this problem involved the operating software and not the hardware. The software was written in such a way that everything on the backing store was stored as blocks or 'pages' each exactly the same size. Thus a file was made up of many blocks or pages of information. These blocks were quite small and, when a block was loaded into volatile memory, it did not take up too much memory.

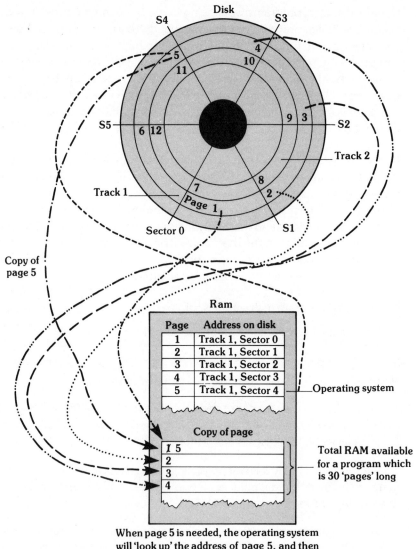

When page 5 is needed, the operating system
will 'look up' the address of page 5, and then
copy page 5 from disk into one of the RAM pages.

How a virtual storage operating system works

When the machine was switched on the operating system was also designed to
load into the RAM a table or index to the backing store blocks plus an index for
everyone who uses the system. The computer operates by looking at this table
to find out where the next block of information required is stored. The operating
system will then fetch that block into volatile memory. Because the blocks are
small it is possible to load many blocks into the memory at once.

The idea is not unlike using a reference book. The book contains far more information than you could ever fit on one page and therefore has an index which
informs you of the contents of each page. By keeping your finger in the index –
the machine's table in memory – you can look up a topic, turn to the first refer-

ence and so on. Clearly, if the book was a file of data – say a name and address book – and you wanted to change something on a page you would turn the page and change the information before going to the next reference. The operating system does the same thing. If you change information on the page loaded into memory, the operating system will write this page back on to the backing store, overwriting what was already there. If no changes are made, the operating system does not need to rewrite the page on to backing store because, as you know, information in memory is *only* a copy of the information stored on the backing store.

This type of operating system is now common on mini and mainframe computers. Since it appears that there is no limit to the size of the volatile memory, it is called virtual storage.

A similar form of operating system is even found on small word processors. With these the program is loaded into RAM: it is not paged in and out as with bigger machines. The document being worked on, however, is split into blocks or 'pages' (not A4 pages). Each block is quite small, perhaps 256 bytes, and so it is possible to read into RAM several blocks at once. As the blocks in the RAM become full of text, the operating system automatically stores on disk several of the blocks that have not been edited for some time. The next series of yet unedited blocks are then loaded into memory.

SUMMARY

Operating systems control and manage the CPU and all peripheral devices. They comprise a number of programs and, as different computers have different operating systems, it is usually difficult to transfer data from one system to another and almost impossible to transfer programs.

A major function of any operating system is the control, management and storage of data, particularly on disks. Often the programs that control data filed on disk are called disk operating systems.

- Every new disk must be initialized or formatted.

- Hard-sectored disks have a series of holes in the disk. As the disk rotates a light shines through each hole in turn, indicating the start of a new sector.

- Soft-sectored disks have only one hole which indicates the start position of the tracks. The computer will then place evenly spaced sector markers around the tracks.

- The operating system always keeps an index on the disk. This index, also called a VTOC, catalogue or directory, has details about all the files on the disk.

- Other information about the file may also be shown in the index including type of file, library, date of creation and modifications, identity of the person who created the file, and a password.

- Most data held on magnetic storage is held in files – this includes programs.

- Often systems have two disk drives referred to as the system and work drives. This configuration makes it easier to use the system because all the computer programs can be stored on the disk in the system drive and all the data files can be stored on the disk in the work drive.

  This allows data disks to be changed without having to remove programs. Additionally, the system responds more quickly owing to the reduced movement of the disk heads which is shared between the two disk drives.

- Files on their own are not the best way of storing data because the same data may be stored on many files (data duplication).

- In addition, use of files demands that every program using the file must have a full description of all the items in the records in the file, even if the program only needs to use one small field in the record. Thus, if an extra field is needed in the record, every program using that file must be changed.

- To overcome these limitations, special types of disk operating systems called database management systems (DBMS) have been written. These allow programs to access only the data they require and most data is held only once thus avoiding duplication.

- Database management systems will play an increasingly important role in future information processing systems.

- The amount of memory which can be addressed or used is limited by a special device in the CPU called an address register. Each storage location in memory has a unique address number and usually the largest number that the address register can hold determines the computer's memory size.

- In addition, memory is relatively expensive and therefore cost also limits the memory available on many computers.

- To overcome the restrictions imposed by having limited RAM, special operating systems called virtual operating systems have been developed. These systems use the disk as an extension of RAM and divide all files and programs into small, equally sized blocks or pages.

- With everything divided into pages it is possible to load only a few pages into memory at any time and, by having an index to every page also loaded into RAM, the operating system can immediately read pages into memory as they are needed.

- Virtual operating systems make it appear to everyone using the system that they have unlimited RAM.

- Simpler operating systems that use this paging technique are found on some word processors. These programs only treat the data files (documents) as paged files thus allowing the creation of documents that are much larger than the RAM available.

SELF-CHECK QUESTIONS

1. Give three functions of operating systems.

2. Why is it often awkward or impossible to use programs from one machine on another?

3. What does DOS stand for?

4. What has to be done every time you use a new disk?

5. What is a track on a disk and how many tracks are there?

6. The computer divides each track into s_____.

7. To divide a track into s_____ two methods are used:
   hard-sectored, and
   soft-sectored.
   Explain the difference between the two.

8. What three items of information does the software need to know to retrieve a file of information from disk?

9. The software needs an index to be able to find files on disk. Give three other names for this index.

10. Give seven items of information that might be contained in an index.

11. Microcomputers and word processors often have two disk drives. What are they called?

12. Into which disk drive is the application software usually loaded?

13. Why is it good practice to put the programs and data files on separate disks?

14. What is the name given to the special software that manages all the data for many different applications?

15. Why is information more likely to be up-to-date when using a DBMS?

16. New developments allow DBMS to file and manage not only files of text and numbers but – what else?

17. Why is it difficult to increase the size of volatile memory?

18. Explain what is meant by 'virtual storage'.

19. What do you understand by a program 'paging in and out'?

20. A form of 'virtual storage' is found on some word processors. Explain:
    a how this operates
    b what the advantages of this type of system are for an operator.

9

CONFIGURATIONS

Chapter Objectives

After studying this chapter you should be able to:

1. Describe and compare the following configurations:

- stand-alone
- shared-resource
- shared-logic.

2. Define the terms 'dumb terminal' and 'intelligent terminal'.

3. Describe multi-tasking and list the functions that may be undertaken using a multi-tasking system.

4. Prepare and label diagrams to demonstrate an understanding of the different types of configuration.

END OF OBJECTIVES END OF OBJECTIVES END OF OBJECTIVES END OF OBJECTIVES

INTRODUCTION

As we have already discussed, the arrangement of a computer and its peripheral devices is called a configuration. Now we look at the various system configurations and discuss the advantages and disadvantages of each.

STAND-ALONE SYSTEMS

Stand-alone simply means that the system is entirely self-contained. It will stand alone without the need to be connected to anything other than a mains power socket. It usually consists of:

- the keyboard
- the VDU
- the CPU
- the backing store (often disk drives)
- and probably has the exclusive use of a printer.

As an example, a stand-alone word processor is frequently a dedicated machine (designed just to do word processing), which often results in the configuration being more efficient and 'user friendly'. However, a microcomputer with several application programs can also be a stand-alone system in that it will be entirely self-contained.

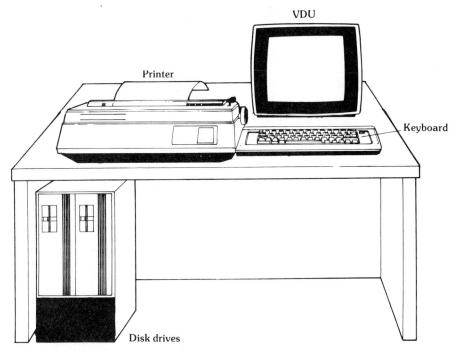

A typical dedicated stand-alone word processor configuration

SHARED-RESOURCE SYSTEMS

Shared-resource systems, as the name suggests, are individual CPUs sharing the same peripherals. The most common form of shared-resource configuration involves different computers (that is, keyboards, VDUs and CPUs) sharing expensive peripherals such as disk drives and printers.

As an example, microcomputers are often configured in a shared-resource way so that several computers will use one floppy-disk drive or printer. However, even large mainframes or minicomputers are sometimes configured to share disk drives. Clearly the most sophisticated shared-resource systems are LANs (local area networks) in which not only are resources shared but computers can freely communicate with each other, share databases, link (via GATEWAYS) to other computer networks, etc.

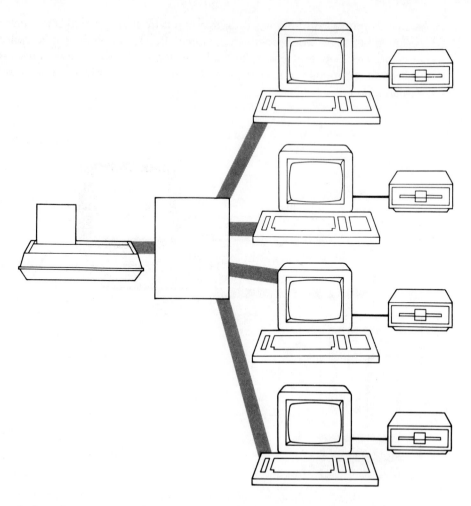

A shared-resource configuration: separate terminals sharing a common printer

SHARED-LOGIC SYSTEMS

Shared logic means that several terminals share the same CPU. This type of system is typical of a mainframe or minicomputer system and, because the CPU is so sophisticated, it is usual for a shared-logic system to share peripherals also.

It may involve the use of 'dumb' terminals (those with no processor of their own) or 'intelligent' terminals (in which some processing can be done at the terminal by its own processor).

Usually a shared-logic system:

- has a large CPU
- uses hard disk storage

- often allows data processing (DP) and word processing (WP) to be carried out simultaneously

- may support printers for differing needs, for example, a high-speed matrix printer and a letter-quality printer.

Sometimes the differences between shared-resource and shared-logic systems seem blurred. For instance, it is possible for all the microcomputers in a shared-resource configuration to do word processing at the same time thus giving the impression that they are 'sharing' the logic of the word processing program. However, each microcomputer has a CPU of its own – these are not shared – and the word processing program plus the documents (or files) are loaded individually into each machine. A shared-logic system, however, has only one CPU and it 'shares' both the CPU and the memory between the various terminals. Obviously, by using virtual memory (as discussed in Chapter 8) it is possible for a shared-logic system to have many users of the same limited memory.

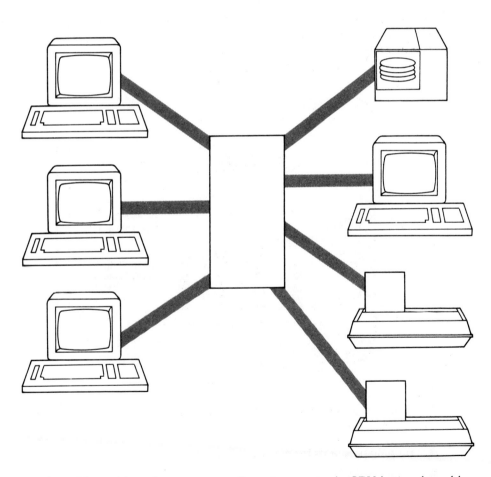

A shared-logic/shared-resource configuration: a single CPU being shared by many devices

MULTI-TASKING

Since CPUs operate at high speeds, a stand-alone system which performs only one task at a time is inefficient because the CPU is spending most of its time waiting to do something. Accordingly, most CPUs – other than the most basic – allow the person using the computer to perform more than one task at a time. The simplest example of this multi-tasking occurs when the CPU allows keying to be done at the same time as printing.

Most word processors do this – it is possible to be editing a document at the same time as printing another one. This feature is called BACKGROUND PRINT-ING. Larger CPUs will allow many different background tasks to be done while the computer is also running programs (such as WP) which are allowing input. There is a growing demand for computers to perform more than one FORE-GROUND TASK – meaning that the person using the computer can see, on a screen, more than one program. The screen is divided into 'WINDOWS' with each acting like a screen on its own. So on one window you may have a word processing document while on another a spreadsheet and you can easily 'jump' from editing the document to adding figures to the spreadsheet. This function is useful for information processing systems since information is often of most value when we can compare it or combine it with other information.

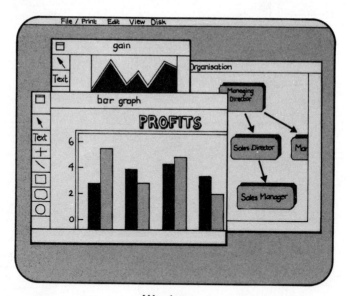

Windows

You should now realize some of the complexities of shared-logic multi-tasking systems. The CPU is:

- running programs for many different terminals
- controlling files
- printing

- perhaps running a large batch processing program such as a wages program
- controlling the memory utilization
- keeping a log of everything done on the machine
- and often carrying out 'checks' on itself (to make sure that there are no problems).

Advantages and disadvantages of the preceding systems are summarized below:

	Advantages	Disadvantages
Stand alone	often dedicated and thus easy to use	wasteful of CPU time
	rapid responses	expensive to expand
	relatively cheap	difficult to communicate with other machines
	relatively portable	expensive way to use peripherals
Shared resources	cuts costs by sharing peripherals	may need to wait while other machines are using resource
	Most of the advantages of stand alone	lack of flexibility
		if shared resource breaks down the whole system is out of use
Shared logic	high speed	if too many users, response time may be slow
	workstations can be remote	initially expensive
	expansion relatively cheap	if CPU breaks down, all computing power is lost
	good control and house-keeping	difficult to operate
	greatly increased memory capacity	
	Does more than one job – effective way to allow a number of users to use different programs	

Table of comparisons between microcomputers, minicomputers and mainframe computers.

	Microcomputers	Minicomputers	Mainframe computers
Stand-alone	common	not common	never
Shared-resources	fairly common	not common	not common
Shared-logic	uncommon but, as CPU power has grown, more are becoming multi-user or shared-logic	always	always
Speeds – (instructions per second)	1000 ips	15-800 000 ips	1 million ips or more
Cost (approx.)	£100–£4000	£20 000–£150 000	£100 000–£1 million plus
Advantages	easy to use	easy to install	very powerful
	flexible	easy to operate	powerful software
	portable	large pool of software	can support large number of users
	software cheap	large memory	does many different jobs at once
	no special environmental conditions	good upgrade paths	flexible
	fast responses	flexible	extensive growth paths
	large volume of software	good data storage (up to gigabytes)	huge data storage (up to hundreds of gigabytes)
	user programmable		

	Microcomputers	**Minicomputers**	**Mainframe computers**
Disadvantages	often difficult growth paths	costs	costs
	rapidly out of date	incompatibility between machines	special environmental conditions
	limited memory size	need for environmental control	difficult to operate
	incompatibility between machines	relatively slow to program	heavy use of power
	restricted data storage capacity		not user programmable

SUMMARY

The arrangement of a computer and its peripheral devices is called a configuration.

A stand-alone system is entirely self-contained and usually consists of a VDU, a keyboard, a CPU, backing store and, in some systems, a printer.

Shared-resource configurations are made up of individual CPUs sharing resources such as disk drives and printers.

A shared-logic system comprises several terminals sharing the same CPU. This system is common with mainframes and minicomputers. It may involve the use of either 'dumb' or 'intelligent' terminals. Shared-logic systems usually have a large CPU, share peripherals and allow word processing and data processing to be carried out simultaneously.

Many CPUs allow the user to perform more than one task at a time – multi-tasking. The simplest form of multi-tasking is background printing. This is common in word processing.

There is a growing demand for computers to perform more than one 'fore-ground task'. The screen is divided into 'windows'. One window may show a word processing document and on another window a spreadsheet may be viewed. It is possible to 'jump' from one program to the other to compare, edit and combine information.

Shared-logic, multi-tasking systems are complex in that many different functions are carried out simultaneously.

A table illustrating advantages and disadvantages of the above configurations is provided in this chapter.

SELF-CHECK QUESTIONS

1. What is the name given to the arrangement of the computer and its peripheral devices?

2. Explain the term 'stand-alone'.

3. A stand-alone system comprises four, or in some cases five, pieces of hardware. List these five items.

4. a What is the name given to the configuration where more than one CPU share the same disk drive and/or printer?
  b What would be an advantage of this type of configuration for a company installing, say, microcomputers?

5. a Explain the meaning of 'shared logic'.
  b Where is this type of configuration typical and why?

6. What is the difference between a 'dumb' terminal and an 'intelligent' terminal?

7. What type of disk storage does a shared-logic system usually use?

8. Why might a stand-alone system be regarded as using the CPU inefficiently?

9. What do you understand by the term 'background printing'?

10. How is it possible for someone using a computer to see two programs, for example, word processing and a spreadsheet, at the same time?

11. With a shared-logic, multi-tasking system it is possible for the CPU to be doing many different tasks at once. List six of the tasks that might be carried out simultaneously.

12. List two advantages and two disadvantages of the following configurations:
  a stand-alone
  b shared-resources
  c shared-logic.

13. Draw a diagram of each of the configurations mentioned in this chapter and label the parts.

14. The following features apply to either a microcomputer, a minicomputer or a mainframe computer. Write next to each feature the computer(s) to which it applies.

  a easy to use
  b need for environmental control
  c can support a large number of users
  d user programmable
  e heavy use of power
  f relatively slow to program
  g operates at approximately 15 000–800 000 ips
  h good upgrade paths

i   very fast responses
j   does many different jobs at once
k   limited memory sizes
l   rapidly out of date

10

COMMUNICATIONS

Chapter Objectives

After studying this chapter you should be able to:

1. Explain how data is transmitted over distances.

2. Describe the hardware necessary for transmitting data.

3. Compare Telex and Teletex.

4. Explain how facsimile transmission operates and list its uses and facilities.

5. Discuss Videotex:
   - who provides the services
   - what type of information is provided
   - what equipment is required
   - costs.

6. Describe the 'teleconferencing' facility and the benefits a company might expect to gain from using such a facility.

7. Explain the term 'telesoftware'.

8. Describe the functions of LANs and WANs.

9. Explain what is meant by 'data encryption' and why it is necessary.

END OF OBJECTIVES END OF OBJECTIVES END OF OBJECTIVES END OF OBJECTIVES

INTRODUCTION

In our discussion of the various kinds of system configuration it was assumed that processors, terminals and their peripheral equipment could be linked together. In this chapter we shall be dealing with some of the ways by which this communication is made possible as well as with some of the more traditional means of machine-to-machine communication.

DATA NETWORKS

Data is usually transmitted over distances by using the public telephone network or lines leased from British Telecom. The use of ordinary telephone lines requires special devices called MODEMS (modulating/demodulating devices) in order to change the digital signals from the computer into analogue signals which can be transmitted down a telephone line. Clearly, modems are required on each end of a line transmitting data: the modem at the receiving end reconverts (or demodulates) the analogue signal into a digital signal before passing it on to the computer.

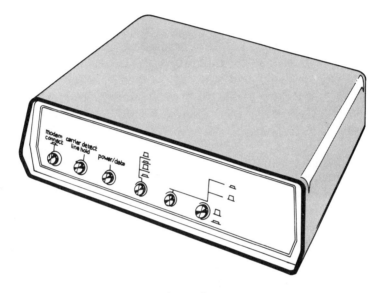

A modem

One way of connecting a computer to the public telephone network is via an ACOUSTIC COUPLER – a modem into which a telephone receiver can be placed – which enables signals to be transmitted and received. This system also allows the destination to be varied so that, wherever there is a telephone, a data terminal or computer may be contacted, provided that the necessary equipment is also present.

Leased lines are dedicated to a specific route and a specific use. Almost always this means a telephone link which is continuously connected between one building and another. Data transmitted down a leased line is not as subject to corruption as on public telephone lines. However, as they link one site with another, they are less flexible since they cannot be used to access many destinations.

Speed of transmission on public data networks can be from 200 to 9600 bits per second (bps) or baud: the faster speeds are provided on the leased lines.

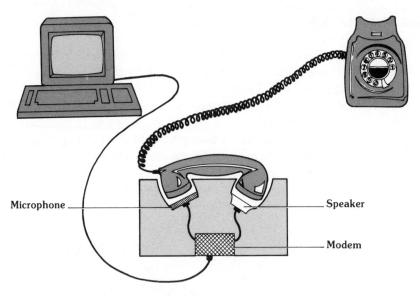

An acoustic coupler

These speeds of transmission are satisfactory when limited amounts of data are being transmitted – such as between a terminal and a central processor. However, when high-speed responses are required or large quantities of data are being transmitted – often the case between computer and computer – much higher speeds are necessary. Currently British Telecom offers two special services to meet this demand:

- Kilostream – provides guaranteed transmission at 19 200 bps– usually used for transmissions between computers and remote peripherals

- Megastream – at present guarantees transmissions at 1.2 Mb/s – only available between major cities – higher speeds of up to 14 Mb/s will soon be available – usually used for links between computers.

TELEX

The Telex service is a telegraph system which has its own exchanges and uses teleprinters instead of telephones. It was the first digital transmission network. The Telex terminal may be used to punch a tape which can be verified before transmission takes place. Before a message can be sent, a direct link between the transmitting machine and the receiving machine must be established. Without the transmitting terminal receiving an answer code from the receiver, no message can be sent. On receipt of a message the receiving terminal sends back a code which confirms that the message has been received by the correct place. Messages can normally be sent at any time of day or night. The received message is printed at the receiving terminal by means of an auto-answer facility if this is available.

The Telex system:

- is supported by British Telecom's Datel 100 service

- transmits data at the rate of 50 bps

- transmits data at the rate of 110 bps on private telegraph circuits

- is relatively slow, resulting in a printing speed of about 66 words per minute

- is limited in its character set (upper case only and no pound, dollar, percentage or fraction signs).

Equipment is now available that will allow the word processor to be linked to the Telex system. As an example, one relatively simple product:

- allows the production of punched paper tape compatible with the Telex system

- is capable of converting some of the special characters on the word processor for use on Telex, for example, the dollar sign is converted to 'DLR'.

While such products currently cost in the region of £3000 they do allow text to be edited using the far superior facilities of the word processor.

More sophisticated products directly interface into the Telex system so that word processing documents can be automatically converted into a Telex form and then transmitted. These products also allow Telexes to be received, converted into a word processing document and then stored for later review.

TELETEX

Teletex is a new service offered by British Telecom and falls within the category of 'electronic mail' systems. The service allows an addressed message to be delivered automatically to a receiving terminal where it can be stored. In order to be classed as electronic mail, a system must be capable of enabling addressed messages to be sent without the sender having to contact the recipient before the message is dispatched.

The Teletex system:

- is much faster than Telex with transfer rates being in the order of 2400 bps

- has a much more extensive character set including all the roman typefaces and a large number of other symbols

- allows transmission to take place automatically between terminals so that they can be used for other work during transmission

- is compatible with most computers and word processors

- can be linked into the Telex network.

The CCITT (The International Telegraph and Telephone Consultative Committee) is currently discussing proposals for a set of international standards for a world-wide Teletex network.

FACSIMILE TRANSMISSION

Facsimile transmission (fax) has been in existence since the beginning of the twentieth century and is used for the transmission of any image that is difficult to translate into a code for transmission purposes.

These images include:

- pictures

- documents

- drawings

- handwritten manuscripts.

The document to be transmitted is scanned and its image is converted into electrical signals. These signals are then transmitted and converted back to a copy of the original on arrival at the destination.

Some international standards for fax machines now exist. These standards have been agreed with the CCITT. There are three standards which are briefly described in ascending order of speed and cost:

- Group 1 machines transmit an A4 sheet in four to six minutes. Transmission is analogue

- Group 2 machines take two to three minutes. Transmission is analogue

- Group 3 machines should transmit an A4 sheet in less than two minutes (normally less than one minute). Group 3 machines work digitally.

There is a fourth class (Group 4) for which standards have not yet been agreed. This class will be digital and considerably faster than Group 3.

These standards however, do not cover all the facilities offered by some machines, such as:

- automatic dialling and answering

- encryption (scrambling)

- paper-size selection

- automatic loading

- repeat print option.

This means that a machine that has some of these facilities cannot be used to full advantage if it is communicating with one that does not have these enhancements.

The great advantage with facsimile transmission is that it allows the transmission of any image, which can include handwritten documents and signatures. It is used a great deal in Japan as Japanese does not lend itself to the limited character set of European languages. Developments in facsimile transmission mean that it will soon be possible to link fax machines to word processors. Although such equipment is not yet readily available, prototypes have been demonstrated by at least one manufacturer. Such developments would allow the storage of both written and image documents and could play a significant role in information and DOCUMENT DELIVERY systems in the future.

British Telecom offers an over-the-counter service called Bureaufax. This service allows companies or individuals to send facsimile images to most parts of the world, using any of the three international standards, at a small cost. The Post Office offers a similar service called Intelpost.

VIDEOTEX

This is simply the generic name for all forms of computer-based information systems which make available information to a dispersed and numerous number of users.

VIEWDATA

The most well-known Viewdata system in the United Kingdom is 'Prestel'. This service is offered by British Telecom and gives access to information that is stored on computer.

The terminal equipment consists of either a modified television set with a numeric or alphanumeric keypad and a telephone, or a normal colour monitor and a computer with suitable software. Users can access the service by dialling their nearest Prestel number which then allows them to consult hundreds of thousands of 'frames' of information. Frames are 'called up' by means of codes which are entered via the keypad (a directory is available). 'Response frames' allow the user to transmit a limited amount of information back to the computer (for example, credit card number, address, etc.). The providers of information on the other hand, can obtain a licence which allows them to enter their infor-

Viewdata screen

mation to the system. Users pay for their telephone call to the system and for each page they access: the fee per page varies from nil to as much as 50p but a typical charge would be between 2p and 5p.

The information-providers rent frames from British Telecom: they pay a fixed annual rental plus a charge per frame.

While the information currently provided by Prestel is limited to such things as news, timetables, financial guides, etc., it may be possible in future for users to make use of the computational facilities of the Prestel computers. It is possible to use microcomputers as Prestel terminals which then have access to data and programs. It is also possible to use the Prestel system for communication between different users: the message is sent to the Prestel computer and stored and accessed by the addressee at a convenient time.

Viewdata systems similar to Prestel are found in most western countries now and there is a growing number of private specialist Viewdata services becoming available.

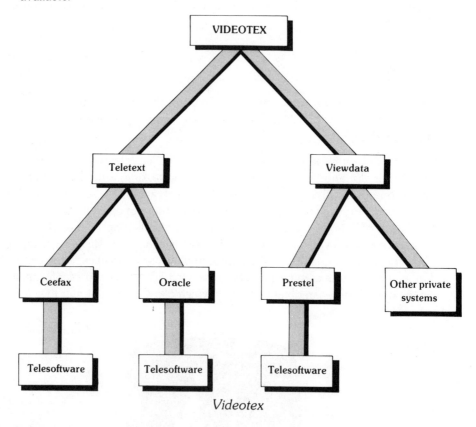

Videotex

TELETEXT

Teletext (nothing to do with Telex or Teletex) is a means of transmitting information along with normal TV programme broadcasts. Both the BBC and the IBA offer these services which are known as 'Ceefax' and 'Oracle' respectively.

Teletext information is provided free of charge but is essentially one-way communication: the user cannot transmit a reply as is possible with Viewdata. A TV set with a Teletext decoder is capable of displaying information from several 'frames' which are accessed by keying numbers on a numeric keypad. Text and picture can be mixed if so desired. The type of information provided includes news, stock prices, food prices, racing results, etc. In addition, the BBC is now transmitting computer program listings as part of its computer-literacy project and with a special adaptor these can be downloaded on to cassette tape for use on most microcomputers.

Teletext is designed for domestic use and, because of its inability to allow the user to send a return message, is likely to be of limited use in the 'electronic office'.

TELESOFTWARE

One spin-off of the increasing availability of communication channels has been the rapid growth in telesoftware or, in other words, programs transmitted over a communication link. Prestel, for example, has a special 'club' called Micronet for home microcomputer users. People can join the club which supports a variety of services such as:

- hardware and software reviews

- electronic mail

- bulletin boards

- swap shops

- teleshopping

- telesoftware.

Some of this telesoftware is free while other programs can be bought. Teletext also broadcasts programs over the air and, with a special adaptor, it is possible to save these programs on a disk or tape and then load and run the saved programs.

Finally, not to be outdone, radio stations have started broadcasts of software. A special language 'BASICODE' has been developed which allows different microcomputers to 'translate' the broadcast software into the BASIC they use: different types of microcomputers use slightly different versions of BASIC.

TELECONFERENCING

Many organizations or groups arrange meetings at which people from various locations nationally or internationally must attend. This requires travelling over long distances and is usually costly and time-consuming. Using telecommunications, it is possible to arrange meetings to which the participants do not have to travel. This is done using techniques called TELECONFERENCING.

One form of teleconferencing involves the use of computer or word processing terminals linked into a computer network. It is then possible for one person to send a communiqué to several others who can, in turn, respond by sending messages back to the 'originator', with copies being sent to everyone else involved, if necessary. This is called COMPUTER CONFERENCING.

A much more revolutionary arrangement called VIDEO CONFERENCING involves the use of closed-circuit television and special meeting rooms. These meeting rooms are equipped with video cameras and special large-screen video displays. It is possible to establish high-speed links between rooms in different cities with up to three or four rooms being linked at any one time. Participants need only go to their local meeting-room to take part in a meeting at which they can see, hear and talk with people in locations remote from their own. This facility, coupled with the VIDEOPHONE currently under development, will make significant differences to work in the future.

British Telecom offers a video conferencing facility called CONFRAVISION.

LOCAL AREA NETWORKS (LANs)

Local area networks are networks that link together computers and peripherals in such a way that a user on the network will not be aware of which CPU or disk is being used. They are called local because the network only covers a small area, for example, a building. It is possible to 'plug' numerous devices into the network.

The lowest level of network operates on a shared-resource basis, that is, each CPU on the network will share disks or printers. There is, however, no facility to share logic. Thus the various CPUs will not 'talk' to each other.

Higher-level LANs have fully integrated features in that CPUs are networked together and it is possible to be connected to one computer while using a program on another computer in the network.

It is foreseen that buildings in the future will be constructed to have sockets in the walls not only for telephones and electricity but also for the LAN. It will then be very simple to 'plug in' your own terminal or microcomputer to the LAN.

High-level local area networks already form the basis for automated offices as it is possible to send voice, pictures (TV-type), data, electronic memos, diary entries, etc., all through the network.

LANs operate at high speeds ranging from 19 200 bps to 4-5 Mbps.

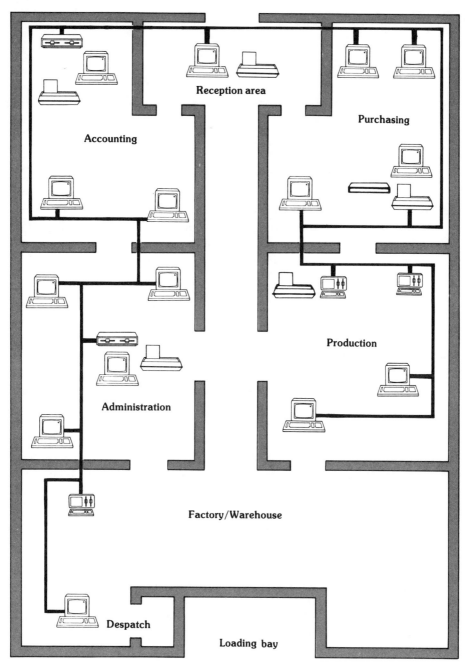

An example of a local area network (LAN)

WIDE AREA NETWORKS (WANs)

With the growth in communications many manufacturers now offer networks which allow simple communication between computers over hundreds of thousands of miles. Speeds are usually quite low – in the order of 9600 bps or less. This linkage allows such facilities as:

- using a large central computer from a local small word processor or micro-computer

- operating programs on one computer which uses data from several other remote computers

- transmitting files freely from one computer to another

- electronic mail and diaries.

Indeed, the growth in demand for wide area networking capabilities has now prompted manufacturers to develop software which will even allow documents to be transferred between computers of different manufacturers. Thus, for example, documents created on an IBM computer can be transferred to, and edited on, a Wang or DEC system.

Future electronic offices will rely heavily on networks, whether local or remote, because communication of information forms a major part of any organization or business.

ENCRYPTION

All forms of communication have one thing in common – the information being transmitted is vulnerable to interference. Thus, bank computers linked together in a network, for example, when transferring funds electronically from one account to another are just as susceptible to robbery as money being transported by a van or train. Indeed, the difficulty in tracing a robber where a telephone line is tapped is much greater than trying to trace a gang who hold up a van or train.

To protect information from illegal tampering or spying, much sensitive or confidential information is stored or transmitted in code and the techniques for changing information into coded form (and back again) are called DATA ENCRYPTION.

Particularly with money transactions and information relating to country security, there is a great deal of effort continuously being put into developing more and more 'uncrackable codes' with some recent techniques thought to be virtually impossible to break, even by the most powerful computers.

SUMMARY

The majority of communication links are telephone lines. To transmit digital data from machine to machine via a telephone line requires devices called modems. Modem stands for modulating/demodulating. These devices change digital signals into analogue signals for transmission and convert received analogue signals into digital.

126

An acoustic coupler is a modem into which a telephone receiver can be placed.

Leased lines link two buildings and are continuously connected. Dial-up lines only link sites when contact is made.

Special services are available for high-speed communications. Kilostream from British Telecom guarantees speeds up to 19 200 bps while Megastream allows communication at speeds up to 1.2 Mbps.

Telex is a widely used slow-speed (50 bps) messaging facility. It requires a direct link between the transmitter and the receiver and only allows a limited character set to be used.

Some word processors and computers can be linked to the Telex network. These allow messages to be stored and forwarded and viewed on terminals.

Teletex is a much enhanced form of Telex. It allows most computers and word processors to link to the Telex network but also allows the transmission, at high speeds, of messages using both upper and lower case, etc.

Facsimile transmission allows the transmission of any image. The item to be transmitted is scanned and its image is turned into electrical impulses. These are transmitted and reconverted by the receiving device to produce the image. Three standards have been agreed for facsimile transmission. Groups 1 and 2 use analogue signals and an A4 page takes between two and six minutes to transmit. Group 3 machines use digital signals and an A4 sheet takes, at most, two minutes. A fourth standard is under discussion: it will be for digital transmission at speeds higher than Group 3.

Viewdata refers to a service by which numerous users can link, via telephone lines, into an information database using special modified televisions with keypads or microcomputers/VDUs. Most information is free although a subscription charge must be paid to join the service. Prestel is the most widely known service in the UK.

As Viewdata is interactive, it is possible to place orders, etc. and pay by quoting your credit card number. Additionally, telesoftware is available whereby computer programs can be downloaded from the Viewdata computer to the user's microcomputer.

Teletext (that is, 'text on the tele') is a service offered by both the BBC and the IBA. These services, Ceefax and Oracle respectively, are transmitted along with normal television programmes. They provide information but do not allow the interaction available with Viewdata.

Local area networks (LANs) are communication networks which link together a range of computers and peripherals in a relatively small area.

Wide area networks (WANs) allow linkage of computers over hundreds of miles and will allow users linked to one computer to use another freely and to transmit data from one machine in the network to another.

As so much information is being transmitted, and as much of this information relates to money or Government or industrial secrets, transmitted information is often coded. This process of coding data is called encryption.

SELF-CHECK QUESTIONS

1. Name the two methods that are used to transmit data over distances.

2. If data is transmitted using ordinary telephone lines, what is needed to change the digital signals from a computer to analogue signals?

3. a What is an acoustic coupler?
   b What is the main advantage of using an acoustic coupler?

4. If a leased line is being used to transmit data, is a modem needed?

5. Which of the following two methods of data transmission is more susceptible to corruption and which one transmits data more quickly?
   a leased lines
   b public telephone network

6. In what respect are leased lines less flexible than the public telephone network?

7. British Telecom offers two special services that increase the speed of data transmission.
   a What are they called?
   b Which one is faster?
   c Which one is currently only available between major cities?

8. What is the name of the telegraph service that uses teleprinters instead of telephones to transmit and receive messages?

9. The T_____ system transmits data at about 50 bps which is relatively _____ and is limited in its c_____ s_____.

10. Can Telex equipment be linked with word processors? If so, what would be the advantages of this link?

11. Teletex is a new service offered by British Telecom and falls within the category of electronic mail. What must a service be capable of before it can be classed as 'electronic mail'?

12. List four benefits a company might expect by using the Teletex system instead of the traditional Telex.

13. Explain how documents are transmitted using facsimile transmission.

14. For what is fax particularly useful?

15. There are international standards for fax machines. These have been agreed with the C_____T.

16. Which group of fax machines transmits an A4 sheet in:
    a   less than 2 minutes
    b   2 to 3 minutes
    c   4 to 6 minutes?

17. List four facilities available on some fax machines.

18. Developments are taking place to link fax machines with word processors. What would such a development allow?

19. Who provides the Prestel service?

20. What terminal equipment is required to access Prestel?

21. What costs can a Prestel user expect?

22. Can a Prestel user transmit information back to the computer? If so, what type of information might the user transmit?

23. What type of information is provided by Prestel?

24. Teletext is a service provided by both the BBC and the IBA. What are the names of these services?

25. What equipment is required to receive Teletext?

26. What type of information is provided by Teletext?

27. What is the generic name for Teletext and Viewdata?

28. Explain how 'computer conferencing' operates and how a company might use such a facility.

29. In a video conferencing meeting room what equipment would you expect to find?

30. What benefits would a company expect from using video conferencing facilities?

31. British Telecom offers a video conferencing service. What is it called?

32. What is 'telesoftware'?

33. a   What is the name of the 'club' on Prestel for microcomputer owners?
    b   What services are available to members of the club?

34. Radio stations broadcast software. How is it possible for users of *different* micro-computers to use this software?

35. What do the following abbreviations stand for?
    a   LAN
    b   WAN

36. How does the lowest-level LAN operate?

37. Higher-level LANs have fully integrated features and already form the basis for automated offices. What types of information can be sent through the network?

38. WANs allow communication between computers over great distances. What facilities does this linkage allow?

39. What is data encryption and why is it necessary?

COMMUNICATION LINKS

Chapter Objectives

After studying this chapter you should be able to:

1. Explain what advantages a business might accrue from linking its computer systems.

2. Define 'serial' and 'parallel' transmission.

3. Explain how it is possible to send many signals at once down a communication carrier.

4. Define simplex, half duplex and full duplex transmission.

5. Distinguish between asynchronous and synchronous transmission.

6. Explain why transmission rates are increased by using optical fibres.

7. List three 'non-physical' methods of transmitting information.

8. Describe the functions and advantages of a packet switching network.

END OF OBJECTIVES END OF OBJECTIVES END OF OBJECTIVES END OF OBJECTIVES

INTRODUCTION

Hopefully by now you will be realizing some of the potential for information systems in all aspects of life. We have discussed how computers can:

- perform many different tasks simultaneously

- share devices

- store and rapidly retrieve vast amounts of information

- communicate one to another

- be made so small and cheap that it is possible to include them in almost any mechanical function such as operating a cooker, landing a space craft on the moon or telling you to put on your seat belt.

However, unless all the functions one may require in a particular system are available on one computer configuration, much of the value of the system is lost. Let us consider a business in simple outline. The business wants to:

- receive and send mail
- manage its accounts
- send and receive accounting information to its bank
- control stock levels
- place orders for new stock when supplies get low.

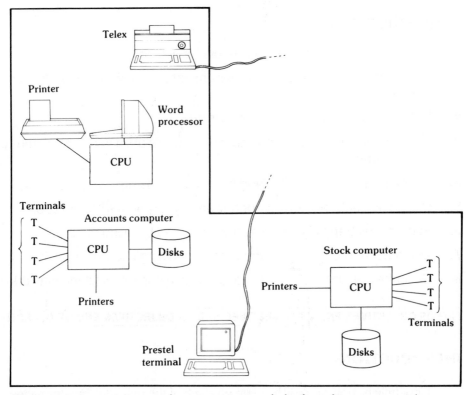

The current, non-integrated communication links found in many modern businesses

It may use Telex, have telephones and make use of public data networks such as Prestel.

Now, if it has:

- a word processor to produce letters
- a computer on which an accounting system is operated
- a different computer to control stocks

- a telex machine
- a television to receive Prestel

and all these machines operate without communicating, then much of the value of the computer is lost. Currently, this is how many businesses do work. There is only limited communication between different functions and their computer systems.

However, with the development of cheap, powerful computers (micro-computers) and the falling cost of computers in general, it is being increasingly recognized that it is (or should be) possible to link different machines:

- in different areas within an organization or building (Local Area Networks)
- between different organizations such as the business, its bank and its suppliers (wide area networks)
- to the public data banks such as Prestel or the telephone and Telex systems.

Before we move further into this area of integrated information systems we must look at how machines are physically able to communicate, that is, how they are linked together.

WIRES

Obviously wires are the most common way of linking machines of any type together. The wires are usually copper and come in many different forms. For very high-speed transmission – say between a CPU and a disk drive – a number of wires are placed next to each other in a protective coating. These types of wire look something like a thick plastic ribbon and are called BUSES. Often eight wires are found in a ribbon and allow one byte to be transmitted at a time – one bit down each wire. This is called PARALLEL TRANSMISSION.

Obviously, wires of this type are very expensive and are therefore used only over short links. Longer links, but still usually within a building, often use a form of wiring called coaxial. Coaxial cable is basically two wires but is special in that

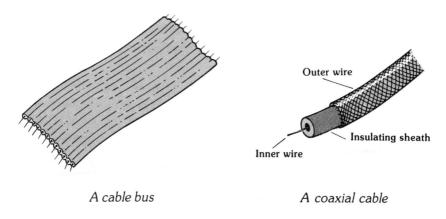

A cable bus   *A coaxial cable*

one wire runs through a sheath formed by the second wire – your television aerial is made from coaxial cable. This type of wire is used because it helps prevent transmitted signals from becoming corrupted.

As it is possible to send only one bit at a time, transmission rates are usually lower than those obtained using ribbon cable. This is called SERIAL TRANS-MISSION. Printers, VDUs and LANs are often linked by coaxial cables or by a simple twisted pair of wires.

Remote wired links are most frequently made by using the telephone/Telex networks. These use copper wires which are simply twisted together into thick bundles of wires. You may have seen them when you have passed men working on telephone wires in the street. It is possible to rent what is called a 'dedicated line' which means that instead of having signals passed through all the normal telephone switching exchanges – each of which will find and use the first available wire for your signal – your signal will be sent down the same line and through the same switches all the time and, even when you are not transmitting, no-one else can use that wire.

To use the telephone network it is necessary to use a modem, whereas to use the Telex network no modem is necessary although the transmitted signal must be converted into a Telex format which uses, for example, five bits for a character and transmits at slow (about 50 bps) rates.

At present most transmission over telephone wires is done at between 300 and 9600 bps which is slow when you consider how fast the CPU works (millions of bits per second).

To increase transmission rates (and the number of different signals which can be sent at one time) a great deal of money is being spent on improving signal carrier networks. It is possible to send many different signals down a communication carrier at one time without each signal becoming muddled with others.

How is this done? Well, imagine two pairs of people in a dark room with one person from each pair on one side of the room and the partner from each pair on the other side. If one pair had red torches and the other pair had blue torches and all knew morse code, it would be possible to transmit different messages between the pairs at the same time because one pair would only be interested in red signals while the other would only be interested in blue. Similarly, if one pair used high sounds (treble) while the other used low sounds (bass) it would be possible to do the same thing.

What actually is happening is that each pair is 'agreeing' what 'frequency' they will use for their transmission and are then only recognizing those signals that are in their agreed frequency band.

If you realize that even we poor humans will recognize sounds across a frequency range from about 20 Hz (that is, low bass sounds) to about 20 000 Hz (that is, high treble sounds) you can see that by using frequency bands it is possible to transmit many signals at once, so that even we could recognize them. Machines are much more able to recognize different frequencies across much greater band widths and copper wires – even those used for telephone systems – have wider band widths than we can hear. Thus, while your telephone conversation is being transmitted down a wire at between 200 and 10 000 Hz, a computer signal using 25 000–30 000 Hz can also be going down the wire, but as its sound is so high you cannot hear it.

Thus, the wider the band width of the carrier the more signals it can carry. So telephone companies such as British Telecom are today using carriers which have very wide band widths and only a small fraction of this band width (20–15 000 Hz) is used for telephone transmissions.

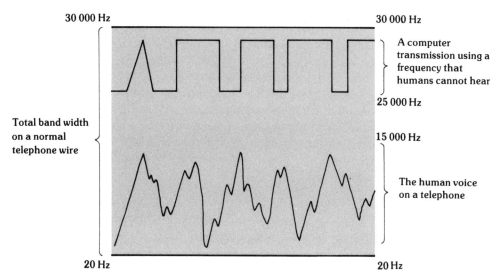

Signals within a bandwidth: an example of two signals being transmitted on the same carrier using different frequencies

FORMS OF COMMUNICATION

Data can be sent from machine to machine via three different types of connection. These are:

- simplex.
- half duplex.
- full duplex.

A SIMPLEX link allows data to be transmitted in one direction only, much as with a book – you receive information but cannot respond. A HALF DUPLEX link allows data to be transmitted in either direction but only one way at a time, like a question and answer session. FULL DUPLEX links allow data to flow in both directions at the same time – a telephone link, for example, is full duplex as people at either end can talk at the same time.

However, being able to link systems does not mean that machines will communicate successfully. What is needed is agreement on the formalities of communicating, such as how the communication session will start and end, how data will be sent, how the transmitter will 'know' the receiver understood what was sent, etc. This agreement on how two machines will communicate is called their communication PROTOCOL.

With a full duplex link it is simple for whole messages to be sent as the receiver can constantly 'tell' the transmitter, 'I understand your message', or, 'Sorry, please say again'. In this way the transmitter starts the message with a start-of-message sequence that enables both machines to set themselves up ready for communicating and synchronize their clocks. This method of sending whole messages is termed SYNCHRONOUS transmission.

With half duplex links it is more common for ASYNCHRONOUS transmission to be used. Messages are sent character by character (characters, as we know, consist of 7 or 8 bits). With synchronous transmission, once the message starts, every bit forms part of the data. With asynchronous transmission each character has one or two start bits and one or two stop bits. Thus each eight bit character can take 10 or 11 bits to send. Synchronous transmission can be compared to our normal conversation – we talk in whole sentences. Asynchronous transmission is akin to spelling out a message – letters are said with a pause separating each one.

FIBRE OPTICS

A new type of carrier is the optical fibre. This is just a fine thread of special plastic material or glass down which light can be shone. You have probably seen fibre optic lights which look like a mop with pin pricks of light glowing (and changing colour) at the end of each fibre. As light travels at enormously high speeds and it is possible to use a very wide band width – infrared through reds through blues to ultraviolets, etc. – these carriers can transmit tens of thousands of signals at speeds up to 10 billion bps!

Fibre optic cables are currently being installed and, in the United Kingdom, form the basis for the Megastream service offered by British Telecom.

MICROWAVE, INFRARED AND RADIO

Transmissions are more and more frequently being sent using non-physical links. Over short distance these may be microwaves (as with the British Telecom Tower) or infrared waves (like those used for remote control of televisions or video recorders). Nationally or internationally, radio waves are used.

All of these are similar but of different frequency. They must be 'aimed' directly from transmitter to receiver which is why satellites are being launched in large numbers.

Signals are transmitted directly at the satellite which then gathers the signals and retransmits them to earth. (An offshoot of this enormous growth in communication technology using satellites is satellite TV which uses a dish aerial to collect signals from many – maybe hundreds of – different channels.)

PACKET SWITCHING NETWORKS (PSNs)

Most of these carriers are also being combined with new ways of transmitting information called PACKET SWITCHING. This form of transmission relies on computers which control the route taken by transmitted information, that is, along which line or wave band the information is transmitted. However, these computers are even more sophisticated in that they 'chop' a long message into evenly sized 'packets' and then label each packet in sequence with its number. This is something like taking a long dictated letter, typing it on to A4 pages (each page is then the same size packet), numbering each page and noting, on each page, the letter reference.

The computer then sends each packet down the first available route. Thus one packet may get to Glasgow via Birmingham, the next packet may go via Newcastle, the next via Bristol, etc. At the receiving-end the receiving computer collects each packet and by using the label and the packet number, re-assembles the whole message. This could be compared to sending each page of the letter separately and then, at the other end, having someone to collect each page together as they are received and to collate them to form the whole letter.

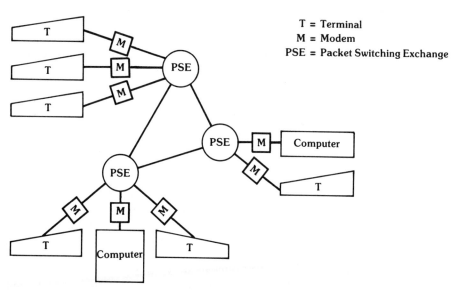

A packet switching network (PSN)

The advantage with packet switching comes from its ability to use all the available carrier lines. This means that the PACKET SWITCHING NETWORK (PSN) will not ever have to wait for a direct line between two areas but will work out the best route to send a packet each time.

Thus the first packet may go directly. However, because all the direct lines are busy when the computer is ready to send the next packet, it will work out the next best route and send the packet via that route.

Overall, this system will increase the speed by which information can be transmitted and make the best and therefore most cost-affective use of the communication networks.

Now we have all the ingredients for a revolution in life-styles: cheap powerful computers, capabilities to store vast quantities of information and rapid, inexpensive (or becoming so) communications. In the next chapter we shall look at how these are now being used and suggest future developments.

SUMMARY

For a business to get the full value from its computer systems it is necessary for all the functions within the business to be able to communicate.

Copper wires are the most common way of linking machines. For high-speed transmission 'parallel' buses are used. These allow one byte to be transmitted at a time. As this form of wire is expensive it is only used for short links.

Longer links, usually within a building, use coaxial cable. Transmission rates are slower as only one bit at a time is transmitted. This is termed 'serial transmission'.

Remote wired links are usually made by using the telephone/Telex networks. To use the telephone network a modem is necessary whereas to use the Telex network no modem is needed but the transmitted signal must be converted into a Telex format.

Current speeds of transmission using the telephone wires are between 300 and 9600 bps. Using the Telex network, the speed is 50 bps.

To increase the speed of transmission, carriers are being developed which have a very wide band width to allow more signals to be carried.

One of these new carriers is the optical fibre. As light travels at enormously high speed, and it is possible to use a wide band width, these carriers can transmit at speeds up to 1 billion bps. Fibre optic cables form the basis for the Megastream service offered by British Telecom.

For machines to be able to communicate they must have agreed protocols. There are three forms of communication between machines, simplex, half duplex and full duplex.

Data can be transmitted either asynchronously or synchronously, i.e. character by character or whole messages.

Transmission using non-physical links involves the use of microwave, infrared and radio. Microwave and infrared are used over short distances; radio waves are used nationally and internationally.

Packet switching networks rely on computers which control the route taken by transmitted information. These computers chop a message into evenly sized packets, label the packets and send each packet down the first available route. The receiving computer re-assembles the whole message. Using the PSN ensures that all available carrier lines are used and no delays are encountered.

SELF-CHECK QUESTIONS

1. Explain the term 'integrated information system'.

2. Wires are the most common way of linking machines. What are they usually made of?

3. What type of wire would be used between a CPU and a disk drive?

4. What is the wire called that consists of two wires with one wire running through a sheath formed by the second wire?

5. Explain the difference between 'serial' and 'parallel' transmission.

6. What is the advantage of using a dedicated line to transmit data?

7. Explain how it is possible to send many different signals down a communication carrier at one time without the signals becoming muddled with each other.

8. What is an optical fibre?

9. Why is transmission via optical fibres very fast?

10. Fibre optical cables form the basis for a new service being offered by British Telecom. What is the name of this service?

11. Give three non-physical methods of transmitting data.

12. What is the function of a satellite when used for data transmission?

13. What does PSN stand for?

14. What is the main advantage of the PSN?

15. What is the difference between asynchronous and synchronous transmission?

16. Explain what is meant by simplex, half duplex and full duplex communication links between two machines.

INFORMATION PROCESSING

Chapter Objectives

After studying this chapter you should be able to:

1. Define the term 'information'.

2. List the features of an information processing system.

3. Identify aspects of the current office environment that may be replaced by an information processing system.

4. Briefly explain the main purpose of the Data Protection Act.

END OF OBJECTIVES END OF OBJECTIVES END OF OBJECTIVES END OF OBJECTIVES

INTRODUCTION

The previous chapter provided all the ingredients for information processing but without actually giving the 'recipe' by which the ingredients are to be combined or even saying what the finished product, an information processing system, actually is.

INFORMATION PROCESSING

Firstly, what do we mean by information processing and why is it different from data processing or word processing?

That is a difficult question but let us try to answer it simply. Data may be thought of as items of information which on their own have little use. An example would be a student's name. On its own it has no real value but on a register, an exam entry, a class list or a piece of work, it does have a real ability to 'inform' someone of something.

Data processing is therefore part of information processing. However, it is only concerned with certain types of information.

Words too, are forms of data but word processing, as you know, is not really concerned with individual words but with words joined together into 'text'. It would probably have been better to call word processing, 'text processing'.

Word processing, therefore, is concerned with improving the informational qualities of text such as getting the right spellings, good presentation, etc., as well as aiding in the creation of text by copying, moving, etc. Thus, word processing too forms part of information processing.

Let us just stop and think for a moment about 'information' and this may help us to come to grips with the idea of what processing information means.

If we picked up a book in Japanese, or read a mathematician's degree thesis, most of us would find it almost totally meaningless – a jumble of data and text. However, to a Japanese the book may well be highly informative or to another mathematician the thesis may prove most useful. Information, therefore, must mean that what is presented is both understandable and useful to the receiver of the information.

Thus, when we use information processing systems we should find it easier and quicker to obtain the 'information' we require. Prestel, for example, can provide an enormous amount of information and it will also allow some two-way flows of information: it is possible to book an airline flight via Prestel – you can therefore 'inform' the airline of your order for a flight reservation.

At present, true information processing systems – at least as we would describe them – are not fully functional. However, they are coming rapidly. So what do we mean by an information processing system? Well, it should allow text and data processing with widespread communications using voice, image (TV-type and facsimile), data and word transmissions and access with little difficulty the public data banks such as Prestel. It should also be sufficiently portable to use the information system anywhere and be expandable.

An expandable system is useful because as we become more used to its powers we may, for example, decide that we want to be able to turn on our oven while still at work. That is, we want to 'inform' the oven (which will have its own computer) that we want it to turn on to a specific temperature at a specific time and thus we need to expand the information processing system.

Initially, the drive to install information systems will be commercial. Offices, will (some already are) be linked into an information system whereby each office worker (and many factory workers) will have his or her own terminal. This will replace the:

- telephone
- Telex
- mail
- diary

- workpad
- dictaphone
- filing cabinet
- TV/Prestel set
- photocopier
- waste bin

and perhaps even the desk itself. Many people believe that eventually these systems will replace the office itself.

DATA PROTECTION ACT

With the burgeoning use of electronic systems for the storage and retrieval of data, many countries have recognised the need for laws to control the use of this data and to protect the individual from improper use of information. In the UK an Act of Parliament, the Data Protection Act, was introduced in 1984. Under this Act individuals are provided with the right to know what data is being stored relating to them, by whom it is being stored and for what purpose the information will be used. Additionally, the Act allows individuals to claim damages when they are adversely affected by disclosure of inaccurate information or disclosure to unauthorized persons or organizations.

With some exceptions, any individual organization that stores personal information electronically is required to register with the Data Protection Registrar details of information stored, how this information is protected, how it is maintained, what is the purpose for storage and who has access. Individuals who request details of information stored about them must be given all such information.

THE FUTURE

For much of the rest of the book we shall be concentrating on word processing as it forms a major part of the work environment. However, before we leave this area we shall consider briefly the future – not the distant future – but the not-so-far-off future.

Only a few years ago, calculators were not allowed in examinations as examiners feared that candidates would not be able to do maths without the help of machines. However, increasingly, society has realised that to use a machine to obtain an answer does imply that the user knows what he or she is doing.

We said earlier that information is only information when *it means something*. Therefore, if you can use a calculator to find out that $1+1=2$ and 2 means something, then why not use calculators? Do you use a telephone? Do you know how it *all* works? Probably not, but even so the results of using a telephone *are* meaningful. With the advent of the microchip, development of mass storage devices and the growth of communication facilities, technology is approaching the point where science fiction can become science fact.

To finish, here are two simple examples of what is and may be.

The first concerns greetings cards. It is already possible to buy greetings cards (for birthdays, Christmas, weddings, etc.) that contain a microchip. When the card is opened the chip plays an appropriate tune – the 'playing card'.

The second concerns virtually anything; for example, a lawn-mower. Lawn-mowers look the way they do because their shape allows them to be controlled and operated by a human. If the mower controlled itself, however, perhaps it would be the size of a cigarette box and it would be put into the garden and left alone. Then, like a tortoise, it would wander endlessly around the lawn 'eating' the grass. However, the computer in the mower would ensure that the lawn-mower never left any part unmown or did one area twice while leaving another area undone.

Try this. Just add the word 'intelligent' to anything and then describe how that intelligent object would look, what it would do, how it would do it, what would be its use, etc., etc.:

- intelligent typewriter
- intelligent cooker
- intelligent car
- intelligent make-up mirror
- intelligent washing machine
- intelligent telephone
- etc.

SUMMARY

Information processing involves the processing of data, text, graphics, etc. into a form that is meaningful to the receiver of the information.

Information processing systems, in the context of this book, refer to systems that have input devices to gather information, processing devices to process information, storage devices to store information and output devices to disseminate information.

These systems must be able to grow and take on new functions. Related to offices, information systems may replace most of the aids currently used to help process information such as telephones, diaries, etc.

The Data Protection Act has been introduced in recognition of the need to protect individuals from erroneous or misleading information being stored about them.

Much of the groundwork has been laid for a future dominated by information.

SELF-CHECK QUESTIONS

1. What is the difference between data processing and word processing?

2. What do you understand by 'information'?

3. List the features that you would expect from an information processing system.

4. List eight aspects of the current environment that information processing systems may replace.

5. Add the word 'intelligent' to anything and describe:

   - what it would look like

   - what it would do

   - how it would do it

   - what would be its use.

   You may use one of the examples mentioned in this chapter, or choose your own.

6. In what year was the Data Protection Act introduced?

7. Explain the main purpose of the Data Protection Act.

8. List four aspects of the Data Protection Act.

THE ELECTRONIC OFFICE

Chapter Objectives

After studying this chapter you should be able to:

1. List the features that are likely to be found on an office automation (OA) system.

2. Describe how these features are integrated.

3. Describe the following features of OA systems:

- spreadsheets
- graphics
- voice-enhancement features
- diary
- electronic mail
- notebooks
- text-checking
- information retrieval
- telephone facilities
- communications.

END OF OBJECTIVES END OF OBJECTIVES END OF OBJECTIVES END OF OBJECTIVES

INTRODUCTION

We have reviewed many of the features that together could comprise an information processing system. In addition, we have projected what may lie ahead for us in the future. This chapter looks at one type of information processing system which is most likely to affect you as potential office workers. This type of system is called one of the following:

- office automation (OA)
- the electronic office
- the office of the future.

Many of the large computer manufacturers already offer 'electronic office systems'. While the facilities offered vary, general trends are emerging and here we shall cover the features that could comprise a complete office automation system.

WORD PROCESSING

As offices are still heavily reliant on the creation and editing of text as the basic source of information, good word processing lies at the heart of office systems.

Included in the system as part of the word processing will often be a programming language which allows most of the use of the word processor to be automated. Single keystrokes will then produce the effects of a whole series of key depressions.

DATA PROCESSING

The second corner-stone of an office information system is data processing. Much of the work within offices involves collecting data from files and combining or processing this data to produce answers to specific questions. Office automation systems must, therefore, provide data processing capabilities. As these systems are intended to be used by non-data processing people, it is usual to find the data processing language is some form of BASIC (often referred to as OFFICE BASIC) – the language most widely used by untrained users of computers who have not undergone professional training in data processing. As newer, more powerful and easier to use 4th-generation languages are introduced, these will undoubtedly supersede BASIC to become the standard languages in office automation systems.

An integral part of the data processing capabilities of these systems is file management. At present, this tends to be a limited card index-type of filing system. However, with the growing use of relational databases, newer systems offer a full relational data manager.

SPREADSHEETS

Another basic function undertaken in most offices involves the production of spreadsheets. These are very common in financial departments but are used in almost every area within organizations.

A spreadsheet is, essentially, the computer's equivalent of a large sheet of paper on which are written tables of information. It is basically:

- a series of rows and columns with

- each row and each column having a heading, and

- generally having some form of relationship between different rows or different columns.

For example, a spreadsheet may have individual employees' names as the row headings and gross salary, tax, pensions, national insurance, net salary, etc. as column headings. Clearly, for each employee there is a relationship between his or her gross salary and tax, national insurance, pension and net salary.

PROFIT FORECAST

		1984	1985	1986	1987
		---1---	---2---	---3---	---4---
A	SALES	200,000	240,000	288,000	345,600
B	COST OF SALE	£50,000	£60,000	£72,000	£86,400
C	GROSS PROFIT	150,000	180,000	216,000	259,200
D	R & D	200,000	150,000	80,000	5,000
E	WAGES	32,000	33,800	35,600	37,400
F	OTHER O'HEAD	35,000	35,000	35,000	35,000
G	TOTAL O'HEAD	£267,000	£218,800	£150,600	£77,400
H	NET PROFIT	(117,000)	(38,800)	65,400	181,800
I		0	0	0	0

		1988	1989	1990
		---5---	---6---	---7---
A	SALES	414,720	497,664	597,197
B	COST OF SALE	£103,680	£124,416	£149,299
C	GROSS PROFIT	311,040	373,248	447,898
D	R & D	2,000	2,000	2,000
E	WAGES	39,200	41,000	42,800
F	OTHER O'HEAD	35,000	35,000	35,000
G	TOTAL O'HEAD	£76,200	£78,000	£79,800
H	NET PROFIT	234,840 .	295,248	368,098
I		0	0	0

A spreadsheet

These sheets are used a great deal when planning for business decisions. The salary chart prepared may be re-done giving everyone a five per cent increase to see what the total effect is on the company's wages bill. Done manually this is time-consuming. However, electronic spreadsheets can be created very quickly. When all the relationships and rules have been defined the chart is often referred to as a MODEL. Data can be entered into the model which will do all the calculations necessary. The greatest strength of these models is that they allow 'what ifs' to be done.

A 'what if' is a change to the basic model. For example, a 'what if' could be:

● what is the effect on total profits if an increase in sales of 15 per cent takes place

● what effect will the strike have if it lasts 12 weeks

● what if one-third of our key production workers leave, etc.

Most office automation systems provide electronic spreadsheets. Increasingly these, plus data from the database (or files) and word processing documents can be combined together. Thus data can be used from the database in a spreadsheet which, in turn, can be included (or merged) into the word processing document. This is often referred to as INTEGRATION OF FEATURES or SOFTWARE INFORMATION.

GRAPHICS

A relatively new feature within office systems is the business graphics facility. This feature allows the user to produce:

● pie charts

● bar charts

● line graphs

● histograms, etc.

using data from the data files or from spreadsheets. These graphs may be:

● coloured

● integrated into the word processing

● produced as hard copy by plotters or matrix printers.

VOICE-ENHANCEMENT FEATURES

Many systems are offering abilities to integrate voice recordings with text. The simplest feature is a VOICEGRAM. This allows the author of a document to:

● review the text on screen

- mark within the soft copy places at which he wishes recorded messages to be replayed

- then record the message.

The messages recorded are filed with the document. When the document is later reviewed by anyone, the voice message will be replayed when the appropriate page is displayed on the screen. Voicegrams could be used to emphasize particularly important items within the text. When reviewing sales targets, for example, the voicegram may say:

> 'Make damn sure that every customer is made aware of this special promotion. It's costing us £25 000 to put on and everyone's bonus is riding on a good response to it.'

A more advanced voice feature is a voice document. This allows the author to dictate in front of a VDU. Each word is digitized and recorded. The author can then review the voice document and perform all the functions one might expect from word processing, except that he does no keyboarding. Thus he can:

- insert words in the recording

- delete whatever he wants from the recording

- move or copy whole sections of the recording

- copy or move recorded speech from previous voice documents into his current document.

Upon completion, the voice document would represent exactly what the author wished to say without his having to record and re-record the whole message until it was right.

(If you ever do audio dictation or typing, you will appreciate how useful this would be as a tool for authors who do most of their work via audio dictation.)

DIARY (OR CALENDAR)

Every office information system will include electronic diaries (or calendars as the Americans call them). These will allow secretaries or their bosses to record their appointments and notes on the system. The major advantage with electronic diaries, apart from *ad hoc* enquiries such as: 'How many meetings have I with Lion and Lamb?', lies in the ability of other system users to schedule events or meetings in your diary.

Clearly, most people would not want anyone to be able to read or amend their diaries, so every system will offer some form of security to preserve confidentiality.

Another use of this feature revolves around the booking of conference or meeting rooms. Most companies have special rooms available and these must be booked in advance. Electronic booking makes this easy.

ELECTRONIC MAIL

Electronic mail is a standard feature on all office automation systems.

This feature allows:

- letters or memos to be created using standard word processing
- these documents then to be 'posted' electronically to a 'mail-box' address, either on the same configuration or via a telecommunications link to another machine anywhere in the world
- letters in your own mail-box to be reviewed on the screen or printed.

The great advantages of electronic mail are:

- speed
- accuracy
- accessibility – by using portable microcomputers you can see what is in your mail-box from any telephone, anywhere.

COMMUNICATIONS

Clearly, any system that offers electronic mail must support telecommunication links. Most office automation systems have a wide range of telecommunication features including:

- local area networking
- wide area networking
- mainframe links
- data file links.

An increasing number of systems also offer document interchange which allows word processing documents to be transferred and converted from one type of system to another.

NOTEBOOKS

Often we need to make notes about something which we want to keep and refer to in future. Many systems provide an electronic notepad or 'scratch pad' on which notes can be typed and recalled and reviewed later.

TEXT-CHECKING

Most office systems will provide a spelling-checking feature. A document or piece of text can be electronically checked for spelling against a dictionary containing thousands of words (80 000 is not an uncommon size). Individual lists or dictionaries can be created and used to check for only those words you most commonly misspell.

A less common feature is a 'readability' or 'fog index' checker which will check text to see how 'readable' it is. Text that has long sentences full of complex words is considered difficult to read and understand while simple, clear prose is thought to communicate effectively. A readability checker provides indexes, based on standard tests, of how readable the text is.

INFORMATION RETRIEVAL

All these systems provide powerful information retrieval features which allow information to be obtained from virtually any stored file.

Facilities include:

- Keyword retrieval – when entering text you can mark words as keywords and the system will automatically create an index to the word.

- Random 'searches on string' including 'wild-card options' – this allows you to search your notebook for all entries of 'plays golf' or every letter for 'market*' (the * is a wild card). The search for market * would find every occurrence of the words market, markets, marketing, marketed, marketable, etc.

This information retrieval facility is often linked to the word processing allowing you to select from the database records meeting particular selection criteria and merging these into the standard letters.

TELEPHONE FACILITIES

Although estimates vary, it is generally accepted that much of the average office worker's time is spent in making telephone calls. A high percentage of these calls are abortive calls in which:

- the number dialled is engaged, or

- the person you are trying to contact is out or on another line.

Often they phone you back only to find that you have gone out. You then return their call and they are in a meeting . . .

Office systems aim to improve this process by:

- storing your private list of numbers

- automatically dialling numbers and retrying if the line is engaged

- ringing your extension when the call being tried is answered

- acting as an answering machine when you are out of the office.

PHOTOTYPESETTING

Just as many systems offer direct lines into the Telex network, so there is a growing demand for direct interfaces to phototypesetters. Typesetting is a specialist form of producing print which provides:

- highest-quality print

- greatest variety of typefaces

- largest range of print sizes – from the tiny print on contracts to the large print on headlines.

Most printed material you see, such as sales brochures or equipment manuals that look really good, will have been produced using a phototypesetter.

Modern typesetters are digital machines employing laser technology. However, the majority of typesetters currently in use are called phototypesetters (or photo-mechanical typesetters).

These machines have a VDU with a keyboard and disk drive. Text keyed in is displayed and edited just as with word processing. However, inserted into the text is a series of typographical commands which the software uses to define the type and size of the print required.

On sophisticated machines it is possible to display mixes of text and graphics and to experiment with layouts and type-styles before finalising the layout.

Once finalized, the material undergoes one of the following processes:

- The material is transferred on to light-sensitive paper which is processed and cut up into sections called galleys. These are assembled together to form a page. The page is photographed and a printing plate is produced from the negative.

- On modern laser systems the image of the whole page is produced directly on to a plate which is used for printing.

The similarities between the front end (or beginning) stage of typesetting and word processing has stimulated demand for companies to be able to produce their own material for printing which is then sent, via disk or telecommunications, to the printer's phototypesetting configuration where the typographic commands are added and the text printed.

OTHER FACILITIES

Other facilities offered include:

- Microcomputer operating systems like CP/M, MS DOS or CPM-86 which allow simple, cheap programs to be used with the office system.

- Telex interfaces which make it possible to create and send Telexes from any terminal linked into the system and to receive Telexes into your own mailbox as if they were electronic mail.

- Image-digitizing hardware which will scan, using a digitizing camera, any document or picture. The resulting digitized image can be displayed on a screen. This facility allows all correspondence to be converted into electronic form thus making the paperless office a real possibility. It will also herald the demise of facsimile transmission as a non-integrated office function.

There are many pilot or trial installations of office automation systems. However, as the technology is still reliant on keyboard skills and also tends to be somewhat laborious to use, it has not yet made a significant impact on the office environment in general. As software improves and becomes easier to use and technology makes computer use simpler, so the use of this form of information technology will increase.

Well-implemented office-based information systems should:

- make the average office worker much more productive

- allow more people to work from home or local neighbourhood 'work-sites' rather than having to commute long distances to work each day.

SUMMARY

Information systems relating specifically to offices are called office automation (OA) or electronic office systems. No OA system yet offers all the functions described. In addition, some systems are much harder to use than others.

Good word processing is one of the fundamental functions offered by OA systems.

A second essential element is the ability to perform data processing. Often BASIC is the standard language although, with the development of new powerful 4th-generation languages, it is probable that these will replace BASIC.

The ability to create, very easily, simple card index-type files is common in OA. As relational databases are developed, so it will become the standard to have a full relational data manager.

Spreadsheets which allow calculations based on rows and columns are often featured in OA systems. These allow models of financial transactions, etc. to be created and then, by simply changing a few numbers, it is possible to see 'what would happen if . . .'

Data from spreadsheets or data files can be directly fed into graphics programs which will produce various charts and graphs.

Many systems offer the ability to add recorded voice messages to soft copy text. These messages, called voicegrams, are then replayed whenever the soft copy is displayed on a screen.

A few systems offer an advanced feature called a voice document. This feature allows speech to be digitized and recorded and then reviewed and edited using editing functions similar to those offered by word processing.

Every system offers electronic diaries. These can be looked at by date or by random inquiries.

The ability to send electronic messages (or 'mail') from one system user to another or to other machines anywhere in the world is a key feature of all OA systems.

Good telecommunications features that are easy to use are common, as are notebooks which allow notes to be entered into the system and reviewed later.

Most good OA systems currently offer a facility to check text for spelling mistakes electronically. More-advanced systems also offer facilities which will check text and give an indication of how easy it is to understand.

An important function in any office is the retrieval of information and OA systems are providing increasingly good facilities to retrieve information.

Simple telephone assistance, in the form of personal telephone directories, are common. More advanced OA systems will automatically ring numbers and keep trying until an answer is received, store your personal numbers and act as an answering machine.

There is a growing demand for word processors to interface directly with phototypesetters. As the initial stage of typesetting is similar to word processing, companies are producing their own material for setting, and sending this text to phototypesetters via disk or telecommunications.

Other features include the ability to operate microcomputer operating systems, direct Telex interfaces and image-digitizing cameras.

SELF-CHECK QUESTIONS

1. List ten features that are likely to be offered by OA systems.

2. What lies at the heart of all office systems?

3. Many systems offer, as part of their word processing software, a programming language. For what might this programming language be used?

4. What is the second 'corner-stone' of OA systems?

5. Why is a form of BASIC usually provided on OA systems?

6. What is a spreadsheet and for what is it likely to be used?

7. Give an example of a 'what if' statement.

8. Systems are increasingly offering the facility to combine data from spreadsheets and files with word processing documents. What is the name often given to this facility?

9. Many systems allow graphics. What use might an office make of this feature?

10. Could you use a graph within a word processing document?

11. How would you produce a hard copy of a graph?

12. What is a voicegram and when might a voicegram be used?

13. What is a voice document?

14. What benefits might be gained by an author using a voice document?

15. List four uses that might be made of electronic diaries.

16. Electronic mail is a standard feature on all OA systems. What are the advantages of electronic mail?

17. List three telecommunication features you would expect on an OA system.

18. Most systems provide a facility for spellings to be checked against a dictionary. How many words might a dictionary contain?

19. It is usually possible to create your own dictionary. In what instances would this be useful?

20. What is the purpose of a readability checker on an OA system?

21. All OA systems provide powerful information retrieval features. What do these features include?

22. With many information retrieval features there is a 'wild-card' option. What is a wild card and when would this option be useful?

23. List four ways in which an office system may improve telephone facilities.

24. What does a Telex interface allow?

25. Why will good OA systems allow people to work from home?

14

INTEGRATED SOFTWARE

Chapter Objectives

After studying this chapter you should be able to:

1. Define the term 'integration'.

2. Identify the main features of integrated software.

3. List the features and facilities offered by:
   a spreadsheets
   b graphics software
   c databases.

4. Distinguish between a database system and a file management system.

END OF OBJECTIVES END OF OBJECTIVES END OF OBJECTIVES END OF OBJECTIVES

INTRODUCTION

In the previous chapter we looked at the range of features that may be expected in an office automation system. Inherent in virtually all office information systems will be:

- word processing software

- database management software

- spreadsheet software

- communications software

- graphics software.

Before we look at word processing in depth, let us look at the other facilities and how increasingly these facilities are being integrated together.

156

INTEGRATION

Until the middle to late 1970s most computer technology was used, at least in business environments, to perform large-scale clerical-type functions such as payrolls, accounting, stock control, etc. The use of computers for processing information was limited particularly as most office workers did not have ready access to computing power. However, with the rapid growth in the availability of powerful microcomputing, the falling costs of computers in general and the improvements in communications, it has become common for almost anyone in a business to have some computing facility. Suddenly, as more people began to use computers they found that the information provided was often inappropriate for their needs. As a result they had to reprocess the information, often combining information from various sources. In general, this 'reprocessing' was (and is) done using microcomputers and, unfortunately, it usually involved 'keying-in' data that had been entered into another computer, processed and then produced as printed output.

Why, you may ask, should it be necessary to re-input information into a computer when it was already held on another computer system in electronic form? Well, as we mentioned earlier, different machines operate in different ways with little standardization between them. Even worse, different programs on the same machines file their data in different ways, thus making it difficult to use data from a database in a word processing letter for example.

As an example of this entering and re-entering of data, let us cite an example which occurred in a large multi-national company comprising several manufacturing plants, a number of group co-ordinating functions and a head office. Every month the plants would report on their performance to their group function. The group function would consolidate (join together) the performance figures from the plants and send these to head office. In head office all the group reports were consolidated to show the company performance. To get this information in the form that was required:

- The data on plant activity was keyed into four systems operating on a mainframe computer – a payroll system, a stock system, a manufacturing system and an accountancy system. (In fact, output from some of these systems had to be re-keyed as input to other systems.)

- Output from these four systems (as paper reports) was then used to provide input data which was keyed into a microcomputer at each plant and reports produced.

- These reports were sent to the group office where they were used to provide input to another microcomputer system. In one case, this system produced some reports which were given to another person in the same building, who, because he had a different microcomputer, had to re-key most of the figures again. (So far the same data had, in various forms, been typed in five times!)

- The reports produced at group level were posted to head office. Here they were used by different departments, each keying figures in until finally a report giving the information required by the company was produced.

(In total, data was keyed in at least seven times, and in one case twelve times!)

All the microcomputer systems had been developed by people with little training in computing using packages such as spreadsheets or databases. Thus, while it was technically feasible to transfer data from one system to another electronically, the complexities of doing so made this impossible for the people involved.

Clearly, to make information systems really efficient, it should be simple to use data from one computer system in another and from one set of software to another. This ability to share resources, whether they be hardware devices (hardware integration) or data files (data integration) or software (software integration), is what integration is all about. In particular the sharing of data files means that data need only be keyed in once and duplication is eliminated because only one source of data is used.

CURRENT DEVELOPMENTS

To provide integrated software, many companies have begun marketing integrated products. Developments are currently either microcomputer-based or mini/mainframe-based. The first suites of truly integrated micro/mainframe software are now on the market.

Basically, these products allow a computer user to manipulate data using any one of the standard software types (that is, word processing, spreadsheets, graphics and databases) and then to combine together output from these programs in a single form. For example, a word processing report can have a table of numbers and calculations produced using a spreadsheet incorporated wherever needed, graphs produced from data extracted from the database merged into the text and all printed out together on the final document.

Most of the present microcomputer software of this type (for example, Lotus 1-2-3) which, while being easy to use on data that the user has keyed in, does not allow simple integration with large databases of information held on mini/ mainframe computers.

Products for larger systems are generally not as simple to use as microcomputer products and, because this type of integrated processing uses large quantities of CPU power, performance of the computer system can noticeably deteriorate when a number of people are using this software.

The ideal solution is to have distributed microcomputers connected to a powerful central CPU which has the ability to store large volumes of data on a central database. These microcomputers should then be easily able to select and extract data from the central database, DOWNLOAD it on to their own disks, process it locally (using integrated software) and then UPLOAD it to the central machine for other users to have access to, if needed.

This type of software (for example, Lotus Symphony, Peachtree's Decision Management/Xiton Open Access) is available now but still requires a degree of technical experience higher than is common with most microcomputer users.

So now we know what integration of facilities will provide, let us look a little more closely at the standard components of spreadsheets, databases and graphics.

SPREADSHEETS

As we said before, a spreadsheet is an electronic 'sheet of paper' ruled into a series of rows and columns. This form of representing information, in rows and columns (or tables) is common and electronic spreadsheets make working with this form of data arrangement easy.

With a spreadsheet program, each row will have a reference (such as row A, B, C, D, E, F . . . etc.). Similarly, each column will have a reference (such as column 1, 2, 3, 4, 5, 6 . . . etc.). The point at which a row and a column cross is referred to as a cell or box – it is the place where something can be written or stored on the spreadsheet. Thus every cell will have a unique reference such as A1 (row A, column 1) or F20 (row F, column 20).

Various types of information can be stored on the spreadsheet. This information may be:

- labels
- numbers
- formulae.

Labels

Labels are the words or titles used for headings on the spreadsheet or on individual rows or columns. A good package will allow you to format these labels in several ways such as:

- left, right or centred within the cell
- fixed so that for example, as you move down the rows the titles on the columns do not disappear off the screen
- upper or lower case
- spread over a range of cells.

Some spreadsheets allow you to search through a spreadsheet for a label or to use a label as part of a cell reference, for example: 'sales, 20' refers to the row labelled 'sales' in column 20, or 'cost of sales, 1986' refers to the row labelled 'cost of sales' and the column labelled '1986'.

```
                              PROFIT FORECAST


                        1984        1985        1986        1987
------------------------------  ----1----   ----2----   ----3----  ----4----

A  SALES
B  COST OF SALE      ................  ................  ................  ................
C  GROSS PROFIT
D  WAGES
E  R & D
F  OTHER O'HEAD
G  TOTAL O'HEAD
                     ==========  ==========  =========  =========
H  NET PROFIT
I
```

Labels on a spreadsheet

Numbers

These can be entered as either positive or negative. The software will often
allow you to:

- fix the number of decimal points to be used

- format a cell as a percentage so that numbers within the cell will be shown
  as percentages

- have a minus sign in front or behind negative numbers or to put brackets
  around negative numbers

- express numbers as exponentials (e.g. 1.2×10^2 instead of 120).

Formulae

The real strength of electronic spreadsheets lies in their ability to have cells
defined as being the result of formulae. This means that any cell can have the
result of calculations displayed in it. Thus cell C1 might be defined as $+A1-B1$
– in other words whatever number is placed into cell B1 should be subtracted
from whatever number is placed into cell A1 with the answer placed into cell C1.

```
           1
    A      6
    B      2
    C      4(+A1-B1)
```

Using labels, this could be expressed as (sales – cost of sales), and this formula
entered into the cell C3 – gross profit.

160

Clearly, as most mathematical functions can be used, it is easy to do complex calculations once the spreadsheet with all its formulae has been completed. A spreadsheet, defined in this way, is referred to as a model.

```
                            PROFIT  FORECAST


                     1984         1985         1986         1987
   ---------------  ----1----   ----2----   ----3----   ----4----

A  SALES            200,000     240,000     288,000     345,600
B  COST OF SALE     £50,000     £60,000     £72,000     £86,400
C  GROSS PROFIT     150,000     180,000     216,000     259,200
D  R & D            200,000     150,000      80,000       5,000
E  WAGES             32,000      33,800      35,600      37,400
F  OTHER O'HEAD      35,000      35,000      35,000      35,000
G  TOTAL O'HEAD    £267,000    £218,800    £150,600     £77,400
                   =========   =========   =========   =========
H  NET PROFIT      (117,000)    (38,800)     65,400     181,800
I                         0           0           0           0


                     1988         1989         1990
   ---------------  ----5----   ----6----   ----7----

A  SALES            414,720     497,664     597,197
B  COST OF SALE    £103,680    £124,416    £149,299
C  GROSS PROFIT     311,040     373,248     447,898
D  R & D              2,000       2,000       2,000
E  WAGES             39,200      41,000      42,800
F  OTHER O'HEAD      35,000      35,000      35,000
G  TOTAL O'HEAD     £76,200     £78,000     £79,800
                   =========   =========   =========
H  NET PROFIT       234,840     295,248     368,098
I                         0           0           0
```

A spreadsheet

A good spreadsheet will allow:

- rows or columns to be inserted (in case you forgot a particular month, etc.)

- a range of cells to be copied or moved

- formulae and titles to be edited

- rows and columns from other, filed spreadsheets to be added to or merged into the spreadsheet being worked on (consolidations)

161

- calculations to be turned off, allowing many numbers to be changed before the spreadsheet recaculates

- look-ups and conditional statements (for example [lookup] the table to find the month of January or if the value in cell A27 equals zero multiply . . .)

- macros to be defined whereby one or two keystrokes will cause multiple statements to be carried out

- 'windows' to be defined – these allow an area of the spreadsheet to be 'held' on the screen while moving around the rest of the sheet or to have various parts of a large sheet displayed on the screen together.

GRAPHICS

Graphics software will produce business graphs either from figures keyed in or from a spreadsheet or database. The graphics produced include:

- pie charts
- bar charts
- line graphs
- stacked bars
- X/Y graphs.

Some software allows the pie charts to be manipulated and sectors of the pie removed.

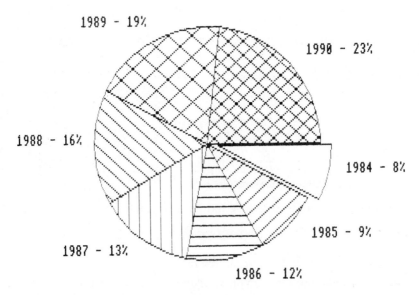

A pie chart

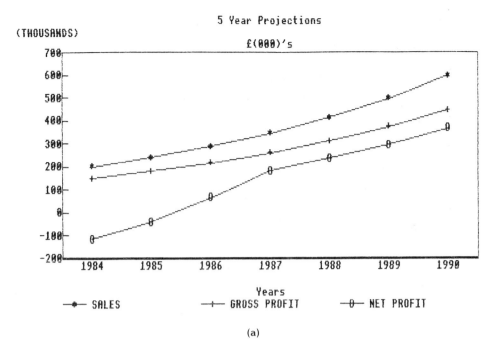

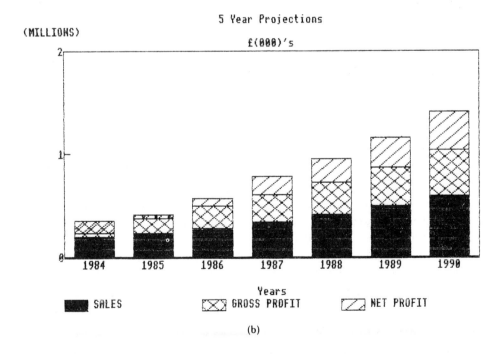

Examples of (a) a graph, and (b) a stacked bar chart

It is usually simple to:

- give the graph a title

- label the X and Y axes

- define a legend (that is, what each line or bar type is)

- select the range of figures to be used

- have the system 'scale' the graph or choose your own scale

- automatically colour or 'hash' the graphs so that one may be distinguished from the other

- include more than one set of variables in a graph (for example, budget, forecast and actual figures – these would give three lines on a line graph and are three sets of variables)

- combine graph types allowing a line to be produced for one set of variables and bars for another

- produce printed output using either a matrix printer or a plotter.

DATABASES

A database, as we said before, is a file or collection of files arranged in such a way that it is easy to store and retrieve data without needing to know how the data is stored by the computer. Unfortunately, many microcomputer products that are sold as databases are no more than file management systems and do not provide the benefits of a good database system. A database system should offer:

- Data independence so that fields in a record (or columns in a row) can be increased or decreased in size, or new columns/fields added without affecting the programs using the data or data already stored on the computer.

- Limited data duplication – ideally no item of information in a database should be stored twice. This means that, as there is only one occurrence of the data item, it must always be the most up-to-date value for that data item. Inevitably, some information is held twice and the software should ensure that both occurrences are updated at the same time.

- Data protection or security so that individual items in a record can be marked as being 'confidential' or private and only certain people able to access this information.

- Physical data protection so that if anything should happen to the computer while the database in in use, the data within the database is still recoverable (that is, it can still be used).

- A measure of data integrity whereby only accurate and valid data can ever be stored on the database. In this way, a program may try to store, for example, characters in a number field – the database software would reject the request and would not store the data. This is a key feature in database software.

- Ease of use with programs that allow screens to be easily created for data to be maintained on the database, query languages that make it easy to find the information required from the database and report writers that make it easy to produce reports using data stored.

While database software for mainframes and minicomputers offer these facilities, most microcomputer 'databases' do not. However, as the power of microcomputers has increased, some true database software is now to be found on microcomputers.

Most current microcomputer 'databases' are, in reality, file management systems. These allow:

- A record layout to be created easily on the VDU. This layout will have the headings as they will appear on the screen plus the titles of the fields on the actual file (often these are the same).

- Field sizes to be specified.

- Masks to be created which only show some of the fields on the file.

- Multiple screens for any one file.

- Searches to be made using the screens defined and specifying what you are searching for in the correct field. For example, you can find all the records for Smith by typing Smith in the surname field.

- Records to be sorted on any field.

- Records to be input, updated or deleted using the screens defined.

- Calculations to be done on the numeric fields within the file.

- Reports to be created with headings, etc. using the data file.

These systems are, however, often limited in that they only allow one (or sometimes two) files to be used at once and are difficult to program to achieve results more than the 'file and retrieve' function.

As the software offered improves, it will become more usual to find integrated packages which provide a database management system, with spreadsheets that can extract or store data on the database, graphics which can use data stored either within the database or on spreadsheets and all of these sources of information readily used when preparing word processing text. Finally, all of these capabilities will be linked to powerful communications software which will allow you to select data from many different sources or machines or to transfer your information freely from your 'local' computer to another machine.

SUMMARY

Integration of data and programs is designed to reduce the amount of re-keying required when using different programs or files of data.

Developments are currently aiming to integrate microcomputers with larger systems so that it will be easy for non-technical people to extract data from large databases to use in local microcomputer applications.

Most integrated products offer spreadsheets, graphics, word processing, database and communications facilities. This is particularly true on microcomputers.

Spreadsheets are electronic 'sheets of paper' ruled into rows and columns. Each row and column will have a reference and the area where they cross is called a cell.

A cell can have labels, numbers or mathematical formulae stored in it. By placing labels in some cells, numbers in others and formulae that do calculations on the stored numbers, it is possible to create complex models. These models will then do multiple calculations whenever numbers are changed within the spreadsheet.

Graphics software uses data that has been keyed in or extracted from a spreadsheet or database. With this software it is easy to produce pie charts, bar charts, line graphs, stacked bars and X/Y graphs. Graphs may be coloured, labelled and scaled. Printouts are often produced using matrix printers or plotters.

Database software allows simple definition of files of information which, once defined, can be used for many different applications. The data is stored in such a way that programs need only use the data they require, rather than all the data stored on the files. Stored data can be extracted to be used in spreadsheets or graphs or to be included in a word processing document.

SELF-CHECK QUESTIONS

1. What type of software would you expect to be provided in virtually all office information systems?

2. Explain what is meant by the term integration.

3. What facilities should integrated software provide?

4. Give an example of when an integrated package would be useful.

5. When several terminals are sharing one CPU and using integrated software
   a Why might the performance of the computer deteriorate?
   b How could this problem be overcome?

6. Give three examples of integrated software packages.

7. A spreadsheet is an 'electronic sheet of paper' made up of _____ and
_____.

8. On a spreadsheet what is the name given to the point at which a row and a column cross?

9. What types of information can be stored on a spreadsheet?

10. A good spreadsheet package will allow you to format labels. What format options might you expect to be able to perform?

11. Give three ways in which it may be possible to display numbers using a spreadsheet.

12. What is it about spreadsheets that makes them so useful?

13. Once a spreadsheet with all its formulae has been completed, it is referred to as a _____.

14. You have been asked to select spreadsheet software. What are the features you would look for?

15. To produce business graphs, figures can be keyed in or taken from a
_____.

16. What types of graph would you expect to be produced from graphics software? Illustrate your answer with examples.

17. What types of facility would you expect to find in graphics software?

18. What is a database?

19. What do you understand by the term 'data independence'?

20. List five features of a good database system.

21. List four limitations of most current microcomputer 'databases'.

WHAT IS WORD PROCESSING?

Chapter Objectives

After studying this chapter you should be able to:

1. Describe and compare the various approaches adopted in the design of word processing software.

2. Explain the differences between a dedicated word processor and a word processing package on a general-purpose computer.

3. Explain how a word processor keyboard differs from a typewriter keyboard.

4. List the special keys found on a word processor keyboard and explain their purpose.

END OF OBJECTIVES END OF OBJECTIVES END OF OBJECTIVES END OF OBJECTIVES

INTRODUCTION

Several years ago we went to our local bookshop and asked the assistant whether there were any books on word processing. 'What would that be about,' the assistant replied, 'English grammar?'. We were, of course, quite amused by this but word processing was relatively new then. We explained that word processing was beginning to be introduced into offices to aid the production of text – it made typing easier, for the following reasons:

● When you press the keys on the keyboard the characters appear on a screen rather than on paper.

● The characters on the screen are not 'fixed' as they are on paper so, if you make a mistake, you can just overtype to change the characters.

● Whole words, sentences and paragraphs can be deleted or inserted without adversely affecting the rest of the text on the screen. Further, blocks of text can be moved or copied from one place in a document to another.

- You can change the entire layout of the document on the screen. For example, you may start the document with margins of one inch on each side. When the document is finished you might decide that margins of one-and-a-half inches on each side would be more suitable. This can be done by pressing a few keys and the text rearranges to the new margins.

- All the documents (letters, reports, etc.) can be stored on backing store and recalled at a later date to be modified or printed out.

- Standard letters can be created and different names and addresses automatically inserted in each letter to provide a personalized letter for every recipient.

- It is not until you are happy with the text on the screen that it is committed to paper. You can thus be certain of a perfect copy every time. (Even then, you need not commit it to paper but can store it for printing at a later date or else, in some cases, transmit it directly to another machine.)

This description of word processing may have been reasonably accurate in the past, and although it is still basically true, a word processor is much more than an 'advanced typewriter'.

Word processing is now commonplace in offices and as time has progressed so have the facilities available.

In the next four chapters we shall be discussing in some detail the basic functions already mentioned as well as the more advanced features of word processing.

WORD PROCESSING

Throughout the remainder of the book we shall be concentrating on word processing. We hope that you will be able to build upon the topics covered earlier and especially to make use of any equipment that you may have to gain 'HANDS-ON' EXPERIENCE. We aim to:

- allow you to become conversant with the terminology used

- illustrate the many functions and features found on word processors

- compare the relative advantages and disadvantages of dedicated word processors and microcomputers operating word processing software.

The design approach adopted for word processing software will determine how the word processing 'looks' to the operator. There are three areas in which different approaches will noticeably affect how the word processor is used. These areas are:

- document or page word processing

- menu-driven or command-driven word processing

- on-screen or embedded formatting.

We shall initially look at the differences between these types of word processing. Our overall aim is to provide you with sufficient understanding of word processing so that you will be able to face any new word processor with the confidence that at least you know what it is meant to do.

PAGE VERSUS DOCUMENT WORD PROCESSING

Whether the software comprises a package on a general-purpose computer or dedicated software on equipment designed solely for word processing, the approach used will fall into one of two categories. The word processing will be either page-orientated or document-orientated.

A PAGE MACHINE treats each page of text as a separate file. You can only type in one page with a maximum number of lines – often about 256. The wider you make the page – say A4 landscape – the fewer lines you will be able to type. Once you have reached your page limit you must store that page on disk before you can start a new page. Each related 'page' stored should have some form of sequencing, for example, Letter 1, Letter 2, Letter 3, etc. in order to allow all the document to be printed or easily edited.

A DOCUMENT MACHINE treats the whole document as one file. Thus it is possible to type a multi-page document without stopping. The size of the document is limited by some physical factor such as memory or disk capacity.

Both designs have their champions. Page machines, it is claimed, are easier for typists to grasp as 'each page is like a page of paper'. Similarly, you can make numerous changes to a page displayed on the screen then 'print the screen' or else decide that you do not like what you have done and clear the screen without saving any of your amendments.

Document machines usually allow greater flexibility in deciding just what goes where and in moving from one place in the document to another. However, unless the moving from page to page is well implemented, it can be slow and frustrating to travel through long documents. Another disadvantage with many document machines results from the continuous updating of the document files on the disk. Thus, should you make several changes and then decide that you do not want the changes after all, with many of these machines your stored or filed document will have already been changed.

However, both authors of this book by far prefer document to page word processing. We hope that our bias does not show too clearly!

MENU VERSUS COMMAND WORD PROCESSING

A menu on a word processor (or any information system) provides you with a list of options you can choose. You choose the option in a variety of ways such as:

- typing the option number

- moving the cursor to the option required

- typing the first letters of the option.

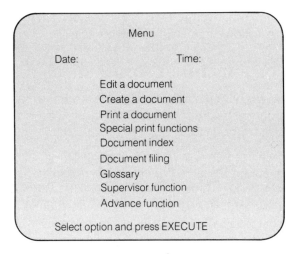

Menu

Date: Time:

Edit a document
Create a document
Print a document
Special print functions
Document index
Document filing
Glossary
Supervisor function
Advance function

Select option and press EXECUTE

A menu

Menu-driven systems often have more than one layer of menu. For example, the main menu may offer the option to 'print a document'. Choosing this option gives another menu of all the features you can select when printing the document. Thus a menu driven system relies on the operator selecting options and answering questions.

Command-driven systems adopt a different approach. No question-and-answer prompts or options are given. The operator must remember the commands to be given to fulfil a particular function. These commands are usually a set of keystrokes which begin with a control or command keystroke.

All word processors will have a key by which the operator can instruct the computer to carry out instructions. This key is often called the 'execute', 'control' or 'command' key.

Again, both approaches have their advocates. Menu-driven systems are usually easier to operate for the novice user but the expert operator frequently finds that being forced to go from menu to menu is slower than being able to issue commands immediately.

This can perhaps be illustrated by using an example. If you go into a take-away restaurant for the first time you will:

- read the menu

- select the item you want

- give your order by number.

You have used a menu-driven system. Now you go to the same restaurant often and so get to know just what you want by number. What you will then do is:

- give your order by number.

This is a command-driven system. You have not been forced to read the menu, make your selection and then give your order.

ON-SCREEN OR EMBEDDED COMMANDS

Word processors have many features that relate to the appearance of the printed text. For example, it is possible to centre text on a line, to right-justify margins or to underline headings, etc.

One approach used is to show on the screen all the special effects such as emboldening or underlining. When and where you place them in the text is edited on the screen. This is quite common with dedicated word processors. The other design approach is to show these effects only when the text is printed. To achieve the required effects you must place a special command in the text which will 'tell the printer' to underline, justify or embolden, etc. These commands are called embedded commands.

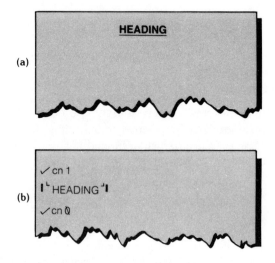

A centred, underlined and emboldened heading produced by (a) onscreen commands, and (b) embedded commands

It is more common to find embedded commands being used with word processing packages on general purpose computers because the developer of the software cannot be sure that the terminal being used will be able to show underlining or emboldening, etc. and therefore he or she must try to write the software to work with any machine, terminal and printer.

DEDICATED VERSUS PACKAGE

The term 'dedicated', as you already know, means 'designed to do one job' and much word processing equipment falls into this category. Until quite recently, dedicated word processors were much easier for operators to use than non-dedicated machines because the keyboards were designed to facilitate and aid the use of the software. For example, keys with special functions such as deletion or insertion would be etched with the function on the key. Thus the key read 'DEL' or 'INST'.

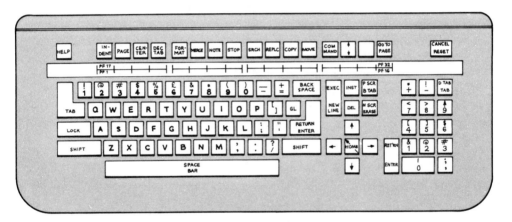

A keyboard with etched keys

In addition, the software had features not found on word processing packages used on general-purpose computers.

However, the major advantage with dedicated machines arose from being single-user, stand-alone or 'distributed-logic' systems (where every terminal had some processing power much like that found in a microcomputer today). This approach allowed each user to have rapid responses and the machine could keep up with even the fastest typist.

Often packages on mini and mainframe computers, while having many of the features found in dedicated word processing, could not make as effective use of all the keys on the keyboard because many different keyboards could be connected to the same computer.

173

Additionally, if the machine was being heavily used by many different users, word processing operators would find the system slow to respond to editing commands and they could type much faster than the machine. It is quite funny watching a good typist using one of these machines. Every time the operator pauses letters keep appearing on the screen as if by magic as the computer 'catches up'. (It is unlikely that anything typed would be lost by the computer as the characters typed are stored in a keyboard BUFFER until sent to the CPU, and then on to the screen.)

It is only since the widespread introduction of microcomputers that word processing packages have begun to rival dedicated machines. Many of the earlier packages were very crude: with some it was faster to type and retype using a typewriter than to use the word processing package!

The task of 'tailoring' packages for particular microcomputers has been made simpler with modern 16-bit microcomputers as many of these machines incorporate keys which can be programmed to perform special functions such as insert, delete, centre, etc. – these are often termed 'SOFT KEYS'.

Finally, minicomputer and microcomputer packages are now offering functions other than just word processing. These packages, which integrate many different functions including spreadsheets, graphics, word processing, database management and communications, give the general-purpose computer a significant advantage over the dedicated machine in a multi-functional environment. Examples of such packages include Symphony, Supercalc 3, Jazz and Apple, Lisa, Mackintosh, Info and Infotext.

THE KEYBOARDS

A final word about word processors generally. As discussed previously, a word processor allows:

- text to be typed in an electronic rather than a printed form

- typed text to be changed, edited, corrected and modified virtually at will

- printing of typed text in many different formats and with numerous special print effects such as emboldening, underlining, etc.

- typed text to be stored magnetically on a disk and to be retrieved for editing or reprinting whenever required.

To perform these functions, a word processor will have:

- a QWERTY keyboard

- an 'EXECUTE', 'RETURN', 'DO' or 'GO' key

- cursor-control keys

- editing keys

- function keys.

Occasionally it will also have numeric keys.

Some word processors have different sets of keys on QWERTY KEYPADS for all these functions, while others use the keys for different things by using a CONTROL KEY or COMMAND KEY to signal a function change. For example, the sequence CONTROL followed by 'C' causes text to be centred, or COMMAND followed by 'B' moves the cursor to the bottom of the page or document. These keys are sometimes given colour coding and are then referred to as the 'gold' or 'red' keys.

Looking at each keypad in turn, the functions they perform are:

- QWERTY keys, on their own, operate just like a typewriter except that text appears on the screen rather than on paper. Many of these keyboard layouts also include a backspace/rub-out key which acts just like a self-correcting key on a good electronic typewriter.

  Many keyboards have an auto-repeat action which will cause the key to repeat if it is held down – very useful for inserting spaces, etc.

- There is always a special key that is used to communicate with the machine, that is, to 'tell' it the operator is ready to perform some action. This key is often referred to as the EXECUTE, RETURN, DO or GO key.

- Cursor-control keys move the cursor around the screen in the direction shown by the arrow on the key. Some machines use a flat pad which is pressed in the direction you wish the cursor to move. Other machines, without 'FULL-SCREEN EDITING' that is, the ability to make changes to text anywhere on the screen, have cursor keys that only move the cursor along the bottom line of the screen which is the line that can be edited.

The editing and function keys characterize word processing. Virtually every machine will have basic editing keys which allow:

- characters to be inserted

- characters to be deleted

- a 'rub-out' or backspace and erase.

However, depending on the method used to provide word processing functions, the keyboard may have many more editing and function keys. These keys will be marked to show the action they perform such as:

- CENTRE (to centre text on a line)

- MOVE (to move a block of text from one part of a document to another)

- GO TO PAGE (to move from one page to another)

- SWAP CASE (to change upper to lower case characters and vice versa)

- FIND (to search through a document to find a particular word or phrase).

The numerous functions available will be discussed later but remember that these functions will either be obtained by using a special function key *or* by using a command or control key followed by a letter from the keyboard.

Machines using the latter approach will tend to have fewer keys on the keyboard than 'function key' machines. It could be said that the special command or control key is the only 'function key' available.

Numeric keys are found on some machines. These are usually placed in a separate keypad to the right of the keyboard and consist of keys marked 0–9, often with other keys for $+$, $-$, $\times$, $/$ and an EXECUTE or RETURN key. On microcomputers, these keys are often 'soft keys' and are used by the word processing package as extra function keys.

SUMMARY

Word processors are either document or page machines. Document machines treat many pages as a single file. Page machines treat every page as a file with a multi-page document consisting of many files.

Menu-driven word processors use menus showing the options available and the operator selects the option required from the menu. A command-driven system requires the operator to enter in the relevant command sequence for the machines to perform the functions required.

On-screen formatting shows the text as it will be printed while text produced using word processing based on embedded formatting commands can only be judged after it is printed.

Dedicated word processing has generally been easier to use than word processing packages on general-purpose computers.

However, microcomputers have allowed the development of packages which rival the word processing found on dedicated machines. Soft or programmable keys make the implementation of word processing easier.

Word processors have different sets of keys including:

- QWERTY keys
- cursor-control keys
- editing keys
- function keys.

Some machines have numeric keys.

- QWERTY keys allow text to be typed in.
- Cursor keys control the movement of the cursor about the screen.

- Editing and function keys simplify the modification and formatting of text as well as moving around long documents.

- Word processors usually have function keys which describe the actions they perform or a special control or command key which changes the normal QWERTY keys into function keys.

SELF-CHECK QUESTIONS

1. What is the main difference between page and document word processing?

2. If using a page machine, what must you do when you reach the bottom of the page?

3. Why is it claimed that page machines are easier for typists?

4. What could be regarded as a disadvantage with a document machine?

5. What do you understand by the term 'menu' in connection with word processing?

6. List three methods of selecting an option from the menu.

7. How does a menu-driven system differ from a command-driven system?

8. Why might an *experienced* operator prefer a command-driven system to a menu-driven system?

9. Explain the difference between 'on-screen commands' and 'embedded commands'.

10. Why is it common to find embedded commands being used with word processing packages on general-purpose computers?

11. What do you understand by the term 'dedicated'?

12. Give two advantages of dedicated word processors.

13. **a** What is a 'soft key'?
b Why has the introduction of soft keys on microcomputers made word processing packages more like dedicated machines?

14. What are the cursor-control keys used for?

15. List four function keys that may be found on a word processor keyboard and explain the function that each key performs.

16. If a word processor does not have 'full-screen editing' how will you correct an error that appears near the top of the screen?

17. There are numerous functions available to a word processor. On some machines these can be obtained by using a special function key. How do you obtain these functions on machines that do not have specific function keys?

16

FIRST DRAFT

Chapter Objectives

After studying this chapter you should be able to:

1. Describe the 'three-phase document-production cycle'.

2. Explain the procedures to be undertaken before keying-in of text commences.

3. Define default format, format line, status line.

4. Describe the various tabulation facilities offered on most word processors.

5. Explain the difference between full-screen editing and bottom-line editing.

6. Explain how different machines handle the insert and delete functions.

END OF OBJECTIVES END OF OBJECTIVES END OF OBJECTIVES END OF OBJECTIVES

INTRODUCTION

This chapter, plus the next three chapters, will be considering word processing in detail. To assist us we shall be using throughout the example of the production of a report from manuscript to final copy.

BASIC PRINCIPLES

We believe that effective use of word processing needs a disciplined approach by both operators *and* authors. This approach is built on the following procedure:

- The operator types a first draft copy. Only basic proof-reading is done on screen. The text is formatted either to the author's/organization's standard or to the operator's preference.

- A draft copy is printed in double-line spacing. This is returned to the author for type-checking and revision. The text is stored on a disk.

- The revised manuscript is returned to the operator who recalls the original from disk. Major editing is done, work is formatted as required and the document is paged.

- The revised document is printed in single-line spacing, with page numbering, headers, footers, etc. It is also filed on disk.

- The revised printed copy is returned to the author for final type-checking and minor revisions. The author should retain this copy until ready for the final product.

- When the final copy is due, the revised copy is returned to the operator. The document is recalled from disk, final edits are made and the document is printed.

One important consequence of word processing has been the tendency for authors to make repeated changes to scripts each time they are produced which often results in five or more 'versions' of the script being printed. In addition, many authors (and operators) do not proof-read diligently which again results in unnecessary modifications.

Thus, it is important to:

- proof-read before printing and to type-check printed material

- encourage a three-phase document-production cycle: draft, first version, final copy.

Our approach will be to follow this cycle. Therefore this chapter will look at the basics of typing an initial draft.

GETTING STARTED

As you know, word processors are computers that are using a special program. Computers are electrical and therefore the first operation must be to switch on the system. With dedicated machines and microcomputers there will usually be a switch for the:

- CPU

- disk drive/s

- VDU

- printer.

On some systems the VDU and disk drives use the same switch as the CPU.

Clearly, on a multi-user, shared-resource system it is unlikely that you will need to switch on the CPU – these systems only need the terminal and printers to be turned on by the word processing operator.

It is always good practice to turn on the CPU before the disk drives (and to turn off the disk drives before switching off the CPU).

Another point to note is that, like most electronic equipment, word processors are generally very reliable and it is often turning on and turning off the machine that causes problems. Thus it is advisable to leave the system on until you are sure that you have finished with it for the day. It is also good practice to remove the disks from the disk drives before switching them off.

LOADING THE SOFTWARE

The word processing software will usually be stored on a disk (although some machines have it stored on ROM chips). It is therefore necessary to load the software into RAM. With floppy-disk machines the program disk (or the operating system disk) is placed into the system drive (usually drive 0 or A). If the system has an automatic boot, the program will load into memory automatically, otherwise you will need to load the program using the commands for the system you are using.

Hard-disk machines, and particularly multi-user computers, will automatically load the operating system. Frequently you will need to enter a special user identification and a password even to start using the system. This personal password ensures that only 'authorized' people can use the computer.

Once the word processing programs are available, we are ready to type in the first draft of the report.

CREATING A DOCUMENT

If the word processor is menu-driven you will have a menu of options, one of which should allow you to create a document or file. If no create option exists then the edit option is used and, when asked for the name of the document to be edited, a new unused name will cause the system to create a new document.

With page systems (which are usually command-driven) the approach differs. You are presented with a blank screen and it is only after you have completed your first 'page' that you create the file on disk.

Again, the order of actions often varies between models. However, generally when you 'create' a document or page you must name it. Some systems also:

- automatically give a reference number
- ask for the operator's name and the author's name
- store the date when the document was created (and the date when the file was last modified)
- record the number of times that changes have been made
- record the total number of keystrokes (some operators earn bonuses on the number of keystrokes during the day).

SETTING FORMATS

The first action the operator must do on most word processors is to set the format required for the text – just like setting the margins and tabs on a typewriter. Most systems will have a DEFAULT format, that is, a format the system assumes you will require. You can change this format, if required.

Often a FORMAT LINE or RULER is displayed on the top of the screen. This line shows the position of the left and right margins of the document plus tab stops. It may also control print-line spacing.

```
DOCUMENT  TEST  PAGE 1  LINE 1  POSITION 1  INSERT  JUSTIFY

  L ............. I .......... T ................................................. R
  _
```

A status line and a format line

Additionally a STATUS LINE is frequently displayed, either at the top or bottom of the screen. This line shows such items as:

● name of document

● line and character position of the cursor (which is a small line or flashing block displayed on the screen to indicate where the next character to be typed will appear)

● page number (on document machines)/page length (on page machines)

● prompts for the operator

● modes of operation, for example, insert, justify, etc.

A point to note is that with page machines it is usual to find that the longer the page the narrower the document must be.

To modify the format line there is often a function key or command sequence. Once on the line the cursor is moved and the tab stops and margins changed as required. If the text required is wider than the screen display (this is usually 80 characters although some microcomputers display less), it is usual for the software to allow wider formats. Often the screen will SCROLL sideways up to the maximum width allowed, while on some systems the screen display changes to show 132 characters across the screen.

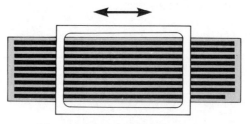

Horizontal scrolling (panning)

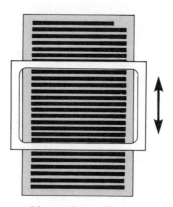

Vertical scrolling

Scrolling means moving the document displayed so that a different part may be seen. Thus, horizontal scrolling or PANNING means moving across a wide document, while vertical scrolling means moving up or down a document or page.

Other than standard tab stops, many word processors have special tabs which allow easier formatting. These include:

● Right-hand margin justification. This creates 'blocked' text.

● Decimal tabs – sometimes called numeric tabs. These are useful for 'lining up' columns of numbers around the decimal point, for example,

10.1
101.2
202.25

- Right alignment. This will align text from this tab setting to the left for such things as addresses, for example,

Mr D. O. Ag-Ain

Many Modes Ltd

All Change Road

INSTABLE

- Indent.   When using the indent tabstop all the text entered is indented. That is instead of returning to the left margin for each new line the cursor only moves in line with the indent tab causing a blocked paragraph like this one. Pressing a return will cancel the indent function.

- Centre. Normally when the centre function is selected the text entered will centre between the left and right margins. However, placing a centre marker on a format line causes text to be created around this marker rather than centred between the left and right margins when the 'centre' function is selected. This facility is ideal for the typing of headings above columns.

Some machines will have dedicated keys (for example, a DECIMAL TAB key, an INDENT key, a CENTRE key) or command sequences to perform these functions while others use the STANDARD TAB key and different tab markers on the format line.

ENTERING THE TEXT

Now we have defined our format requirements we can start entering our text. The report starts with a three-line space – three returns. Next we have a centred and underlined heading. Both are functions found on most word processors either via command sequence or function keys – an option to centre followed by an option to underline. With on-screen formatting you will see the heading centred and underlined. With embedded commands, the commands are placed into the text (usually at the left margin) and the heading will remain at the left of the screen.

The heading should be in upper case (or all capitals). A SHIFT-lock key 'locks' the keyboard into upper case. On many microcomputers this key only causes the QWERTY characters to be displayed as upper case and does not affect any other keys (such as the number or punctuation keys).

We now start KEYING-IN the report. This is the actual typing of the report and is sometimes called inputting, keyboarding or typing!

With most word processors you will notice that there is no need to operate the carriage return at the end of each line. When you reach the right-hand margin the words 'wrap around' to the beginning of the next line. On some machines we do not have true word-wraparound, because words are split at the end of the line. True word-wraparound takes the whole word to the beginning of the next line. If, for example, you are typing the word 'the', some machines would leave the 't' at the end of the line and carry on with the 'he' at the beginning of the next line but true word-wraparound would take the 't' to the beginning of the line as well. Machines without on-screen wraparound will normally wraparound words when printing.

Word-wraparound works as follows: every time you operate the space bar between words, you type what is known as 'a written space', as opposed to 'a blank space' which is what the screen is full of when you start. As you already know, a written space is a character as far as the machine is concerned, because a space character has a unique code of bits which the machine will recognize as a space. If the last character typed at the end of the line was a written space, the machine moves to the beginning of the next line and carries on from there. If there is not a written space telling the machine that a word has been completed, it searches back along the line until it finds one – at the end of the previous word. It then moves everything after that to the start of the next line.

Now is the t	Now is the
ime for all g	time for all
ood men to c	good men to
ome to the	come to the

No wraparound and the wraparound

To avoid right-hand margins being too ragged there is a facility which will allow you to insert a hyphen.

MINOR EDITING

As you are typing you may make a mistake. If you realise this as you make it you can often use a 'RUB-OUT' or 'BACKSPACE AND ERASE' key. This key causes the cursor to move back one space and remove the character there. It acts just like the erase key on self-correcting typewriters.

Should you notice a typing error when proof-reading on the screen, this may be corrected using an INSERT or DELETE function. With full-screen editing, the cursor is moved to the error while with bottom-line editing machines, the line to be edited must be moved to the bottom of the screen by scrolling the text.

The insert function allows extra text or characters to be inserted at the cursor position. It is obtained with a special function key or a command-insert instruction. The effect on the displayed text varies enormously between machines:

- With some, everything after the cursor 'vanishes' only to reappear when the insert function is cancelled.

- With others, characters before the cursor 'shuffle along' as text is inserted.

- With others, a gap of several lines appears after the cursor and this gap is maintained as long as text is inserted.

Some word processing is always in 'INSERT MODE', that is, it will always insert text at the cursor position. Others allow you to select insert or OVERTYPE MODES. When in overtype mode you simply type over the text that is already there.

The delete function is similar to the backspace and erase function *except* that the cursor does not move backwards. Thus, when you press the delete key the character above the cursor disappears and the remainder of the line to the right of the cursor moves back one space, for example:

- 'a' delete this character (text before deletion)

- move the cursor under the letter 'a' (action)

- press DELETE (action)

- delete this character (text after deletion).

There are also differences between machines in the way text is adjusted after deletion:

- With some, only the line to the right of the cursor moves back each time the DELETE key is pressed.

- With others, every character in the paragraph moves back one space causing words to split over lines (see 'wraparound').

- With the best word processing, reverse-wraparound is provided. Thus every time a character is deleted the program checks to find whether the first word on the next line can be 'pulled back' one line. If it can, the whole paragraph is adjusted.

Some word processing allows you to delete any one of the following:

- a character
- a sentence
- a word
- a paragraph
- a line
- a page.

Others prompt you to mark the text to be deleted by either:

- moving the cursor, or

- setting special markers at the beginning and end of the text.

This is sometimes referred to as DEFINING A QUANTITY.

We shall return in a later chapter to deletion. However, our report has now been typed in and proof-read. It will have the format we have defined.

Again, we shall discuss later how the format may, on some word processors, be changed. We must now save our document (or page) on to disk. This process is given many different names including:

- saving

- memorizing

- storing
- writing to disk
- filing.

We shall use the expression 'filing' because, as you will remember from earlier chapters, everything stored on a disk is a 'file' and therefore our document or page is a file that should be filed. So our next chapter will discuss how to file text on to a disk.

SUMMARY

It is believed that for word processing to be effective a disciplined approach by both authors and operators must be adopted. A three-phase document-production cycle – draft, first version, final copy – is suggested. It is important that proof-reading is carried out diligently.

When starting up the word processing system it is good practice to turn on the CPU before the peripherals and to switch off the CPU last.

The word processing software is likely to be stored on either disk or ROM chips. If the program is on disk this will be placed into the system drive. On some systems it is necessary to use a special password to ensure that only 'authorized' staff can gain access.

Once the word processing programs are loaded, a document can begin to be created.

Generally, when you create a document you must give it a name. Some systems automatically assign a reference number.

The first action of a word processing operator must be to set the format required. Some systems also display a status line showing the name of the document, cursor position, page number, mode of operation and prompts for the operator.

It is possible to create documents that are wider than the screen. By using the scroll facility it is possible to scroll both horizontally and vertically.

In addition to standard tab stops most machines allow:

- right-hand justification
- decimal tabs
- right alignment
- centring
- indenting.

Having defined format requirements keying-in can commence. If the document requires a centred heading which is to be underscored, this can be performed by either a command sequence or a function key. With on-screen formatting the heading will be seen centred and underscored. With embedded commands, the commands are placed into the text and the results will not be seen until the document is printed.

Most word processors have a 'wraparound' facility which avoids having to operate the carriage return at the end of a line. If the last word typed will not fit, it will be 'wrapped around' to the beginning of the next line.

As we are inputting text we may need to make use of some minor editing features, such as the:

- 'rub-out' or 'backspace and erase' key
- insert function
- delete function.

The document, when completed, is filed (saved) on disk.

SELF-CHECK QUESTIONS

1. The authors feel that for word processing to be effective a 'three-phase document-production cycle' should be adopted. List the phases in this cycle and explain why such an approach is recommended.

2. When switching on equipment, which piece of hardware should you switch on first?

3. Why is it often advisable to leave the equipment on until you have finished with it for the day?

4. Where is word processing software usually stored?

5. Where is the software loaded into?

6. Into which disk drive is the word processing program placed?

7. What is an 'automatic boot'?

8. Some systems require the operator to enter a personal password. Why?

9. You wish to create a document. How will you do so if you are using a menu-driven word processor?

10. You are using a 'page' word processor. You have typed the first page of text. What must you do now?

11. When you create a document or page you must give it a name. What other information might the system require?

12. Some systems automatically assign additional information to the document. Give two examples of such information.

13. What information does a format line or ruler show?

14. What is a default format?

15. List five items of information that might be displayed on a status line.

16. Explain what is meant by horizontal and vertical scrolling.

17. What is a decimal tab?

18. When might you use the right-alignment facility?

19. What is the difference between a standard tab stop and an indent tab stop?

20. You have centred and underlined a heading. What would you expect to see on the screen if you are using a machine that provides:
    a on-screen formatting
    b embedded commands?

21. Give three different names for 'typing' when using a word processor.

22. Why is it unnecessary to use a carriage return at the end of lines?

23. Explain how 'wraparound' works.

24. How can you avoid having right-hand margins that are too ragged?

25. Explain the function of the 'rub-out' or 'backspace and erase' key.

26. You have a screen full of text and notice that you need to insert a word on line two and delete a word on line seven. How will you carry out this task using a machine that has:
    a bottom-line editing
    b full-screen editing?

27. Machines vary in the way they deal with the 'insert' function. With some, everything after the cursor vanishes and reappears when the insert function is cancelled. What are the two other methods adopted?

28. What do you understand by the term 'defining a quantity' and when might this be used?

29. The process of filing a document on disk is given many different names. List four of these names.

STORING A
DOCUMENT

Chapter Objectives

After studying this chapter you should be able to:

1. Explain the disk-filing functions available with some systems.

2. Describe the methods used for protecting files on disk.

END OF OBJECTIVES END OF OBJECTIVES END OF OBJECTIVES END OF OBJECTIVES

INTRODUCTION

Now that we have created a draft copy of our document (or with a page machine, a draft copy of each page) we must save the work done so that, after any changes are made by the author, we can re-edit our original draft.

Some document machines that are designed to use disk drives will automatically have saved much of the text as we typed it in (using a paging technique like that discussed in Chapter 8). However, even with this type of software, it is still important to 'file' everything on completion of text entry.

FILING THE REPORT

With some systems there will be an option which refers to filing a document. Command-driven systems have specific command sequences which allow filing and retrieval of text. The filing process may involve having to give the file a name, or to decide on which disk drive you wish the file to be stored. Document machines generally assume that the name you used when you created the document is the name that you will use for your file and they automatically file the document when you have finished editing it.

OTHER DISK FUNCTIONS

Most systems allow you to carry out other filing functions on your disk. These include:

- Copy a document file – this will take an exact copy of your document from one disk to another or from one area to another with a different name on the same disk.

- Rename a document/file – this allows you to change the name of a stored file.

- Delete a document/file – this option allows you to 'scrap' or to get rid of files you no longer need. Often (because losing a long file can be disastrous) the software will make you confirm that you really do want to destroy all that work!

- Recover a document/file – when you delete a file all that happens is that the software removes the file name from the index. The file still exists on the disk (it is like taking a library index card out of the index: the book is still on the shelf but there is no record of it). As long as no further work has been done on the disk, the recover option allows the index entry to be re-created.

- Compact or reorganize documents/files – this option allows you to 'tidy-up' the disk, filling up all those sectors where documents that you have deleted were stored, etc.

- Back-up (or archive) documents/files. As floppy disks tend to have a limited life and can become corrupt without warning, it is possible to lose many pages of work which cannot be recovered. To protect against this, BACKING-UP is important. This means either taking a complete copy of the whole disk (on to another disk) or, more usually, taking a selective copy of just a group of documents on a disk. Hard disks, although much more reliable than floppy disks, should also be backed up as they store large quantities of text which would be lost if the disk corrupted.

PROTECTING FILES

With many systems it is possible to protect files/documents against accidental deletion using some form of software protection. This may be a password (which also prevents anyone without the password from editing or printing a document) or a file lock, which just stops accidental deletions or updates after editing.

The ultimate level of protection in floppy disk systems involves the use of hardware. Each floppy disk will have a WRITE PROTECT NOTCH. The way this works will vary according to the word processing system.

If you want to protect the information stored on a 5.25-in disk, you stick a tab of silver over the notch. This allows you to access the information but not to store or erase information.

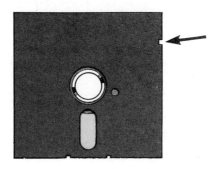

A write protect notch on a floppy disk

On 8-in disk drives, the reverse applies, that is, you need to cover the notch to store and erase information – when the notch is *not* covered the information on the disk is protected.

3.5-in drives use a little plastic plug rather like a cassette tape. With it in, data can be read but not written; with it out, data can be read and written.

Finally, all disks must obviously be labelled to give an indication of what they contain. Since disks must handled with care, it is advisable to write on the labels before applying them to the disk. However, should it be necessary to write on the labels after they have been affixed, it is important that you use a felt-tip pen and press very lightly. There are now special pens for writing on disk labels. You must *never* use a pencil or ball-point. This label plus a print of the document index (which should be placed into each disk sleeve with the disk) should ensure that no document is 'lost' because you cannot find where you stored it.

RÉSUMÉ OF FLOPPY DISKS

We discussed floppy disks and disk drives earlier in the book. This résumé covers the main points mentioned there:

- Floppy disks are made of flexible plastic coated with a magnetic material and enclosed in a cardboard or plastic sleeve.

- The sizes of floppy disks are 3.5 in, 5.25 in and 8 in.

- The sleeve has a window cut in it through which the heads read and write information.

- The number of bits per sq cm that can be stored on a disk is called packing density.

- The amount of data that can be stored on a floppy disk will vary according to whether the disk is single-density, single-sided, double-sided, double-density, 40-track or 80-track, but will be between 100 K and 2.5 Mb.

- The disk drive contains the mechanism that spins the disk and moves the read/write head across the disk to allow random access of files.

- Access time refers to the time taken for the computer to find and retrieve data from a disk.

- DISCRETE MEDIA is a term used to describe items including floppy disks. It means that they can be removed from the machine and transported or stored away from it.

We have now:

- created our document

- entered the first draft

- stored the text for use later.

Now we must print out a copy for typechecking and editing.

SUMMARY

All work done must be saved or filed on disk so that it can be recalled later.

Some document machines actually save much of the text automatically as it is worked on.

It is possible to copy a document (file) from one disk to another. Alternatively, you can copy a file onto the same disk, but with a different name.

The name of the file can be changed.

Files can be deleted from a disk. As this only involves removing an entry from the index, it is possible to recover a document by re-creating an index entry, assuming that no other work has been done using the disk.

Disks on files can be reorganized which tidies up the disk by filling up all the gaps left where files have been deleted.

Disks or files may be backed-up which involves taking an exact copy of a whole disk or group of files from one disk to another. This is often done as a form of protection.

Other forms of protecting files include placing a password on the file or a file lock which allows the file to be displayed but not updated.

The whole floppy disk can be physically protected by the write protect notch.

All floppy disks should be labelled using a soft flexible-tipped pen.

A résumé of disks is given in this chapter.

SELF-CHECK QUESTIONS

1. Why is it not recommended to store documents on cassette tape?

2. What form of backing store is commonly used with word processors?

3. Some systems allow the following disk-filing functions. Explain what each one is:
    a   copy a document/file
    b   rename a document/file
    c   delete a document/file
    d   compact or reorganize documents/files
    e   recover a document/file
    f   back-up a document/file.

4. Why might you use a password or file lock?

5. What is a 'write protect notch' on a disk?

6. You want to protect information on the following disks. How will you do it?
    a   5.25-in disk
    b   8-in disk
    c   3.5-in disk.

7. All disks must have a label indicating what they contain.
    a   Why should you write on the label before applying it to the disk?
    b   If you need to write on the label after it has been affixed, what writing instrument should you use?

8. Why is it a good idea to print the index of the disk and to keep the printout with the disk in the disk sleeve?

9. What is a floppy disk made of?

10. What are the three standard sizes of floppy disk?

11. How does the read/write head read and write information on the disk?

12. What do you understand by 'packing density'?

13. Define 'access time'.

14. What are discrete media?

PRINTING A DOCUMENT

Chapter Objectives

After studying this chapter you should be able to:

1. Define 'soft' and 'hard' copy.
2. Explain the procedures to be carried out when printing a document.
3. List and describe the print options available on most word processors.
4. Describe 'foreground tasks', 'background tasks' and 'spooling'.
5. Recognize the function of a printer buffer.

END OF OBJECTIVES END OF OBJECTIVES END OF OBJECTIVES END OF OBJECTIVES

INTRODUCTION

The text of our report has now been typed in and some minor corrections made to the SOFT COPY, that is, the text displayed on the screen. The text has been filed. Now we must print out the report or produce a HARD COPY. This stage would be where the actual format of the document was revealed, if your word processor used embedded commands.

Menu-driven systems provide a menu with prompts for you to change, as required, for your printing. Command-based systems rely on you to enter the full sequence of commands required to control the printing. Some command word processors allow you to create a 'command file' which contains the right sequence of keystrokes needed. This file can then be used each time you print.

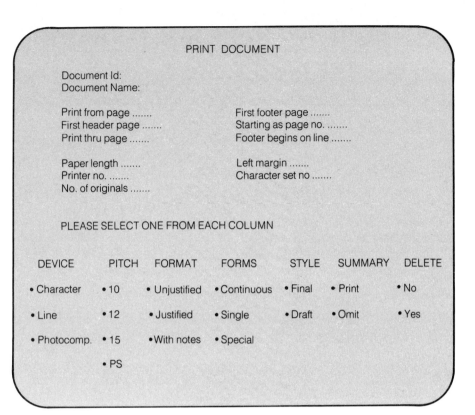

DEVICE	PITCH	FORMAT	FORMS	STYLE	SUMMARY	DELETE
• Character	• 10	• Unjustified	• Continuous	• Final	• Print	• No
• Line	• 12	• Justified	• Single	• Draft	• Omit	• Yes
• Photocomp.	• 15	•With notes	• Special			
	• PS					

A print menu

A final point here. Page machines often allow you to 'screen print', that is to print the soft copy displayed on the screen without saving the text on disk. This is obviously useful for one-page memos and letters, but will not do for our multi-page report.

PRINTING THE REPORT

Initially, we must define the name of the document we wish to print. A document machine will need only one file name. A page machine will need the first and last files to be printed, for example Report 1 and Report 27 (a 27-page report).

Most machines will allow the following options when printing a file. Just how these options are implemented varies so greatly that we shall not endeavour to make generalizations.

- Line spacing – either 0.5 (unusual), 1, 1.5, 2, 2.5, or 3 line spacing. Double or 2-line spacing is very useful when printing first drafts as it allows space for author corrections.

This is an example of text printed in
half line spacing (or 0.5). As you
can see the lines are very close
together.
This is an example of text printed in
single line spacing. This is the
line spacing most commonly used for
letters and memos, etc.

This is an example of text printed in

one and a half line spacing.

Sometimes this line spacing is used

for reports, to make them easier to

read.

This is an example of text printed in

double line spacing. This line

spacing is always used for draft

copies as it is easy to insert

additional text.

This is an example of text printed in

triple or treble line spacing. This

line spacing is not often used, as it

takes up rather a lot of paper.

- Character pitch – the number of characters per inch. 10 and 12 are very common; 15 (compressed) and proportional spacing (theme) are less common. Proportional spacing uses different spacing for each character. Thus 'm' and 'w' will take more space than 'i' or 'l'. Although proportional spacing looks attractive when printed, both tabulations and underlining usually 'go wrong' making it unsuitable for much word processing work unless the VDU is capable of displaying proportionally spaced text and allowing soft copy formatting on screen prior to printing.

This is an example of text printed in
15 pitch using Rockwell Condensed

This is an example of text printed in
10 pitch using Rockwell Expanded

This is an example of text printed in
12 pitch using Rockwell Medium

- Justified-right margin – a straight right-hand margin. On many machines this is achieved by putting extra spaces between words which often leads to a visually disturbing effect. More sophisticated machines, particularly those with proportional spacing, will put extra spaces between characters as well as between words.

- Page numbering and page numbers. Many systems will allow the automatic printing of page numbers. Usually a special character or characters are inserted into the text (or header or footer – see below) and the software replaces this character with a page number. Each time the page number is printed, its value is increased by one. Some software allows you to choose at which page to start numbering.

- Headers and footers. It is possible, with many systems, to include headers and/or footers on pages. A header is defined as something that appears at the head or top of every page while a footer appears at the bottom of a page. The ability to include headers and footers can be very useful. Page numbering symbols, for example, can be placed once in the header and then page numbers will be printed on every page. Some software allows the inclusion of special print features such as sections, footnotes and notes.

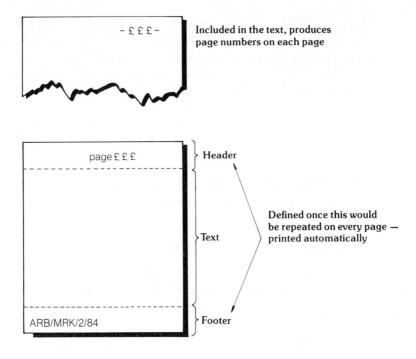

- £ £ £ - Included in the text, produces
           page numbers on each page

page £ £ £ } Header

Text

Defined once this would
be repeated on every page —
printed automatically

ARB/MRK/2/84 } Footer

- Pages to be printed. For document word processing it is usual to find an option that allows the selection of the starting and the finishing page numbers so that only a selected portion of the text can be printed. Page machines achieve this by specifying the start and end file names.

- Number of copies. Frequently the word processing allows more than one copy of the text to be printed by using a 'number of copies' option.

- Left margin setting. With some word processing (particularly page machines) it is necessary to set the left margin (that is, how far in from the left edge of the paper the text appears) when the document is created. If the document is not correctly positioned when printed, this margin setting must be changed by editing the document. However, an option allowing the left margin setting to be selected when printing generally makes this positioning easier.

- Continuous or single sheets (alternatively 'stop on every page'). When using continuous stationery and a tractor feed, or a cut-sheet feeder, it is desirable that the printer prints all the pages without stopping whereas, if friction feed is being used where individual sheets must be fed into the printer, it is important that it stops after every page. There is frequently an option allowing this form of control. With friction feeding a pressure pad holds the paper against the platen as it turns.

- Lines – per page, per top margin and per bottom margin. These options provide a method of automatically controlling the text being printed. The number of lines per page ensures that if the page of text is longer than the actual paper size, the printer will automatically 'throw' to a new page (that is, feed through a new sheet of paper) or stop printing after the fixed number of lines selected by using these options.

A point to note is that fixed page lengths may easily result in 'WIDOWS' or 'ORPHANS', that is, the first line of a paragraph appearing at the bottom of one page (a widow line) or the last line of a paragraph appearing at the top of another page (an orphan line). Some word processing software will ensure that up to three or four lines of paragraph text will override the page length, top and bottom options.

Thus with a setting of:

- page length 66 lines
- top margin 6 lines
- bottom margin 6 lines

the software would expect to print 54 lines of text, that is, the number of lines less top and bottom margins (66 minus 6 minus 6).

With a widows and orphans function, the software will only split a paragraph after 54 lines have been printed if:

- there are more than three lines of the paragraph remaining to be printed, or
- there are more than three lines of paragraph text before the page break length has been reached.

(a)

Page 1	Page 2	Page 3
This diagram shows the effect of orphan lines.	an orphan line.	two lines of a paragraph appear at the bottom of the previous page.
	The opposite effect is when a widow line occurs.	
When a paragraph is printed and only one line is printed on a new page, this line is called	In this case only one or	

Page 1	Page 2	Page 3
This diagram shows the effect of preventing orphan lines.	The opposite effect is found when widow lines are prevented.	In this case the software prevents the first few lines of a paragraph from being printed on the bottom of the previous page.
When a paragraph is printed and only one line is printed on a new page, this line is called an orphan line.		

(b)

Examples of pages printed (a) with widow and orphan lines, and (b) without widow and orphan lines

ALTERNATIVE CHARACTER SETS/ALTERNATIVE PRINTERS

With some word processors it is possible to connect more than one printer. If this configuration is permitted, then it is usual to provide options for selecting which printer and which character set to use. The character set option allows the printing of special print-styles with matrix or laser printers. These styles could be, for example, italic or expanded (large letter) print-fonts. ('Print font' is another term for type-style. Font is the American spelling for the English word fount.)

This covers the most widely available print options. Undoubtedly there are more, such as the ability to print only a selected number of lines of a document but, considering our multi-page report, these options should cover most requirements.

Many of the features mentioned rely on the capabilities of the printer. Most modern printers can be extensively 'programmed' by the software to produce special effects such as:

● superscripts (for example, 2^2)

● subscripts (for example, H_2O)

● bold print or double stroke – double printing of the same characters (for example, **bold**)

- shadow printing or emboldening – printing each character twice with the second printing fractionally to the right of the first (for example, **shadow**)

- underlining

- composite characters – characters joined together (for example ø, or ê).

In addition, line feeds, character pitch, form feeds (page throws), etc., can all be controlled by the software which will send to the printer special CONTROL CHARACTERS which change the way the printer behaves. Many older printers have very limited software-selectable features and it was up to the operator to physically change small switches called DIP switches in order to change character pitch, page lengths, print-styles, etc.

These newer printers, in addition to being software-controlled, can often communicate with the computer. Thus, when the printer detects, via special sensors, an error condition, such as:

- paper jammed

- end of paper

- ribbon out, broken or finished

- daisy-wheel breakage

the printer can signal this condition to the computer causing the machine to prompt the operator to check the printer. A similar prompt can be produced when a stop code or pause command is placed in the text. This code will cause the printer to stop, for example to allow the operator to change the print wheel.

Assuming that we have now selected all the options we want for our report, and that the printer has paper in, we are now ready to print. Here we will encounter differences between configurations and software yet again. On many dedicated word processors, and on a more limited number of general-purpose microcomputers, it is possible to print a document while editing another one. This ability to perform two functions or tasks at once is referred to as multi-tasking. The action of editing the document on screen is a foreground task, that is, a task you are directly involved in, while the printing of the document is a background task, that is, it progresses without your involvement.

Machines that support background printing also often allow SPOOLING, which means allowing several documents to be sent to be printed. The machine then organizes each of these print requests so that they follow each other to the printer. Another term given to spooling is QUEUING and a series of documents waiting to be printed forms a PRINT QUEUE.

So we can now proceed to print our report. Generally, after selecting all our options we must 'tell' the computer that we are ready to print. There is a key on the keyboard with which we can inform the machine that we are ready to go. This may be the '?' key. (If you cannot remember, read the summary in Chapter 15.) Having pressed this key, our printing will start.

Let us suppose that something goes wrong immediately and we stop the printing (an option on many systems). What you will notice with most printers is that the printing does not stop immediately! This is really quite disconcerting and is the result of the printer having a buffer. A buffer is an area of random access memory in which data is stored before printing. Many new printers have 1 K or 2 K buffers which will therefore hold one or two thousand characters. Thus, when you tell the computer to stop printing, the printer will carry on until its buffer is empty.

So we can now print the report and send it – in double-line draft format, remember – to the author who will undoubtedly:

- add new paragraphs, lines, words, etc.

- move paragraphs, lines, words, etc.

- change the layout and format

- change all of one word to another (for example 'company' to 'Company', or 'Burtons' to 'Boots')

- copy sections from one page to another

- paste-in paragraphs from another report

or more! He will then gleefully return it to you with the passing comment that: 'It must be completed, printed, copied and bound by five o'clock tonight'. It is now 2.45 p.m. and this is where word processing is a real aid. Our next chapter considers how we can achieve our deadlines!

SUMMARY

'Soft copy' is the term used to describe the text displayed on the screen.

When printing using word processing there will frequently be a range of options. These include:

- line spacing – 0.5, 1, 1.5, 2, 2.5 and 3 lines

- character pitch – 10, 12, 15 characters per inch and proportional spacing

- justified-right margins – creating a blocked print

- automatic page numbering

- headers and footers

- pages to be printed

- number of copies to be printed

- left margin – this allows the spacing between the left paper edge and the left margin to be selected

- a setting for continuous or single sheets of paper

- lines per page, per top margin and per bottom margin

- alternative character sets/alternative printers – allowing the use of different printers connected to the same machine or printing using various typefaces (available on matrix and laser printers).

All these features, plus special effects within the document such as superscripts, subscripts, emboldening, shadow printing, underlining and composite characters, depend on the software being able to send the printer the correct control codes to program it with the ability to achieve these effects.

Modern printers can often signal an error back to the computer.

Most dedicated word processors and some general-purpose microcomputers allow background printing. This allows the operator to print at the same time as editing which is a foreground task.

Spooling is often possible on systems that have background printing. This allows a number of documents to be queued up ready for printing.

Many printers have a 1 K or 2 K buffer which means that, even when a printer is stopped at the terminal, it often takes some time for the printer to stop.

SELF-CHECK QUESTIONS

1. What is the difference between 'soft copy' and 'hard copy'?

2. Some command word processors allow you to create a 'command file'. What is this?

3. What is the 'screen print' facility provided on most page machines?

4. You want to print the report created. What information will the machine need if using:
   a a document machine
   b a page machine?

5. What is character pitch and what pitches are available on most word processors?

6. What is proportional spacing?

7. Many machines allow justified right-hand margins. Give two ways in which justification is achieved.

8. What is:
   a a header
   b a footer?

9. What type of paper would you be using to print the report if you 'asked' the printer to:
- **a** stop at the end of every page
- **b** print continuously?

10. What is:
- **a** a widow line
- **b** an orphan line?

11. Most modern printers can be 'programmed' by the software to produce special effects. List five of these special effects.

12. Some printers can detect errors and cause the computer to signal to the operator to check the printer. What types of error might occur?

13. If a 'stop code' is inserted in the text:
- **a** what will happen at the printing stage
- **b** why might a stop code be inserted in the text?

14. What do you understand by:
- **a** 'foreground tasks'
- **b** 'background tasks'?

15. What is an alternative name for 'spooling'?

16. What is the name given to a series of documents waiting to be printed?

17. What key will you press to 'tell' the machine that you are ready to print?

18. Why, when you 'tell' the computer to stop the printing, does the printer not stop immediately?

19. What line spacing should be used for the draft report and why?

19

ADVANCED EDITING FEATURES

Chapter Objectives

After studying this chapter you should be able to:

1. Describe the function and purpose of the following:

    - a search
    - defining a quantity
    - copying and moving text
    - global functions
    - search and replace
    - hyphenation
    - indentation
    - pagination.

END OF OBJECTIVES END OF OBJECTIVES END OF OBJECTIVES END OF OBJECTIVES

INTRODUCTION

This chapter concentrates on the more powerful editing features found in word processing. These features make word processors so much more powerful and productive than typewriters and will allow us to produce our report on time. Without these powerful features we would surely miss our deadline!

We shall approach this chapter as though we were actually working on the report, that is, we shall discuss editing, re-formatting and paging.

EDITING TEXT

The range of more advanced editing options available varies enormously between word processors, as does their ease of use. Thus much of what we will discuss in this section may or may not be readily available to you as an operator.

Before we can begin to make amendments to the report we must reload the word processor with the text. As you will remember, we have filed our document (or series of pages, depending on the type of machine) on to a disk. We must therefore:

- Select the correct work disk which contains the document.

- Insert it into the work or non-system disk drive.

- 'Recall' or 'retrieve' the file from the disk.

Often it is possible just to choose the 'edit' option or command and give a document or file name and then to leave the software to recall the text into memory.

Our first correction involves changing a few characters in a word that has been misspelt. To save time finding the word we opt for the SEARCH facility. This allows us to type in a word or phrase and the software will then search through the document until it finds the first match. We type in the incorrect spelling, press the 'execute' key and the cursor moves rapidly to the word.

We OVERTYPE (or STRIKEOVER) the incorrect spelling, Overtyping does what it suggests. It simply places the new letters where the old letters were.

Next we must DELETE a few sentences in a paragraph. Some machines allow deletions of:

- characters

- words

- sentences

- paragraphs

- pages.

Others simply allow you to DEFINE A QUANTITY which means to mark the text you want to delete, either by placing a special mark at the beginning and end, or by moving the cursor from the start position to the end position (often causing the screen to highlight the selected text in some way). In both cases the EXECUTE key will remove the text. Most good word processing will automatically re-adjust the text after a deletion – with some you have to re-adjust or re-format it yourself.

Our next task is to COPY a section of text from one place in the document to another. This function is very similar to MOVING text – our next task. It is usual for the software to allow you to define a quantity to be moved or copied – just like deletion. Having selected the text you wish to copy or move you press EXECUTE. You can then scroll through the report to the place where you wish the new text to reappear and use the INSERT HERE option.

It is very common for prompt-driven word processing to prompt the operator during these operations. For example, choosing the move option results in a prompt:

'Move what?'.

You define the text to be moved and press EXECUTE.

The system then prompts:

'To where?'.

You take the cursor to where you want to insert the text and press EXECUTE.

Moving is often called CUT AND PASTE because, on normal typed work, the way you would have moved a paragraph, etc. would have been to cut it out and then paste it back in where you wanted.

Copying is also referred to as DUPLICATING.

The degree of sophistication available when moving or copying varies. Some systems only allow you to work with lines of text while others allow you to move columns as well. Thus, if we had a table in our report like this:

JANUARY	FEBRUARY	MARCH
10.00	10.25	2.40
20.17	27.25	34.32

and the author wanted it like this:

MARCH	FEBRUARY	JANUARY
2.40	10.25	10.00
34.32	27.25	20.17

a system that allows you to define columns would make such a change easy. Without this ability, changing and editing columns is fiddly.

To move from one page to another, many document systems provide a feature which allows the operator to select the page to go to by page number. (With page machines you move to the desired page by loading the page file by name.)

We have now moved and copied the text marked by the author. He or she wants a paragraph inserted, and so we use the insert function to type this in.

Finally, the author wants a paragraph to be copied from another document into this one. Many machines offer this ability but vary enormously in how easy it is to use. With some you must:

● file your current document

● recall and edit the document containing the paragraph

- cut or copy the paragraph
- file the selected document
- re-edit the document into which you want the text to be inserted
- move to where you wish to insert
- press EXECUTE – the text will then be inserted here.

Clearly, a laborious task but still much faster than retyping a long paragraph.

With other software the task is much easier. These offer a feature termed SUPERCOPY or SUPERMOVE. Using a command key followed by the MOVE or COPY function key the system will:

- Prompt for the name of the document from which you want to take text.
- You enter the name and press execute.
- The new document appears on the screen (but your current one is not lost).
- You are prompted to define or mark the text you require and then press execute.
- As soon as you execute you return to your original document and move the cursor to where you want the new text to appear.
- Pressing execute will insert the new text.

There are two common ways in which copying or moving text is handled by the software. The first involves the use of a COPY or TEXT REGISTER which is basically a buffer in memory into which the marked text is stored. The other method involves storing the marked text on disk in what is essentially a temporary disk file created by the system.

Most of our major editing is complete except that the author wants some occurrences of the word 'company' changed to 'Company', and all occurrences of the word PASCAL changed to BASIC. For this we use GLOBAL FUNCTIONS. Global means throughout the document (as opposed to LOCAL which relates to the text displayed on the screen). These functions are generally much easier to use with document systems than with page systems.

The function we shall use is called SEARCH AND REPLACE. Use of this facility involves:

- entering the word or phrase we wish to search for
- entering the replacement text.

Frequently you are then prompted to say whether you wish every occurrence changed or just some.

With the option to replace 'all' selected, the system automatically scans through the document replacing the target word or phrase with the replacement text.

With the 'some' option, the system finds each occurrence of the target phrase and asks whether you wish to replace. If you do, replacement occurs. If you do not, the cursor moves to the next occurrence.

Which options would we select for our report?

Often people will refer to a STRING search or string search and replace. This is because it is usual to allow more than one word to be selected – a string being a whole series of characters, including spaces and, possibly, special characters like codes for emboldening.

Our editing is now complete. The next task is to format the work as required.

RE-FORMATTING

We saw how the format is controlled (in Chapter 14) with the use of embedded commands or rulers. Other factors that control the format (or layout) include:

● page lengths

● character pitch

● line spacing.

One page of the report is an extract from a book and the author wants this page justified. With all but very good, usually dedicated, word processors, right-justification involves the software adding spaces or PADDING between words. With true justification, as found on phototypesetters, the spacing between characters in a word, as well as between words, is increased, making for a much more visually appealing print.

Given the limitation of our justification, what can we do to improve the appearance? One option is to HYPHENATE long words that have been wrapped round on to the next line. Hyphenation involves splitting a word into two with a hyphen (-) placed between them. One point to note with hyphenation is that some words *should* be hyphenated, for example:

● co-ordinate

● re-format.

When you hyphenate, the software removes all the hyphens before calculating where the new ones should be placed. If the word must remain hyphenated, then it is often possible to use a command function which defines the hyphen as a REQUIRED HYPHEN. Hyphens that can be removed are often referred to as DISCRETIONARY hyphens.

When justifying, it is often possible to define a HOT or HYPHENATE ZONE (the size of which can be adjusted). The software will then use this zone to:

- detect words that begin within this zone, and
- stop wraparound by inserting a hyphen into the word.

This process involves the use of a formula to calculate where to put the hyphen – most of these formulae do not work very well and the results of automatic hyphenation are usually most unsatisfactory and often very funny.

A global function which can be used, should it be required, is RE-HYPHENATION. Selecting this facility results in the whole document being re-hyphenated (and assumes that you have defined hot zones).

A second method of improving justification of text involves the use of REQUIRED OR COMMAND SPACE. Normally, when a word is too long to fit on a line, the software scans back character by character until it finds a space. It will then move all the characters after the space on to the next line. Occasionally, it is desirable to OVERRIDE this automatic wraparound, that is, to stop it occurring.

To do this a special space character is available on some systems. Using the command key followed by the space bar changes the space so that the system will no longer wraparound on this space. For example, No. 5 looks odd as No. 5.

A required space would prevent this happening.

Many systems will only justify when printing, so it is probable that this page will need to be printed, re-edited and reprinted to get it to look all right!

Our next task involves one paragraph. This must be:

- indented from the left margin
- have a narrower right margin, and
- be in double-line spacing.

If our system allows:

- embedded commands
- multiple rulers, or
- indenting

> Then it should be relatively easy to achieve this effect as this paragraph shows. To indent the left margin we can use an indented paragraph or redefine the left margin. To achieve the effect of a narrower right margin we must reduce the position of the right margin from, say, character position 75 to character position 55.

The double-line spacing is more likely to cause a

problem. Some systems do allow embedded

commands or special 'line spacing' commands in

the ruler which change line spacing, giving:

- half

- single

- one-and-a-half, or

- double-line spacing.

Other software only allows different line spacing

for the entire document – no use for our report!

To achieve the double-line spacing, returns need

to be inserted after each line in the paragraph.

Our re-formatting done, our final task is to page the document prior to printing it – and we are still within our deadline.

PAGINATION

PAGINATION or (re-pagination) really relates to document systems. Page-based word processing is already divided into pages equivalent to the paper on which you wish to print. Significant insertion of new text may have resulted in the need to create new pages (that is, new files) and to copy the old pages into the new ones.

However, document systems allow you to decide where in the text you wish one page to end and the next to start. This is done by inserting a special command called a PAGE BREAK or NEW PAGE MARKER which signals to the printer that it must FORM FEED, that is eject the sheet of paper it has been printing.

Global pagination allows:

- you to define how many lines of text you want on each page and then
- the system to go through the whole of the text inserting the page breaks.

Global pagination may have a widows and orphans function which helps reduce the likelihood of page breaks occurring at inappropriate points in the text.

Often, especially for final copy, it is better to move through the document deciding where you wish new pages to start and inserting page breaks. To help with this exercise it may show, on the status line, the line number of the line where the cursor is. Without this assistance it is usual to:

- re-paginate globally
- then advance page by page, changing the position of page breaks as required.

With the report now:

- edited
- re-formatted, and
- paged

all we have left to do is to print the report as a final copy, photocopy it and bind it – and still have time to catch the 5.02 home!

SUMMARY

Text requiring editing must be recalled from disk by inserting the correct disk into the disk drive and then loading the text into RAM.

The word processing facilities used when editing a document include:

- searching – searching for a specific string of characters
- overtyping – replacing displayed characters with the new typed characters
- deleting – either characters, words, sentences or a defined quantity of text
- copying – copying text from one section to another
- moving – moving text from one place to another – either lines or, if the software allows, columns
- search and replace – replacing one string with another. An option exists to replace every occurrence or just some
- re-formatting – this involves changing the layout of the text. Factors affecting format include:
  - page lengths
  - character pitch
  - line spacing
  - right-hand justification
  - required spaces and hyphens.

Most editing is a local function – it is done on the screen. However, some changes can be global. These affect the whole document.

When editing is complete, it is necessary to decide where in the text new pages should start. This can be done automatically using the global pagination facility. This may have a widows and orphans function. Without automatic pagination it is necessary for the operator to move through the text deciding where new pages should start.

SELF-CHECK QUESTIONS

1. What must we do before we can begin to edit our report? List three steps.

2. How does the search function work and when might we use this function?

3. What is another name for 'overtyping'?

4. You want to delete a section of text and your machine allows you to define a quantity. What are the two common methods used for defining a quantity?

5. You have now defined the quantity of text to be deleted. What key will you press to remove this text and what will happen to the remainder of the text?

6. Explain how the 'copy' and 'move' functions operate.

7. Give an example of an operator prompt.

8. Why is moving sometimes called 'cut and paste'?

9. What is another name for copying?

10. List the steps to be taken when moving a section of text from one document to another using the 'supermove' function.

11. What is a 'text register'?

12. What are 'global functions'?

13. Explain the 'search and replace' function and give an example of when this function might be used.

14. Sometimes search and replace is referred to as 'string search and replace'. What is a string?

15. Besides margin settings, what other factors affect the final layout of a document?

16. What is the difference between:
    a   a required hyphen, and
    b   a discretionary hyphen?

17. What is a 'hot zone' and what is its purpose?

18. Why might you use a 'required' or 'command' space?

19. How can a paragraph within a page of text be indented from the left-hand and right-hand margins?

20. Give the two methods by which double-line spacing in one section of text can be achieved.

21. Define the term 'pagination'.

22. When a page break is inserted in a document what does it signal to the printer?

23. What does global pagination allow you to do?

24. Some systems incorporate a widows and orphans function. What is the advantage of this?

FURTHER FUNCTIONS OF WORD PROCESSING

Chapter Objectives

After studying this chapter you should be able to:

1. Describe and explain the purpose of the following functions of word processing:

- help facility
- mail merge
- standard paragraphs
- macros
- records management
- maths
- sort
- spelling
- readability checks
- glossary
- windowing.

END OF OBJECTIVES END OF OBJECTIVES END OF OBJECTIVES END OF OBJECTIVES

INTRODUCTION

Word processing, as you know, has been one of the driving forces behind office automation and some information processing systems. Indeed, as software becomes more multi-functional and integrated, it is difficult to define exactly what it is that one would expect from a word processor.

215

Clearly, it should have the functions and facilities described earlier. However, many word processors have a range of additional functions that are designed to:

- increase the number of uses that the machine can be put to
- reduce the efforts involved in dealing with many aspects of text handling
- improve the quality of information provided, and
- provide that 'something extra' which will help salesmen sell the system!

In this chapter we shall look at some of the more standard offerings provided, starting with the most common. We do not expect this list to encompass everything available, but hope to provide you with a good feel for these extras.

HELP

Every supplier of word processing will provide a manual describing how to use the system and its features. These manuals vary from being clearly presented to being totally incomprehensible!

However, you will often be using the machine and have forgotten how to perform a specific function. Some systems provide on-line help for this reason. Often obtained by pressing a 'HELP' function key, what appears on the screen is information about how to use the word processing or what specific functions mean. The text being edited is not lost, and pressing the RETURN or EXECUTE key returns you to your exact place in the text.

MAIL MERGE

This feature is referred to by a variety of terms including:

- standard letters
- form letters (with merge variable inserts)
- change reader codes, and
- batch infill.

However, the principle remains the same irrespective of the name used. The feature allows the operator to produce many apparently individual documents, the bulk of which remains constant throughout. This is done by creating a standard form or letter. This letter will have all the information needed except for the individual elements such as name, address, salutation, etc. In place of these items special MERGE or VARIABLE MARKS are placed.

Next a list of VARIABLES is created, each separated by a merge or variable mark. For each variable mark in the letter or form there must be a variable placed in the list. Thus, if our form has variable marks in place of name, address and salutation, then in the list must be the names, addresses and salutations for all the forms you wish to produce.

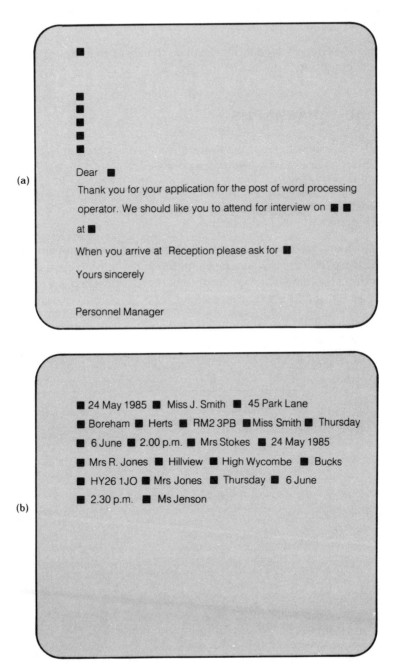

Examples of (a) a primary document, and (b) a secondary document

The standard form is then merged (usually at the printing stage) with the values from the variable list to form a series of personalized forms.

Merging is achieved by the software recognizing the merge character in the PRIMARY DOCUMENT and copying the next variable from the variable list (SECONDARY DOCUMENT) into the position of the merge character. Often, if this facility is used for standard letters, it is possible to use the list of names and addresses for envelopes or labels.

A variation on the merge facility involves the ability to merge or join together two documents to form one new longer document.

STANDARD PARAGRAPHS

Many businesses often use the same wordings and paragraphs on many of their documents. For example, insurance policies, solicitors' letters or overdue accounts letters will have common 'standard' paragraphs.

It is possible to type in and store on disk all these paragraphs. Each paragraph can be given a number or reference.

Then, when the author wishes to write a specific letter or document, he can quote these references where he wants the paragraphs to appear. The operator does the same thing when typing and the word processing will merge the relevant passage into the text being created.

This ability to build-up a document using a series of referenced paragraphs is also termed BLOCK BUILDING or BOILERPLATING.

```
1 =   Thank you for your recent letter
2 =   Thank you for your letter of
3 =   Thank you for your enquiry regarding our 'Highland'
       products.
4 =   We are sorry to inform you that we are unable to meet
       your requirements but  take this opportunity to send
       you a copy of our latest catalogue.
5 =   We have pleasure in enclosing our latest catalogue
       which, we are sure, will  help you decide on the design
       most suitable for your requirements.
6 =   We supply a vast range of household fabrics to suit all
       types of house design.
7 =   We look forward to hearing from you shortly.
8 =   We are returning your cheque with this letter and
       apologise for any inconvenience caused.
9 =   Yours sincerely

       Sales Manager
```

Example of standard paragraphs

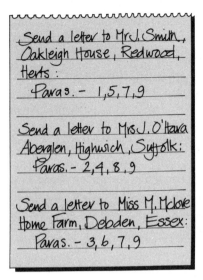

Examples of instructions for creating documents from standard paragraphs

MACROS

Often you will find that a particular phrase or name appears again and again in the text you are typing. A facility may exist which allows you to define a MACRO. A macro is a short command that causes the word processor to do something. For example, a macro could be defined which, when entered, will cause a long phrase to be entered into the text rather like using an abbreviation which the word processing expands to its full form.

Macros can be used for standard letters except that, instead of the variables being typed in as a separate document, they are typed in as part of macro statements.

RECORDS MANAGEMENT

This facility is a source of confusion since some manufacturers call the facility LIST PROCESSING, while others describe list processing as the ability to produce a series of letters using information from lists – what we have described as standard letters!

Records management was one of the earliest examples of word processing being used with other, non-word processing facilities. By using records management:

- It is possible to create a data processing type of file which contains many records.

- Each record relates to a different example of the same thing. For example, each record will be for a different customer in a customer record management list or file.

- Within each record will be items of interest such as name, address, customer number, telephone number, etc. These individual items are called FIELDS.

- It is possible to add to and delete from the list of records as well as to edit the information within each record.

- It is possible to merge fields from the records into word processing documents, just as with standard letters. In addition to being able to merge fields, it is possible to select and sort records before merging which makes this a powerful facility.

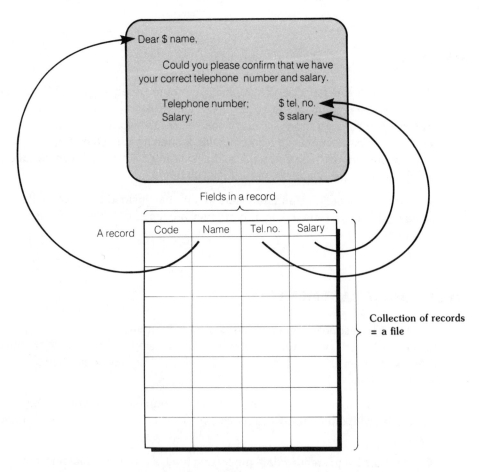

An example of records management showing fields being merged into a letter

MATHS

Many documents contain figures. Usually these need some arithmetic to be done with them such as:

- addition of columns

- subtraction of one number from another

- finding percentages, etc.

Some word processing offers a maths option which allows elementary maths to be done using the figures contained in the text. In its simplest form, only columns can be added, with totals being placed at the base of the column. Better software offers a range of functions including use of figures anywhere in the text and combination of these figures with mail-merge.

As an example, a standard letter sent to all employees notifying them of a ten per cent salary increase could look something like this:

Dear (Name)
I have pleasure in notifying you that your salary of (old salary) is to be increased by ten per cent giving a new salary of (old salary $\times$ 10%).

SORT

This facility allows items of text particularly lists, to be sorted in either ascending or descending numerical or alphabetical order.

SPELLING

Increasingly common are spelling checkers which will check through text for spelling mistakes. These programs use a large dictionary of words and check each word in the text against those in the dictionary.

The facilities offered vary. At a basic level it is possible to:

- add new words to the dictionary

- choose to change words marked as incorrect or to move on – this allows you to leave words not recognized by the software but which are correct.

More sophisticated software offers:

- the nearest words that can be found to the unrecognized word displayed with the option to replace the unrecognized word – often termed a 'thesaurus' function

- the option to add the unrecognized word to the dictionary

- the option to define words to be ignored before checking, so that the program does not stop every time it reaches the name of a company
- the option to create different special dictionaries containing only certain difficult, perhaps technical, terms.

The speed at which these checkers work has improved. When first available they were quite slow, taking a few minutes to check through a long document, especially if the disk contained a large dictionary. It is now possible to scan a document in seconds.

READABILITY CHECKS

A function available on a few expensive word processors is the ability to perform checks on the text which assess the constructions used. These checks, such as the fog or readability index, give some indication of how easy the text is to read.

They work by calculating the length of sentences, number of words, average number of syllables, etc. Particularly complicated sentences are marked, allowing the author to change them into a simpler, more readable form.

GLOSSARY

'Glossary' is another instance where different manufacturers use the same term to describe different facilities. In one form, a glossary is a collection of standard paragraphs. This is also sometimes referred to as a library.

However, the term 'glossary' also refers to a collection of keystrokes which can be stored and recalled with a few simple keystrokes. This facility, alternatively called USER-DEFINED KEYS, KEY CAPTURE or USER PROGRAMMING, can range from relatively simple to very powerful. In its simple form, it is possible to record a limited number of keystrokes including editing strokes such as 'centre' or 'bold'. These strokes can then be recalled when working on any document.

For example, you may store the keystrokes that make up the standard ending to your boss's letters. The recorded form would look like this:

return, return, return, y,o,u,r,s, space, s,i,n,c,e,r,e,l,y,
return, return, return, return, S, space, O, space, G,r,o,s,s, return,
return, bold, M,a,n,a,g,i,n,g, space, D,i,r,e,c,t,o,r.

When used, these recorded strokes would result in:

Yours sincerely

S O Gross
Managing Director

being produced at the end of the letter.

222

In its advanced form, as found with Wang word processing, glossary really is a programming language especially designed to work with text:

- Any keystroke can be recorded.

- Prompts for the operator can be given.

- Conditional tests can be made (for example, if name equals Smith then . . .).

- Branching is possible (for example, GOTO [another page or paragraph]).

- Maths, sorting, merging and records (list) management facilities can be used.

- Printing can be controlled.

With this software many companies have developed complete 'systems', not unlike those usually associated with data processing languages such as BASIC or COBOL.

A relatively new offering is the ability to develop a glossary program 'by example'. Useful for non-technical people, this facility allows the operator to 'tell' the machine that it must record all the keystrokes that follow. This ability to 'LEARN BY EXAMPLE' is appearing with many functions available on information systems.

Many systems now offer a windowing facility which allows two or more documents to be displayed on screen at once. This is achieved by splitting the screen display into separate areas. It is relatively easy to switch from one document to another for editing purposes.

As the boundaries between word processing systems and full information processing systems become blurred, it is increasingly difficult to decide what is word processing and what is not. However, the features we have talked about in this chapter are those more commonly associated with word processing specifically, while Chapter 13 dealt with the features expected in information processing systems in offices.

SUMMARY

Many word processors offer more than the standard editing, printing and formatting functions.

On-line help offers the operator the facility to press a 'help' function key at any time and to have information regarding use of the word processor displayed.

Mail merge allows variable information (such as names, addresses and forms of greeting) to be inserted into a single standard form. The insertion (or merging) usually occurs during printing.

Standard paragraphs can be used to allow frequently used paragraphs to be stored and referenced by either a number or a code. These paragraphs can then be recalled at will and in any order into text as it is created.

Macros enable the operator to define a short command which, when used, will carry out the series of actions defined for that macro.

Records management allows the creation and maintenance of a file of records; each record contains a number of fields. Thus fields from this file can be selected, sorted or merged into a standard letter.

Many word processors offer a maths capability which will perform simple arithmetic on numbers within a document.

The ability to sort lists either alphabetically or numerically and in ascending or descending order is common in word processing.

An increasing number of word processors use spelling checkers which will automatically check text for spelling mistakes.

Some systems offer software that will check text and give an indication of how easy it is to read. The method of testing is based on standard tests called the readability or fog index.

Glossary functions allow the operator to store repeatedly used keystrokes and to recall these at will in any document. Simple functions of this type allow only a limited number of keystrokes to be stored. More advanced versions allow complete programming to be done.

Windowing allows more than one document to be displayed on the VDU simultaneously.

SELF-CHECK QUESTIONS

1. What does every supplier of word processing supply?
2. What is an on-line help facility?
3. How is the help facility obtained and what type of information will it provide?
4. Give two other names for mail-merge.
5. What does the mail-merge facility allow?
6. When creating a standard letter where might the merge or variable marks be inserted?
7. When does the actual merging usually take place?
8. Define the following:
   a primary document
   b secondary document.

9. What are the two other names for standard paragraphs?

10. What type of business might make use of standard paragraphs?

11. What is the advantage of using standard paragraphs to:
    a   the operator
    b   the author?

12. What is a macro and when might macros be used?

13. Give an example of a field in a record.

14. Explain the records management facility and give an example of its use.

15. What is the simplest form of maths found on a word processor?

16. What types of function are available on more sophisticated maths packages?

17. Into what order can lists of information be sorted using the sort facility?

18. What is a spelling dictionary and how does it work?

19. On some systems it is possible to create your own dictionary. When might this be particularly useful?

20. What is a readability check and how does it work?

21. Give an example of when the readability check would be a useful feature.

22. Some manufacturers refer to a glossary as a collection of standard paragraphs. What is this sometimes called?

23. The term 'glossary' is alternatively called 'user-defined keys' or 'user programming'. What is the purpose of this facility?

24. In its advanced form glossary really is a programming language designed to work with text. List four facilities that this offers.

25. How is a glossary program developed 'by example'?

26. Why might windowing prove useful to a WP operator?

21

THE WORD PROCESSING ENVIRONMENT

Chapter Objectives

After studying this chapter you should be able to:

1. Describe the various organizational methods used by companies when installing word processing and the changes that are likely to take place.

2. List the methods used by authors to generate text.

3. Identify the people involved in the creation and production of text and describe their skills and qualities.

END OF OBJECTIVES END OF OBJECTIVES END OF OBJECTIVES END OF OBJECTIVES

INTRODUCTION

We have looked in some depth at word processing – how a word processor works, the different types of software available and the many functions that can be performed using word processing equipment. In this chapter we will discuss the word processing environment, that is, word processing in the workplace – the people involved and the way that companies organize their word processing equipment.

It should be noted that often a company will make its initial entry into office automation by purchasing word processing equipment. Once WP is established and the company sees the benefits that can be gained from 'electronic' equipment, they will seek further enhancements, upgrade their present systems and introduce more electronic office equipment.

The introduction of word processing will involve many changes within the organization. Factors causing these changes include:

- the physical location of the equipment

226

- the training of staff

- the reorganization of work procedures.

WORD PROCESSING WITHIN THE ORGANIZATION

The number of machines purchased and the purpose for which they are required will obviously determine the location. Some companies may feel that all the secretaries will have their own word processors and thus the machines will be sited on the secretaries' desks.

Smaller companies may purchase one machine for use by all secretaries, each secretary booking time on the machine as necessary.

However, it has been found by many companies that the introduction of word processing has reduced the need for each manager to have his own secretary and they have set up, what are often called 'administrative centres' or 'work groups'. With this type of arrangement there might be perhaps four secretaries together, each with a word processor, working for five or six different managers.

Initially, some managers and secretaries were averse to this idea as they felt they both lost a certain amount of status resulting from the manager no longer having his personal secretary and the secretary no longer working for one person. However, once this type of arrangement was under way, certain advantages became evident:

- The company saved money because the number of staff was reduced.

- The work-load was evenly shared by the secretaries: they were able to 'spread the load' when the work of one manager became excessive.

- The managers no longer had the problem of how to cope when the secretary was away from the office (for holidays or sickness) since the remaining members of the work group could carry on as usual.

Larger companies installing word processing will often adopt the 'centralized' approach. Here all the word processors will be installed in one room, rather like the old-fashioned typing pool, and a central word processing service will be provided.

Clearly the size of the company, the number of machines installed and the use that is to be made of word processing will affect the arrangement of the equipment. There are many other factors to be considered besides those briefly mentioned. The furniture, lighting and physical comfort of the staff will all need consideration and these factors will be discussed fully in Chapter 22.

Having discussed the type of set-up that may be used in a company, namely:

- individual machines for each secretary

- one machine to be shared by all secretaries

- work groups or 'administrative centres'
- centralized services

let us go on to discuss the people involved with word processing.

THE AUTHOR

The author, as you know, is the originator of the material. He/she will generate text in one or more of the following ways:

- longhand
- audio dictation
- shorthand dictation
- direct keyboarding.

All authors should attend a training course on word processing so that they are familiar with the capabilities and limitations of the equipment being used. This will allow them to make full use of the capabilities of the word processing equipment without placing excessive burdens on the operator. The ideal author will:

- have clear, neat handwriting
- dictate clearly using audio equipment and give all instructions at the beginning of a tape
- adopt the 'three-phase document-production cycle' discussed in Chapter 16
- not falter and hesitate when using the direct keyboarding approach.

(are we being over optimistic?)

THE OPERATOR

The operator is the person who will require extensive training. (As most word processing operators at present are women we shall talk about operators as 'she' but you must remember that there are male operators and, as more men are becoming familiar with using keyboards, it will become less and less easy to refer to operators as 'she'.)

The operator may be a typist or secretary:

- using a word processor or
- working in a small group 'administration centre' or
- within a large centralized word processing service.

228

The work may come to her from the author via one of the techniques previously mentioned.

The ideal operator will:

- have good keyboarding skills

- have good language skills

- be an excellent proof-reader

- have a logical approach to her work

- be able to follow instructions

- have a knowledge of word processing and how the equipment works

- be able to display and present text in a pleasing manner.

Often with word processing equipment there is more than one way of carrying out a particular function. A good operator will be instantly recognizable by her ability to carry out a task in the shortest, most efficient way.

THE SUPERVISOR

In a centralized word processing department it is usual to have a supervisor to organize and co-ordinate the work of the department. This person's duties and qualities will be many and varied.

The supervisor will need to be:

- fully conversant with the equipment being used as she may be called on to deal with minor technical problems

- responsible for training new staff on the use of the equipment and for providing advanced training for existing staff.

She should keep herself up-to-date on new technological developments as she may be requested by management to recommend further enhancements, expansion or replacement of existing equipment. It is particularly important that she understands the concepts of hardware configurations such as shared-logic or shared resources so that she can advise management on how best to match hardware to the structure and development of the organization.

The supervisor will have the ability to communicate with staff at all levels. She will be liaising with authors, operators, maintenance staff, equipment manufacturers and suppliers.

Good organizational ability is a must. It is the supervisor who will organize the work-flows ensuring that authors receive their work on time and spreading the work evenly and fairly among the operators.

Her aim must be to provide an efficient service with happy staff.

In many companies the supervisor will also be responsible for 'general house-keeping', that is:

- filing diskettes

- ensuring back-up is done regularly

- deleting documents

- ordering and managing consumables

- cataloguing documents on disk.

Some companies employ a 'word processing librarian' who is responsible for cataloguing documents on disk. Standard paragraphs, standard letters, reports and minutes are all carefully catalogued and indexed so that information is retrieved quickly and efficiently.

Having now discussed the way a company might organize:

- its word processing equipment

- the people who are closely associated with the production of text

our next chapter will discuss the ideal environment for word processing equipment. Hopefully, this will ensure that the 'ideal' people we have discussed will find themselves in 'ideal' working environments.

SUMMARY

Introduction of word processing involves changes within companies. These should be recognized and planned for.

The approach to word processing varies. Some companies provide a word processor for every secretary. Others have created administrative centres or work groups where three or four secretaries, with word processors, work together as a team. This team supplies services for several managers. Others have made the word processing function into a central service.

To maximize the benefits of word processing, authors should be trained in methods of text production. This should stress neat handwriting, clear instructions at the beginning of an audio tape, smoothly and evenly delivered dictation, the three-phase document-production cycle and no hesitation when dictating for direct keyboarding.

Operators should be provided with extensive training. In addition they should have:

- good keyboard skills

- good language skills

- good proof-reading skills

- a logical approach

- the ability to follow instructions

- a sound knowledge of word processing and how the equipment works

- good skills in the presentation of typing.

With centralized word processing services it is usual to have a supervisor who should be:

- knowledgeable about the equipment

- responsible for training

- conversant with new developments so as to recommend changes to equipment as necessary

- good at communicating and at organizing the flow of work

- responsible for all the general housekeeping including filing diskettes, backing-up work, deleting documents, ordering supplies and cataloguing diskettes.

A word processing librarian may be employed to catalogue and control documents on disk, especially standard paragraphs, standard letters and long reports.

SELF-CHECK QUESTIONS

1. How does a company often make its initial entry into office automation?

2. List three changes that are likely to take place when a company introduces word processing.

3. Describe an 'administrative centre' and how it operates.

4. Why are some managers and secretaries averse to the idea of administrative centres?

5. What are the likely advantages of an administrative centre?

6. What is meant by the 'centralized' approach to word processing?

7. List the four different types of 'set-up' that might be used by a company installing word processing.

8. What methods might an author use to generate text? Give one advantage and one disadvantage of each method.

9. Why is it recommended that authors attend word processing training courses?

10. List four qualities of an 'ideal' author.

11. List seven qualities of an 'ideal' operator.

12. Who usually organizes and co-ordinates the work in a centralized word processing department?

13. Why is it necessary for the supervisor to be fully conversant with the equipment being used?

14. List six duties that you would expect a word processing supervisor to perform.

15. What does a word processing librarian do?

16. Your company is going to employ a word processing operator and supervisor. Prepare a checklist of the skills and qualities each of these prospective employees should possess.

ERGONOMICS AND HEALTH AND SAFETY REQUIREMENTS

Chapter Objectives

After studying this chapter you should be able to:

1. Explain why the study of ergonomics is important.

2. List the features of correct screen and keyboard design.

3. List the features of good workplace design and explain their relevance.

4. Explain how heat, humidity, noise and static electricity can be controlled.

5. Explain how software can play a part in reducing stress for an operator.

END OF OBJECTIVES END OF OBJECTIVES END OF OBJECTIVES END OF OBJECTIVES

INTRODUCTION

We ended the last chapter by stating that we hoped to create an 'ideal' working environment for our word processing staff and in this chapter we shall look at the various 'ERGONOMIC' and legal aspects which will create such an environment.

We read about 'ergonomically' designed workstations and ergonomically designed chairs, but what is ergonomics?

Basically, ergonomics is the study of people in their workplace. This involves such things as the design of:

● equipment

● the workplace

- the software

- the desk

- the chair, etc.

The study of ergonomics is complex, but very important if we wish to achieve the maximum efficiency from people. If the workplace and the equipment we use are badly designed we become tired and stressful which results in reduced motivation (our desire to work) and this will affect the quality of our work and the amount of work we can produce.

So, let us walk into our 'ideal' workplace and look carefully at every aspect.

THE WORKSTATION

You remember of course that all word processing terminals consist of a screen and keyboard. This is referred to as a workstation or visual display terminal (VDT). This is so whether the configuration is stand-alone, shared resources or shared logic.

When first introduced, the screen and keyboard were housed together as one unit. However, it was soon discovered that this was unsatisfactory as the operator could not:

- easily move the keyboard to a comfortable typing position

- move the screen closer or further away to suit her eyes.

Now most keyboards are detachable. They are connected to the screen by a wire or an infrared beam and can be moved and angled to suit the individual operator.

A visual display terminal screen and keyboard

It is now a regulation in many countries that keyboards are detachable. There are several other features of a keyboard that are required in some countries and recommended in others, these include:

- An adequate palm rest – this is the area between the space bar and the edge of the keyboard. In the 'old' days when typists used manual typewriters they always kept their arms and wrists high. With electronic keyboards, it is necessary to keep the wrists low and let the fingers 'hover' over the keys. A palm rest therefore becomes essential to avoid wrist and arm fatigue. The recommended width of the palm rest area is 50 mm.

- A keyboard with a 'matt' surface is now preferred. A shiny surface reflects light and may be slightly slippery. In some countries it is stipulated that the symbols on the keys should be dark while the keys themselves should be of a light colour.

- The slope or angle of the keyboard also plays a part in its ease and comfort of use. The angle should be between 5° and 15°.

Finally the keyboard must be stable and well-balanced. If you have ever tried typing on a keyboard that wobbles you will fully appreciate why this is a necessity.

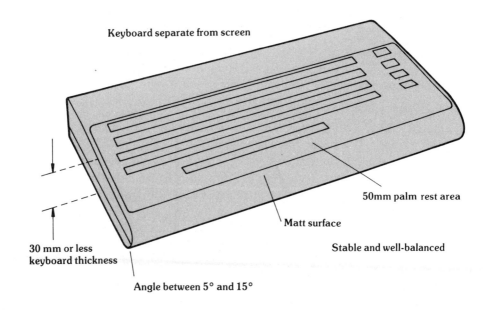

Keyboard separate from screen

50mm palm rest area

Matt surface

30 mm or less
keyboard thickness

Stable and well-balanced

Angle between 5° and 15°

Good keyboard features

Now the screen. There is much talk about the effect on the eyes of looking at a screen for lengthy periods. Some authorities suggest that VDUs do not affect the eyesight while others suggest that there is evidence to prove that VDUs do harm the eyes. However, whichever is true, there are certain features that are essential to the correct design of a screen because the operator does spend a great deal of time looking at it.

We have already said that screens vary in size from a 'thin window' single-line display to a full A4-size screen. However, the most common size displays 80 characters across the screen and 24 lines down.

The colour of the screen display varies from manufacturer to manufacturer. The most common colours are:

- green characters on a dark-green background

- green characters on a black background

- black characters on a white background

- white characters on a black background

- amber characters on a brown background.

It is believed that green characters on a dark-green or black background, or amber characters on a brown background are the most restful on the eyes. Whatever colour display is used there should be adequate contrast between the characters and the background.

If you remember, the characters on the screen are formed by a matrix of dots (called pixels), much like the dot-matrix printer. In order that the characters do not appear 'dotty' a 5×7 (or greater) matrix is recommended.

The line-spacing between the lines of text also determines the ease and comfort of viewing and, in fact, in the United Kingdom it is a regulation that there is 100% character height between the lines.

You may hear or read about the 'REFRESH RATE' of the screen. The image on a cathode ray tube (CRT) is produced by a beam of electrons which are shone on to the screen. The screen has a coating of phosphorescent material which glows when the electron beam strikes it, rather like a luminous watch at night. This glow gradually fades after the beam has passed. The beam starts at the top-left corner and moves down line by line to the bottom before starting at the top-left again. If the speed at which this cycling occurs is low, the screen appears to flicker rapidly causing eyestrain. A cyling of 50 times per second is the minimum accepted in most countries. This cycling is called the refresh rate and is measured in hertz – 50 Hz means 50 cycles per second.

Another factor which affects the use of the CRT is the speed with which the screen loses it phosphorescent glow. If the glow does not fade quickly, a ghost image is left on the screen which affects the clarity of new characters displayed and leads to eye problems.

Further important features of good screen design include:

- Adjustable brightness and contrast controls. It is important that the operator can adjust the luminance of the characters on the screen to suit her own requirements. There are usually brightness and contrast control switches on the front, side or back of the screen.

- Tilt and swivel adjustment. The angle of the screen must be easily adjustable to allow it to be swivelled from side to side and tilted backwards and forwards. This enhancement allows the operator to move the screen to the position she desires and it is important that the adjustments can be made *easily*.

- Anti-reflective screens. Many of the problems associated with VDUs arise from glare and reflections from the screen. Many manufacturers now supply screens that have been treated to reduce glare and reflections. It is also possible to purchase polarized screens that can be fitted over the existing screen to alleviate these problems.

Our operators now have a suitable screen and keyboard, so let us discuss where we shall put the terminal and where our operators will sit. After all, we want happy, comfortable operators.

Obviously we shall place the terminal on a desk and ensure that the desk is sufficiently large to allow room for papers, pens, rulers, etc. but we must ensure that everything the operator needs is easily accessible.

In the United Kingdom it is a regulation that the screen is 450-550 mm from the operator's eyes and, although she can tilt and swivel the screen to suit herself, the recommended height of the screen is approximately at right-angles to the line of sight, or slightly below.

A copy-holder

As the operator will be 'copy-typing' much of the time, we should provide her with a copy-holder. This must be adjustable so that it can be angled to suit the individual. Some copy-holders have a ruler attached which can be moved line by line down the copy manually or by using a foot pedal connected to the ruler to move it.

Any good operator will tell you that when inputting text, the eyes are mainly on the copy and only glance from time to time at the screen. If the copy were flat on the desk it would involve moving the head up and down from copy to screen which would, after a time, become tiring with the eyes continually having to adjust and re-focus to the different distances. However, a copy-holder placed beside the screen means that only slight head movements are made and, if the copy-holder is placed at the same viewing distance as the screen, no re-focusing of the eyes is necessary.

Good posture is a must when operating screen-based terminals. Backache is a common complaint among office/desk-workers. The desk should be of a suitable height and there should be adequate room between the seat and the desk to allow the knees to fit comfortably underneath the desk. Of course, no two people are the same height and build so the chair must be *easily* adjustable to allow 'knee clearance' and a foot-rest should be supplied for short users. Many modern desks now provide mechanisms to adjust the desk height easily.

The chair must also:

- have an adjustable back-rest to give lumbar support
- swivel
- have a sturdy base with castors for easy movement.

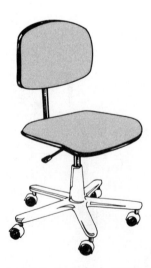

A comfortable chair for a VDU operator

We have said that 'glare' is an important consideration when designing the workplace and this applies not only to the screen. The surface of the desk should be of a non-reflective colour, with a matt surface. Ideally the documents from which the operator is copying should not be of a glossy finish and the characters should be clear.

One last point before we leave our operator's workstation. As you are no doubt aware, one of the requirements of the Health and Safety at Work Act, 1974 is that there should be no 'trailing wires', that is, wires connecting equipment and laid in such a way as to get in people's way. With today's electronic equipment there are more wires than ever to be kept out of the way and certainly we do not want our operator's feet getting tangled up in wires as she sits at her desk!

To overcome this problem, manufacturers of office furniture provide desks that have ducts built in, either at the back or down the side. When the equipment is installed the wires are placed inside these ducts. Not only does this ensure that regulations are complied with but it provides a more attractive work place.

We now have our operator sitting on a comfortably adjusted chair, at a desk of the correct height and with an ergonomically designed screen and keyboard. Let us now place the operator and her immediate workplace in the wider office environment.

First we shall decorate the room in pastel/matt colours that do not reflect light and therefore cause glare. The windows will have blinds to prevent strong sun-light from entering the room and causing reflections on the screen. We shall site the workstation away from the windows and in a position to avoid reflection from any artificial lighting.

The ceiling will have acoustic tiles to reduce the noise in the room and the floor will be carpeted with an anti-static covering. Static electricity which builds up where there is electronic equipment can cause:

- keyboards, CPUs or VDUs to freeze up or malfunction

- diskettes to become corrupted

- operators to get shocks.

Anti-static floor covering will help to prevent this and will also reduce noise.

Noise, particularly in a large centralized word processing environment can be a problem. We said earlier that manufacturers provide keyboards that produce an electronic click when the keys are depressed. Some manufacturers provide keyboards that have a 'sound' control to reduce or increase the 'clicking' sound. If the noise does become excessive it is then possible to 'turn off' the clicking sound. (Similar volume controls are often available for the 'bleep' that sounds if you press the wrong keys.)

Most of the noise however will not be generated by the keyboards but by printers. In our particular environment we shall house the printers in a separate room, away from the work-area. Where this is not possible, an ACOUSTIC HOOD would be placed over the printers to reduce the sound.

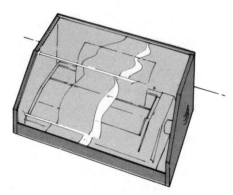

An acoustic hood

An acoustic hood is rather like a box that fits over the printer. It often has a clear perspex lid and the inside is covered with layers of foam to deaden the noise. Usually there is a fan in the hood to keep the printer cool and to blow out printer-dust and paper-dust.

All electrical equipment, as you know, generates heat. In order to keep the work environment within a suitable temperature range, it is desirable to install some form of air-conditioning. The Health and Safety at Work Act, 1974 stipulates that the temperature in the workplace should never exceed 26°C.

Most air-conditioning reduces the amount of moisture in the air. This reduction in humidity can increase the amount of static electricity generated and very dry environments become unpleasant to work in. The introduction of plants or a humidifier help to control the humidity within an office. There is a statutory requirement to maintain humidity within the range of 50% to 70%.

We mentioned at the start of the chapter that the study of ergonomics also involves the software. You might wonder what the software has to do with operator comfort and motivation. If you remember, 'response time' is the time the system takes to respond to a question – how long you have to wait for an answer to your query.

If any of you have used a screen-based terminal you will appreciate that one cannot relax while waiting for a response. If the response time is too short, the operator feels forced to work too quickly. If the response time is too slow the operator becomes frustrated. If the response time is erratic – sometimes fast, sometimes slow – then this is equally irritating. The most common problem is that of response times being too slow. This sometimes happens with shared-logic systems, particularly if the system is overloaded.

You should now appreciate some of the complexities of ergonomics and good workplace design. Of course, all the regulations of the Health and Safety at Work Act, 1974 apply equally to the 'electronic office' as to any traditional office. In addition, some unions have their own regulations for operators of screen-based terminals.

One final point of particular importance is that all operators should be given frequent breaks away from their terminals in order to avoid eyestrain and posture problems. The recommended break is 20 minutes in every two hours worked.

You remember our word processing supervisor? She will of course ensure that operators take sufficient breaks and will organize the word-load to ensure that they are able to do a variety of work.

A comfortable happy work-force will produce more work of a higher quality.

SUMMARY

Ergonomics involves the study of people in the workplace. This involves study of all the factors that surround them and how these affect their ability to work.

Items to be considered include:

Keyboards – these should be detachable, have an adequate palm rest and matt surface and be stable and well-balanced.

Screens – these should be in restful colours and have a minimum refresh rate of 50 Hz, adjustable brightness and contrast, an easily operated tilt and swivel and a filter (or treated screen) to prevent glare.

Desk – this should be sufficiently large to provide adequate working area. It should be high enough to allow the knees to fit under the desk and a foot rest should be supplied for short operators. To reduce glare, the desk surface should have a matt finish. Ideally the desk will be fitted with ducts into which wires from the terminal can be placed.

Decor – in order to reduce glare, rooms should be decorated in pastel shades. Blinds should be used to prevent strong sunlight from entering the room. Workstations should be located away from windows and positioned to avoid reflections.

Noise – ceilings should have acoustic tiles and floors should be covered with anti-static carpet to reduce the level of noice. The noise of the 'click' generated by the keyboards should be adjustable. Printers should be housed in acoustic hoods.

Temperature – the temperature should be kept stable with the use of air-conditioning and central heating if necessary. The temperature should not exceed 26°C and humidity should be kept in the range of 50-70%.

Software – software should be designed to respond evenly at a comfortable pace at which to work.

Operators should not work more than two hours continuously and should have a 20-minute break between each session. The word processing supervisor should ensure that work-flows are designed to promote this form of working.

SELF-CHECK QUESTIONS

1. What does the study of ergonomics involve?
2. Why is the study of ergonomics important?
3. What comprises a workstation?
4. Why is it necessary to have keyboards that are detached from the screen?
5. What are the two ways in which keyboards are connected to the screen?
6. Where is the palm rest on a keyboard?
7. Why is it necessary to have a suitable palm rest?
8. What type of surface material should be used on keyboards?
9. List two further features of a good keyboard.
10. What are the most common sizes of screen?
11. List the common colours of the screen displays.
12. What are considered to be the most restful colours for screens?
13. How are the characters on a screen formed?
14. What does 'refresh rate' mean when talking about VDUs?
15. Why is it important that the phosphorescent glow fades quickly?
16. List three features of good screen design and explain the importance of each.
17. What piece of equipment should be provided for any operator to assist her when copy-typing?
18. How can unnecessary eye movement and re-focusing of the eyes be avoided when typing from copy?
19. What is one of the most common complaints among office-workers?
20. What should be supplied for short operators?
21. How can glare on a desk be avoided?
22. List the features of a well-designed chair.
23. Why do some desks have 'ducts' built in?

24. Explain how a word processing room should be decorated to avoid glare.

25. Give two ways in which the workplace can be designed to reduce noise.

26. Static electricity builds up where there is electronic equipment.
    a Explain how this can be controlled.
    b If static is allowed to build up what problems might occur to:
        i   the equipment
        ii the operator?

27. How can the noise from keyboards be reduced?

28. Printers usually generate a lot of noise. State two ways in which the problem of printer noise can be alleviated.

29. Describe an acoustic hood.

30. How can the humidity in the word processing room be controlled?

31. Explain how the software can reduce or increase stress for an operator.

32. Why is it important that operators have frequent breaks and what is the recommended break?

WORD PROCESSING SUPPLIES AND CONSUMABLES

Chapter Objectives

After studying this chapter you should be able to:

1. List and describe the most essential word processing supplies and consumables.

2. List the rules that apply to the care of floppy disks.

3. Recognize the importance of the care of word processing equipment and explain the procedures to be adopted in its care.

END OF OBJECTIVES END OF OBJECTIVES END OF OBJECTIVES END OF OBJECTIVES

INTRODUCTION

In any office there will always be certain items, such as pens, paper and pencils, that are continuously being used and need replacing. These replaceable items are referred to as CONSUMABLES. Word processing demands its own supplies and consumables, and this chapter looks at the range of consumables one might expect to stock for use with a word processor.

PAPER

As most of the output from a word processor is hard copy, paper is an important stock item. Paper can be:

● cut sheets – like normal typing paper

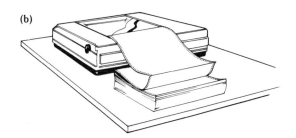

(a) Fanfold paper　　　　　　　　(b) Fanfold paper loaded in a printer

- continuous stationery – a long continuous sheet of paper – may be in a roll or stacked page upon page (called FANFOLD) with perforations marking each page

- mounted sheets – a long continuous sheet of paper on to which individual cut sheets are mounted – they can be easily removed without damaging them

- labels – usually on continuous rolls and after printing can be peeled off and stuck on envelopes.

Most continuous stationery will have holes along each edge which allow the paper to be drawn through the printer by a tractor or pin-feed mechanism.

It is important to keep paper clean and dry and, particularly with sheet feeders, to fan the paper regularly to prevent it sticking together. In addition, paper should not be allowed to become too hot as this will adversely affect how easily it feeds into the printer.

RIBBONS

The large volume of hard copy produced from a word processor will necessitate a stock of printer ribbons being held. Ribbons may be:

- fabric – a nylon cloth impregnated with ink – they can be used repeatedly, back and forth but, as the ink is used, the print image becomes faint

- multi-strike – a plastic film with carbon on – each time the ribbon is struck the printer winds the ribbon on slightly but the amount of movement is less than one character which results in a slightly patchy print

- single strike – identical to multi-strike except that each time the ribbon is struck the printer moves the ribbon one complete character position, ensuring the highest-quality print.

Many newer printers use cartridge ribbons which can be changed very easily unlike the older spool ribbons found on typewriters and early printers.

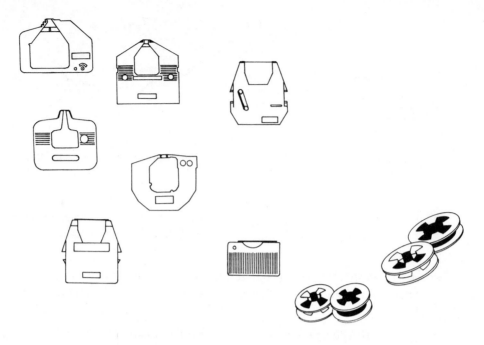

Ribbons on cassettes, cartridges and spools

DISKETTES

With much of the work on a word processor being stored on diskettes, a supply of these should be kept. Although fairly robust, nothing is worse than losing pages of work through a disk corruption. To avoid this, certain simple rules should be observed:

- Do not place diskettes near electrical equipment, including telephones. These generate magnetic fields which can cause corruptions.

- Do not touch the exposed surface of the disk.

- Do not write on the disk sleeve with anything other than a soft felt-tip pen as this can damage the disk.

- Do not smoke near disks or disk drives and try to prevent disks from becoming dusty.

- Do not allow disks to become hot – heat can affect the magnetic recording.

- Always return the disk to its sleeve when the disk is taken out of the disk drive and store diskettes upright in a protective box or file.

- Do not bend or twist diskettes.

- Do not spill drinks on to your diskettes (or anything else for that matter!).

Care of diskettes

DISKETTE STORAGE

As it is important to store floppy disks carefully, it is necessary to provide storage facilities. Types of storage system available include:

- cardboard boxes with slide-off lids which hold approximately five disks

- plastic boxes of various types with hinged lids – these are often lockable and will hold from 10 to about 50 disks

- plastic boxes on which the lid slides back and then hinges to form a stand

- ring binders with plastic wallets to hold disks

- suspension files with plastic-wallet disk holders

- rotating carousel stores into which disks can be slid.

PRINT ELEMENTS

It is sensible to have spare print elements (daisy wheels or thimbles) as the most common printer faults often cause damage to the print element. Additionally, different type-styles can be obtained through different print elements.

Print elements may be either plastic or metal. Metal wheels last longer and are generally more durable but are much more expensive than plastic.

Many print elements must be pushed on to a spindle which, if the fit is tight, can result in accidental damage. To ease the fit, wipe the inside of the spindle socket on the daisy wheel with a cotton bud dipped in oil.

DUST-COVERS

It is sensible to provide dust-covers for word processing equipment. These often take the form of a keyboard-cover, a VDU-cover and a printer-cover, and should be placed over the equipment whenever it is not being used.

WORD PROCESSING RULERS

These special rulers, which have scales for:

- 10-, 12- and 15-character pitches

- 6 or 8 lines per inch

- inches and centimetres

make the formatting and layout of text much easier and are especially useful for tabulation work.

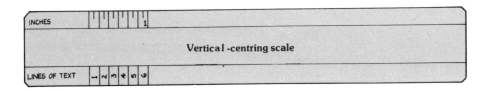

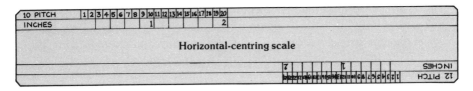

Word processing rulers

COPY-HOLDERS

These devices are designed to hold manuscript in an upright position, close to the VDU, thus making copy-typing more relaxed (see page 240). Various types exist from simple, stand-up holders with a ruler to mark the lines, through versions that can be clipped to the side of the VDU, to de luxe versions with a foot pedal which operates an air pump causing the line-marking ruler to move down each time the foot pedal is depressed.

SUPPLIES FOR CARE OF EQUIPMENT

There are various supplies that should be available for the maintenance of the equipment. These include:

- Floppy-disk drive cleaning kits. Various types exist although all work on the principle of a cleaning disk (usually with a cleaning fluid) which can be inserted into the disk drive and the drive activated. As the disk spins it cleans the disk drive read/write heads and helps to prevent corruption or errors.

- Screen-cleaning kits. VDUs generate static electricity which attracts dust and this dust film, together with finger marks on the screen, can cause eye-strain. It is therefore important to clean the screen regularly. Cleaners may be special cleaning cloths impregnated with a cleaning fluid, foam cleaners which are sprayed on to the screen and wiped off with a tissue or soft cloth or special pads. There are pad-type cleaners which are usually designed for use with screens that have special surfaces designed to reduce glare.

249

- Daisy-wheel cleaners. These cleaners ensure that the daisy wheels are kept clean, thus giving the best possible print. Simple kits comprise cleaning fluid and cotton buds, while better versions provide a special device on to which the daisy wheel is fixed and is then rotated against a cleaning pad impregnated with fluid.

- Anti-static sprays. Static electricity often builds up in air-conditioned or centrally heated buildings. Disks, keyboards and most electronic equipment are susceptible to electrical sparks which can cause anything from a corrupted diskette to a whole system requiring maintenance. Anti-static sprays are used around all word processing equipment and are sprayed on to furniture, carpets and the equipment to prevent the build-up of static electricity.

Generally all word processing equipment should be maintained and looked after at least as well as we are taught to look after typewriters. However, as this equipment is more likely to go wrong if not correctly cared for, it really is essential that you do carry out your housekeeping regularly, rather than to forget it as is the norm with many typists and their typewriters.

SUMMARY

Word processing requires a supply of consumable goods plus some basic stock items.

Paper may be:

- cut sheets

- continuous stationery – either on roll or as fanfold

- mounted single sheets on a continuous backing.

Ribbons are either fabric or film.

A stock of diskettes should be kept. Diskettes should be well cared for. A résumé of the rules for the care of diskettes is given in this chapter.

Various forms of diskette storage units are available and should be kept.

Spare print wheels or thimbles should be kept for printers. As well as keeping a variety of type-styles, it is important to have spare elements of the normal type-style used in the organization because often a faulty printer can damage the print element.

Dust-covers should be kept for all equipment and placed over the equipment when it is not in use.

Word processing rulers, with scales for 10-, 12- and 15-pitch, 6 or 8 lines per inch as well as centimetres and inches make the task of formatting work easier.

Copy-holders should be supplied.

Various cleaning materials should be stocked. These include:

- floppy-disk cleaners
- screen-cleaning kits – either spray-on foam, liquid or cleaning cloths
- daisy-wheel cleaners
- anti-static sprays – aerosols or pump sprays.

As a general rule all word processing equipment should be looked after at least as well as a trained typist looks after her typewriter.

SELF-CHECK QUESTIONS

1. List three types of paper that might be used for word processing.

2. What is continuous paper?

3. Why is it necessary to 'fan' paper regularly?

4. What is the difference between:
   a fabric ribbons
   b multi-strike ribbons
   c single-strike ribbons?

5. List eight rules applying to the care of disks.

6. Give two reasons why spare print elements should be kept.

7. What are print elements made of?

8. Many print elements must be pushed on to a spindle which, if the fit is tight, can result in accidental damage. What can be done to ease the fit?

9. How can the equipment be protected from dust when not in use?

10. What is a word processing ruler and when is it useful?

11. What type of copy-holders are available?

12. How can a floppy-disk drive head be cleaned?

13. Give three methods that can be used to clean screens.

14. Why is it important to clean daisy wheels regularly and how are they cleaned?

15. Why are anti-static sprays needed and where should they be sprayed?

16. Why is it important to look after your word processing equipment carefully?

BUSINESSES USING WORD PROCESSING

Chapter Objectives

After studying this chapter you should be able to:

1. Identify the word processing functions that are particularly useful for certain types of business.

END OF OBJECTIVES END OF OBJECTIVES END OF OBJECTIVES END OF OBJECTIVES

INTRODUCTION

Word processors, as we have seen, have many functions and features designed to make the production and handling of typed text much easier. So what businesses can benefit from word processing and how can they use it?

GENERAL USE

Almost every business will produce written correspondence of a general type:

- letters
- memoranda
- sales invoices, etc.

Clearly, this form of text-production can be produced, quite easily, using a typewriter. However, unless:

- the typist is very good
- authors do not change their minds

simple word processing can improve the speed and quality of general text-production as it allows easy correction and editing of text. Whether it is cost-effective to use a word processor in this way would need careful consideration as the equipment is still considerably more expensive than a typewriter.

SALES AND MARKETING

Business involved in mass marketing or sales promotions should find word processing with a mail-merge or (better still) records-management facility extremely useful. Consider, for example, a large car-dealership. If everyone who bought a car or even expressed an interest in doing so had their details such as name, address, car bought, date of purchase, amount paid, reason for buying or not buying, etc. taken down by the salesman, and then these details were typed into a word processor, it would become very easy to send 'special offer' letters to these people.

Suppose the Sales Manager decides that, to boost sales in July, he will offer all ex-customers a special bonus trade-in on the car they bought. This trade-in will be available to everyone who bought a car more than two, but less than four years ago, and will be worth 35% of the original purchase price.

Using a word processor with mail-merge (and maths to calculate 35% of original value) it becomes relatively simple to produce these letters. In addition, just by changing the standard letter and the criteria used for selecting the variables to be merged, many different offers can be made to different groups.

As most businesses have customers and suppliers, the use of a word processor with mail-merge does not limit itself to specific business types. However, businesses that have adopted word processing for this function include:

- mail-order companies
- mass-market magazine publishers
- real-estate agents
- motor vehicle dealerships and manufacturers
- insurance companies and brokers
- building societies and banks.

REPORT WRITING

Many organizations produce lengthy reports either for internal or external consumption.

Invariably, long reports (or books for that matter) are subject to several revisions as:

- figures change
- new items of commentary are added

- layout is varied

- chunks of text are moved about

- words and phrases are changed and re-changed.

Without word processing, it is often the case that the author retains most of the report in manuscript, writing on the revisions in various colours until the script being presented to the typist resembles a multi-coloured spider's web. The typist then produces a copy which the author edits (hopefully in pencil) and returns for final production. Generally this is not terribly successful and the pressure to meet deadlines places great strain on author and typist. (And, as you know, it is much easier to make mistakes when you are under pressure.)

Thus, any business that has long reports to produce will find word processing a tremendous boon. Businesses associated with this type of text-production include:

- any form of consultancy – medical, design, management, financial, etc.

- medium-to-large manufacturing companies

- authors and publishers

- educational establishments

- government departments

- news reporters and newspaper publishing.

STANDARD WORDINGS/PARAGRAPHS

It is common for many professions to use standard phraseology, particularly where legal implications are involved. Before the introduction of word processing it was common for authors in these types of business to pass to the typist a set of documents taken from file plus the new manuscript. Written in to the manuscript would be instructions such as:

- insert para 3, section 4 from Mrs Phelps v. Crown

- copy indemnity wording used for policy arrangement obtained for CIT.

Word processing that offers standard paragraph facilities (or even merge facilities) has greatly improved the production of this form of semi-standard document.

- Authors can be given a dictionary or catalogue of standard paragraphs or wordings, each paragraph having a reference.

- They select, by reference, the paragraphs they want, in the order they want them.

- The operator then 'builds' the document by recalling the paragraphs into the text where required.

Businesses using word processing in this way include:

- solicitors
- insurance brokers and companies
- estate agents
- consultancies
- banks and stock brokers
- organizations that issue contracts for the supply of goods or labour.

SUMMARY

A word processor can benefit virtually any business although if it is used as a direct replacement for a typewriter, it may be difficult to justify the extra cost of one of these systems.

Businesses that need to produce large volumes of standard letters will benefit from a word processor that supports good mail-merge or records-management facilities.

Many organizations produce long reports or documents. These may be for internal use or as part of their commercial service. Word processing with strong editing features and good printer control will significantly improve this operation.

Professions and businesses that use standard wordings or paragraphs – particularly where legal implications are involved – will benefit from word processing with simple-to-use standard paragraph functions. The business can generate a whole series of approved and checked paragraphs which can be integrated into text in whatever order is required.

SELF-CHECK QUESTIONS

1. What type of general correspondence might a word processor be used to produce?
2. **a** What facility of a word processor would be particularly useful for companies involved in sales and marketing?
   b Give examples of how these facilities might be used.
3. What types of business can make use of the mail-merge function? Give an example of the work they may do using this function.
4. Why is word processing particularly useful for producing lengthy reports?
5. List six types of business likely to produce lengthy reports.
6. What word processing facility would be particularly useful to businesses involved with legal work?
7. Think of a business in your own locality, describe the type of work they do and state what particular word processing functions could assist them.

PROLOGUE TO THE FUTURE

Having reached the end of this book in which we have reviewed information processing and looked in some depth at word processing, we felt that we should discuss the effects of this technology on society. We tried to do this, only to abandon the attempt as all the effects we identified were 'possible effects'. Everything was prediction: 'this is what we think might happen . . .'. In the end we decided to leave the future with you.

It is our belief that humanity is on the threshold of an exciting and challenging period in its history and that the world we all live in will be unrecognisably better for everyone as the new information-based society supersedes the current industry-based society. As has happened before, old skills will disappear to be replaced by new ones.

The changes in society widely predicted – widespread job losses, people working from home rather than from offices and factories, machines controlling our lives, people becoming addicted to screens and machines and forgetting how to talk to other people, society losing the ability to think – may occur and how we cope with these changes makes the next decades both interesting and exciting. Clearly, these changes are already beginning – and we are 'muddling through'! The future lies in our hands and we hope that you will find that this book provides sufficient understanding for you to make informed decisions about where you want your future to go.

GLOSSARY

ACCESS TIME: the time delay between the CPU starting to fetch data from memory or backing store and the data reaching the CPU.

ANALOGUE COMPUTER: a machine that works on data signals that vary constantly (unlike digital signals that are on or off). An example of an analogue signal is the human voice. It goes smoothly up and down in tone and volume. A digital 'voice' would jump from soft to loud, low or high with nothing in between.

APPLICATION SOFTWARE: the set of programs designed specifically to carry out a task such as control and production of wages, storage and retrieval of information, etc.

ARITHMETIC LOGIC UNIT: the part of the CPU in which calculations or logic operations are done.

ASSEMBLY LANGUAGE: a low-level language in which each statement corresponds to a single machine code or CPU instruction. Usually it is written using mnemonics, for example, LD for load, ST for store, JMP for JUMP.

ASYNCHRONOUS TRANSMISSION: transmission in which each data character has start and stop bits.

BACKGROUND PRINTING: when the program that controls printing of a file does not restrict the use of the input terminal while printing is being done, the printing is said to be background printing.

BACKING STORE: the term used to cover all the devices on which a computer may store data and from which it may retrieve it when required.

BATCH PROCESSING: the collection of a large number of transactions and then the processing of them as a batch (that is, all at once) rather than immediately as they arise.

BAUD: a measurement of the speed of transmission of data, usually equivalent to bits per second. Thus a baud rate of 1200 usually means that 1200 bits per second would be transmitted down the carrier channel.

BIT: short for a BInary digiT. Computers that operate digitally, that is, with a series of ons and offs work using binary numbers.

BUFFER: an area of temporary storage usually found between input/output devices and the CPU, or between high-speed and low-speed devices, which allows data to be held until the receiving device is ready.

BYTE: a byte is a unit of measurement containing eight bits, usually equivalent to one character.

CARD: a printed circuit board with the electronics required to achieve a specific function, e.g. a graphics card that allows the computer to produce high resolution graphics output on a screen.

CENTRAL PROCESSING UNIT: the part of a computer that does all the processing of data and controls all the computer peripherals. Its role may be compared to that of the human brain.

CHIP: an integrated circuit etched on to a semi-conducting substance such as silicon.

CLOCK: this device provides the timing which the CPU uses to keep control over all the operations of the computer.

COMPILER: a program designed to translate an entire source program into a machine code version. The CPU will then use the translated version when carrying out the program instructions.

CONFIGURATION: the term used to describe the arrangement of a computer and its peripheral devices.

CONTROL UNIT: the part of the CPU that ensures that the computer carries out every instruction in a program and can fetch and store data from the right area in the memory.

CURSOR: a character (usually a rectangle or line) on the VDU that indicates the current position where information will appear on the screen.

DATA: units of characters that together form the basis for computer processing. When data is combined and becomes useful or meaningful, it is referred to as information.

DATABASE: a collection of files storing data in such a way that very little data is duplicated (stored twice) and the stored data can be used by many different programs – each using only the data they need.

DATABASE MANAGEMENT SYSTEM: a set of programs designed to control and manage data stored in a series of files. These programs make access to information stored much easier and usually ensure that data is stored only once, even though used by many different applications programs.

DEFAULT: a value that is assumed to be correct but which can be changed if required.

DOCUMENT DELIVERY SYSTEMS: electronic systems that allow text to be transmitted, stored and retrieved from one source to central storage facilities – associated with both electronic mail and large-scale information databases.

DIGITAL COMPUTER: a machine that works with digital signals – either on or off. These are called binary signals.

DISK OPERATING SYSTEM: a special set of programs written to control and co-ordinate the use of magnetic disks and disk devices and the storage of data on these devices.

DISK PACK: a number of hard disks connected together on a single spindle.

DUPLEX: a communication link that allows data to be sent in two directions. See also FULL DUPLEX and HALF DUPLEX.

FEEDBACK: the mechanism by which part of the output from a system is re-input to the system in order to regulate the system in some way.

FLOPPY DISK: a flexible magnetic disk on which data can be stored by a computer – usually associated with microcomputers.

FOREGROUND TASK: a program with high CPU priority which restricts the use of an input device while in operation.

FULL DUPLEX: a communication link that allows data to be sent in both directions simultaneously.

FUNCTION KEYS: special keys on a keyboard which, when pressed, will carry out a specific program instruction. Sometimes called program function keys or PF keys.

GATEWAY: a hardware and software link that allows the users of one computer network (usually a viewdata system) to access external computers and their databases.

HALF DUPLEX: a communication link that allows data to be sent in either direction but not simultaneously.

HARD CARD: an ultra-thin Winchester disk which is fitted to a microcomputer as any other printed circuit board would be.

HARDWARE: the physical and tangible parts of the computer – those we can see and touch.

HIGH-LEVEL LANGUAGES: programming languages where a single statement in the source program may translate to multiple CPU instructions. These languages generally resemble psuedo-English. Examples include COBOL, BASIC, PASCAL, SQL and LOGO.

HYBRID COMPUTER: a machine that operates using both digital and analogue signals. Often data is stored digitally but processed as analogue signals.

INPUT: the 'taking-in' of information into a system from the world surrounding the system.

INTEGRATION: data integration describes the process whereby data defined (or input) using one type of program (say a spreadsheet) may freely be used with the output from another program (say a word processing document).

INTELLIGENT PRINTERS: printers that have the capacity to perform certain local functions without the control of the central processing unit.

INTERPRETER: a special program designed to translate a high-level language into machine code instructions. Interpreters always translate the source program one instruction at a time with each translated instruction being submitted to the CPU only after translation (cf. compiler).

KEYPAD: a set of keys not part of the normal QWERTY keyboard, designed to aid input. A numeric keypad, for example, can make the input of numbers much easier.

LETTER-QUALITY PRINTING: the production of printed computer output that is of high quality.

LOW-LEVEL LANGUAGES: languages where each statement in the source code translates to no more than a few machine code instructions.

MACHINE CODE: the actual collection of bits that together form the instructions that the CPU carries out.

MACRO: a single command that will cause the system to carry out several instructions.

MAGNETIC DISK: a disk of either plastic or metal (usually aluminium) covered with a magnetizable surface on which computer data can be stored.

MAGNETIC TAPE: tape covered with a magnetizable film on which data can be stored.

MAINFRAME: a very large powerful computer that can support many peripheral devices. Originally so called because the electronic devices and the memory units were mounted in metal frames.

MEMORY UNIT: the part of the CPU in which data is stored until required for processing. Data in the memory unit can be used directly by the CPU.

MICROCOMPUTER: a small computer of limited power and often capable of supporting only a few peripherals. The CPU comprises a small number of chips.

MINICOMPUTER: a medium-sized computer, with moderate memory and power capable of supporting fewer peripherals than a mainframe.

MODEM: stands for MOdulation/DEModulation. A modem is a device that will either change a digital signal from a computer into an analogue signal suitable for transmission down a normal telephone line, or change an analogue input received via a telephone line into a digital signal for the computer.

MULTI-USER: more than one user can access the central processor at what appears to be the same time.

NETWORK: a series of devices connected by a number of different channels.

OBJECT PROGRAM: a translated version of a source program that is in binary form (a machine code).

ON/OFF LINE: if a peripheral device is connected to the CPU both physically (for example, by a wire) and electronically (that is, so that data can be passed between the peripheral and the computer) then the device is on-line. A disconnected device is off-line.

OPERATING SYSTEM: the set of programs that supervise and control the operation of a computer and all its peripherals.

OPTICAL DISK: a disk onto which data can be stored by laser as pit, or no pit, burned into the disk.

OUTPUT: information from a computer communicated to the outside world.

PACKING DENSITY: a measure of the number of bits stored per unit of measure (e.g. a square centimetre) on a backing-storage medium such as a disk or tape.

PARALLEL TRANSMISSION: a form of data transmission where enough bits to form a character (usually a byte) are transmitted simultaneously.

PERIPHERAL DEVICES: all the pieces of hardware that are not part of the CPU, for example, VDUs and printers.

PIN: Personal Identity Number used as a security code by many systems.

PIXEL (or Picel): PICture ELement – the dots or areas on a visual display which, combined together, form the image. The greater the number of pixels, the higher the resolution (or detail) of the image.

PROGRAM: the set of instructions computers follow when carrying out a task.

PROGRAMMING LANGUAGES: the languages by which users of computers can instruct the computer to carry out a task.

RANDOM ACCESS MEMORY (RAM): volatile memory into which data can be written at any location.

READ ONLY MEMORY (ROM): memory chips that are non-volatile and therefore hold data or programs permanently.

REAL-TIME PROCESSING: the process by which inputs are processed immediately they occur rather than being collected and grouped before processing as with a batch process.

REGISTER: a temporary store within the CPU that can hold a limited amount of data. The accumulator is a special register in which all arithmetic and logic manipulations are performed. The address register maintains a number that corresponds to the next storage location in the volatile memory to be used.

SERIAL TRANSMISSION: where one data bit is transmitted after another.

SHARED LOGIC: terminals sharing the same CPU (and often the same programs).

SHARED RESOURCES: CPUs capable of sharing the same peripherals.

SIMPLEX: a link that allows data to be sent in one direction only.

SOFTWARE: the term used to describe all the programs that a computer uses.

SOURCE PROGRAM: a program in a language form that users can recognize.

SPOOL: Simultaneous Peripheral Operation On Line. A spooler is a form of software that allows spooling, that is, the orderly use of peripheral devices by many users.

STAND-ALONE: entirely self-contained hardware, often comprising keyboard, VDU, CPU, backing store and printer.

SYNCHRONOUS TRANSMISSION: transmission in which data is sent in a continuous stream from the start of a message to the end of a message.

VARIABLE: an item of data that can be changed during the running of a program (for example, names and addresses during the printing of standard letters).

VISUAL DISPLAY UNIT (VDU): an output device, similar to a TV screen, on which output from a computer can be displayed. It is often associated with a keyboard and called a terminal.

VOLATILE MEMORY: any form of memory that loses all its data when the power supply is turned off.

WORD: the unit of measurement used to describe how many bits the CPU can deal with at once. Thus a computer that uses 32-bit words will deal with 32 bits during each operation.

WORM: Write only Once, Read Many times – an acronym given to a special form of optical disk and disk drive that allows data to be stored on disk only once, i.e. non-updateable.

APPENDIX OF QUESTIONS

1. All methods of processing data, in order to provide meaningful information, contain the basic elements of:
INPUT/PROCESSING/OUTPUT/STORAGE/CONTROL. Compare a manual system with a computerized system at each stage, giving examples to aid your explanation.

N.B. It is not necessary to use one procedure (for example, payroll preparation) throughout your answer; examples can be taken from any procedure.

Comparison may be in the form of a three-column table, beginning as follows:

Element	Manual	Computer
Input	Clerks receive data in form of source documents – for example, customers' orders, time cards, invoices, store issue notes.	
Processing		

(from LCCI Information Processing, June 1983)

2. Document readers can read printed or written characters on source documents and convert the data for processing by computer.

Briefly describe three such devices and give one example of each.
(from LCCI Information Processing, PESD/PSC, June 1984)

3. OCR stands for
  a one colour region
  b optical character recognition
  c own cable relay
  d original computer records.
(from RSA Word Processing Elementary (Pilot Scheme), June 1983)

4. The main disadvantage of printed output from computers is the large quantity of paper which is used. Paper is bulky, and becomes increasingly expensive. To overcome these disadvantages, COM has been developed.
Describe what is meant by COM, and how it is used.
(from LCCI Information Processing, PESD/PSC, June 1984)

5. Visual display on screen, paper tape, punched card, line printout, magnetic tape, magnetic disk, documents from printers etc. are all types of computer

_____

(from RSA Word Processing Stage I, November 1983)

6. Describe the following, give one advantage of each:
a an ink-jet printer
b an optical character reader (OCR)
(from LCCI Information Processing, June 1982)

7. Mini diskettes, Winchesters, optic (video) disks, cassettes, magnetic cards are all types of _____?
(from RSA Word Processing Stage I, November 1983)

8. You work in the word processing department in the head office of a travel agent, which has recently taken on a Youth Training Scheme trainee. As the youngest member of the department, you have been asked to introduce the YTS trainee to the word processing equipment, and to the other equipment in your working area.
Select five of the following items and explain to the trainee what their functions are:

a daisy wheel
b dual disk drive unit
c OCR scanner
d floppy disk
e printer
f visual display unit
g facsimile copier
h hopper paper feed.
(from RSA Word Processing Stage I, November 1983)

9. Four of the most popular methods of printing are the golf ball, daisy wheel, dot matrix and ink jet. Briefly describe each of them, mentioning their respective speeds and quality of print.
(from LCCI Word Processing, SSC, June 1984)

10. A stand-alone word processor is one that
a should always be placed in isolation, in a room of its own
b must be separated from all other office equipment by at least one metre on either side
c is linked to a central storage medium, but is not necessarily close to that storage unit
d is comprehensive, having its own keyboard, storage medium and printer.
(from RSA Word Processing Stage I (Pilot Scheme), Summer Series 1983)

11. a By means of a diagram, show the main parts of a shared-logic configuration and label the parts.
b State the advantages of a shared-logic system over a stand-alone system.
(from LCCI Information Processing, June 1982)

12. Describe stand-alone and shared-logic word processing systems, giving the advantages of each.
(from LCCI Word Processing Specimen Paper)

13. a By means of a diagram, show the main parts of a stand-alone system.
   b Briefly describe the functions of each of the parts.
(from LCCI Word Processing, June 1983)

14. Reply to the following Memorandum:

M E M O R A N D U M
To: Information Processing Supervisor
From: Branch Manager
Date: Yesterday's

Subject: VIEWDATA AND TELETEXT

At the Business Exhibition yesterday, I saw some aspects of the above services but owing to pressure of work I was unable to stay long enough to understand fully the differences between the two. Please would you clarify this for me and also let me know how, at this branch, we could use them.
(from LCCI Information Processing, Higher Stage, May 1984)

15. 'Facsimile transmission has been in existence since the beginning of the twentieth century and is used for the transmission of pictures, documents, drawings etc.'
   a How is this possible?
   b What are three current international standards for fax machines?
   c Name and describe the British Telecom over-the-counter facsimile service which individuals, as well as companies, can use for a small payment.
(from LCCI Information Processing, Higher Stage, May 1984)

16. What Viewdata systems are available, and who supplies them? State their uses.
(from LCCI Information Processing, June 1982)

17. If a company intended having an electronic mailing system, what essential computer hardware would be required before messages could actually be transmitted?
(from LCCI Information Processing, Higher Stage, May 1984)

18. a State briefly what is meant by the term 'information processing'.
   b In the office of the near future, it will be possible to originate, transmit and retrieve information in the form of words, numbers or graphics entirely by means of electronic information processing equipment.
   List six of the principal items of office equipment which the new technology comprises.
   c Developments are moving towards a total electronic communication system, where all the equipment is inter-connected or 'convergent'.
   What are the advantages to a firm of installing such an integrated system?
(from LCCI Information Processing, June 1983)

19. a i Describe what is meant by *phototypesetting*, and say how you think it would be of benefit in the office of a manufacturing concern engaged in the production of domestic electrical equipment – say, electric cookers, kettles, etc.

ii How can phototypesetting equipment be used in conjunction with a word processor and what advantage would there be from this link?

b Some word processors are able to communicate with each other within the same room, or across the country. Say how this is possible and describe the procedure for sending a letter by this method from a Head Office to one of its branches. Mention the speed of transmission with/without hard copy at the receiving end.

(from LCCI Information Processing, June 1983)

20. a In the modern office, increasing use is being made of electronic transmission. Describe briefly what is meant by the following:

i electronic mail and

ii facsimile transmission,

outlining how the systems operate, and one advantage of each to an office organization.

b Explain the meaning of 'hardware' and 'software'.

(from LCCI Information Processing, June 1984)

21. Current trends indicate that word processors are increasingly likely to become part of multi-purpose office systems. Name FOUR pieces of equipment which could be interfaced to, or used in conjunction with, a word processor to aid the integration of office procedures, and describe how each could be used when linked to a word processor.

(from LCCI Word Processing, Intermediate Stage, May 1984)

22. Any print on paper of any kind (book, letter, memo, report, continuous stationery printout, etc.) is known as . . .

(from RSA Word Processing Stage I, November 1983)

23. You are employed as a typist/word processing operator at Mather PLC, based in Hampshire. Your boss, Mr Trevor Jones, has a visitor today, Mr Khamil from Saudi Arabia.

Mr Jones has warned you that he will bring Mr Khamil into your office to meet you, and may need you to describe your work and the word processing equipment to him. Mr Khamil has no experience or knowledge of word processing systems.

When Mr Khamil is introduced to you he expresses great interest in your word processing equipment and asks you a number of questions

This is the layout of your workstation.

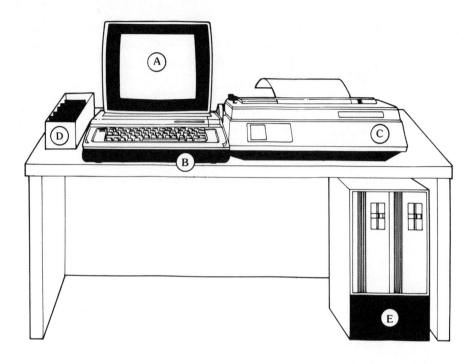

a Identify the parts labelled A, B, C, D and E and explain briefly the function of each in the word processing operation.

b Mr Khamil has been reading some advertising material relating to word processing and has picked out the following terms:
   i wraparound
   ii housekeeping
   iii text retrieval
   iv search and global change
   v daisy wheel
   Explain briefly what each term means.
(from RSA Word Processing Stage I Specimen Tasks, 1982)

24. Explain briefly what is meant by four of the following terms:
   a automatic decimal tab
   b hard and soft copy
   c string search
   d justify
   e scrolling
   f embolden.
(from LCCI Word Processing, SSC, June 1984)

25. One of the main functions that a word processor performs is storing information for retrieval later, for example, a letter on disk may be recalled and a further copy printed.

List six other functions (*not* applications) of a word processor, and give an example of each.

(from LCCI Word Processing, SSC, June 1984)

26. Your tasks this morning include typing the following documents:
  a   a report for consideration by senior management, relating to company policy
  b   minutes of the Social Club Committee meeting
  c   a letter confirming offers of employment to 15 new apprentices
  d   a memo detailing Christmas holiday arrangements for distribution to all staff
  e   a cheque for payment of a hotel bill

Go through each of the tasks you have this morning, stating whether you would use a word processor or a typewriter. Explain the reasons for your choice, referring to the functions available on the word processor where applicable.

(from RSA Word Processing Specimen Paper, 1982)

27. Explain briefly what is meant by four of the following terms
  a   shared logic
  b   wraparound
  c   cursor
  d   boilerplating
  e   CPU

(from LCCI Word Processing, SSC, June 1984)

28. Choose the letter a, b, c or d which correctly completes or answers the sentence. 'Double density' refers to:
  a   emboldening areas of text due to overprinting.
  b   the ability to store twice as much information as usual on a disk.
  c   the ability to store information on both sides of a disk.
  d   altering the line-spacing from double to single for the final copy.

(from RSA Word Processing Stage I Specimen Paper, 1982)

29. a   List the facilities available on a word processor:
    i   as new text is being keyed in
    ii   during the modifying of stored text
    iii   at the printing stage.
  b   Describe what is meant by a 'personalized' standard letter and give one example.

(from LCCI Word Processing, June 1984)

30. a   Name the facility the word processor uses for each of the following operations:
    i   sending an identical letter to large numbers of people, but with individual salutations and addresses on each one

    ii   keying-in additional paragraphs in the centre of a long document

    iii ensuring that words are not misspelled

    iv adding columns of figures

    v   rearranging information into alphabetic or numeric order.

b   Explain why these techniques are attractive functions of word processors.

c   Give an example of the type of document for which they might be used.

(from RSA Word Processing Stage I, November 1983)

31. In each branch of a company there is the following equipment:

    an electronic typewriter

    reprographic equipment

    a facsimile copier

    shared-logic word processing workstations, with electronic-mail link with the other branch offices.

Choose which of the above equipment you would use in the following situations and give reasons for your choice.

a   You are asked to prepare details of a special offer tour (which is due to depart within the next fortnight) in a form which can be sent to all the branches of the company and which will be handed to people enquiring about late-booking holidays.

b   Your boss asks you to write to all the people who enquired about any holiday last year, to tell them that they are entitled to a 5% discount on any holiday booked for 1984 provided they book before Christmas 1983. There is a computer file of all the names and addresses of people who enquired.

c   Complete a special form for booking confirmations which is sent to people booking holidays, before they actually receive their tickets. The layout has already been agreed.

d   Your boss asks you to send a non-personal memo to each of the 60 members of staff detailing the holiday entitlements for 1984, and the special discounts to which they are entitled as employees of the travel company.

e   Prepare a draft document with gaps for specific information, to be used as a legal document for travel insurance. The form will be considered by a solicitor, who will no doubt wish to make numerous amendments to it.

(from RSA Word Processing Stage I, November 1983)

32. Explain what is meant by four of the following terms:

    a   workstation

    b   status lines

    c   variables

    d   text editing

    e   VDU

    f   Teletext.

(from LCCI Word Processing, Intermediate Stage, May 1984)

33. Explain six of the following terms:

    a   configuration

b   CPS

c   megabyte

d   narrow or thin window

e   fax

f   shared logic

g   wraparound

h   OCR

i   format

j   dot matrix.

(from LCCI Word Processing Specimen Paper)

34. You work in the word processing centre of a large company; there is also an electric typewriter. Visits by students from local schools are frequently arranged. Generally the supervisor takes care of these students, but she is absent today and you have been asked to substitute for her.

The visiting students have had a brief theory lesson on word processing but are rather confused on some points. In response to their questions explain briefly what five of the following eight terms mean:

a   floppy disk

b   cursor

c   format line

d   global replace

e   merge

f   archive disk/diskette

g   hard copy

h   wraparound

(from RSA Word Processing Stage I, Summer 1983)

35. 'Housekeeping' refers to:

a   ensuring the equipment is kept in working order

b   ensuring the running costs are within the specified budget

c   maintaining a close check to see that operators are using the system effectively

d   maintaining the system efficiently and deleting all out-of-date material.

(from RSA Word Processing Stage I (Pilot Scheme), Summer 1983)

36. In a word processing department, describe the duties of

a   a librarian

b   the supervisor.

(from LCCI Word Processing Specimen Paper)

37. Describe the skills and qualities required by a good word processing operator.
(from LCCI Word Processing, June 1983)

38. In a centralized word processing section, the supervisor is vital to the efficiency of both the system and operators.

Describe:

a   the role and duties of a word processing supervisor

b the qualities such a person should possess.
(from LCCI Information Processing, PESD/PSC, June 1983)

39. A workstation for an electronic office consists of considerably more than a desk. Seating, lighting, wiring, acoustics and storage capacity must also be given consideration to enable the operator to work efficiently.
Briefly describe a modern workstation, designed to safeguard the operator's health and comfort.
(from LCCI Information Processing, June 1984)

40. The period of time a word processor takes to react to a given command is known as _____?
(from RSA Word Processing Stage I, November 1983)

41. As Health and Safety Representative, Office Services Section, you are concerned when one of the word processor operators in the Word Processor Centre tells you that the operators in the Centre sometimes complain of eyestrain, headaches and fatigue and are worried by frequent mistakes caused by lack of concentration. You, yourself, have noticed how hot and noisy it is in the Word Processor room.
List the recommendations you would make to the Office Services Manager, to minimize the discomfort at present being experienced in the Centre.
(from LCCI Word Processing, Intermediate Stage, May 1984)

42. Centralized word processing services often use a shared-logic system. What would be the advantage and disadvantage to an operator working in such a Word Processing Centre?
(from LCCI Word Processing, May 1984)

43. What aspects of health and safety need to receive care and attention in order to protect VDU operators?
(from LCCI Information Processing, June 1982)

44. You work in one of the branch offices of a large sales organization. The secretarial section of your branch office is about to be given a word processing terminal linked to the company network. The five secretarial staff in your small branch office will share the terminal, each person having access for approximately one hour per day. The system will give access to Videotex via the network.
You are secretary to the Branch Manager and work alone in a small office. There are two shorthand-typists and two audio-typists who work together in a large room, handling all the secretarial work for the branch.
The Branch Manager has spoken to you about three different matters relating to the new word processing terminal. Prepare a short report on each of these three points, giving the advice required in each case.
a The Branch Manager has said that he has heard of Viewdata and Teletext and feels that they would be useful, but would like to know more about them, in particular, the differences between the two and what kind of use

might be made of them by the branch. Explain these services, pointing out the differences, and give three examples of possible uses.

b the Branch Manager has stated that initially all secretaries should use the new word processing terminal for standard tasks only. He has asked you to suggest the standard tasks that could be carried out on the terminal. Prepare such a list, explaining why these are particularly suitable applications for word processing.

c The Branch Manager has to decide where to site the terminal and asks for your advice. He suggests that perhaps you could squeeze a small table into the corner of your room underneath the south-facing window.
Prepare a list of factors that should be taken into consideration when selecting a location for such equipment and make a definite suggestion for a site, justifying your choice. Add a note about any extra sundry items that it might be necessary to order for use in connection with the terminal.

(Case Study from JEB Word Processing Teachers' Diploma, July 1983)

45. A variety of 'consumables' is necessary for effective word processing operation. Describe the items (materials, 'spares', stationery) which it is necessary to keep in stock.
(from LCCI Information Processing, June 1982)

46. a The useful life of a floppy disk can be significantly reduced by subjecting it to careless treatment. Give five points you consider of major importance in the care of floppy disks.

b Describe three methods of storing floppy disks.
(from LCCI Word Processing, Intermediate Stage, May 1984)

47. Outline the advantages to a company of installing a word processor and give an example of each.
(from LCCI Word Processing, June 1983)

48. Describe how the use of word processing would be of benefit in the office of a large hotel.
(from LCCI Word Processing, June 1983)

49. A firm of solicitors, employing six audio-typists and copy-typists, is considering whether to replace the conventional typewriters, at present in the offices, with word processors.

a Describe the benefits the firm could expect as a result of such a replacement, as regards:
  i quality control
  ii filing and stationery costs
  iii electronic mailing.

b In what ways would a word processor improve the typists' jobs?
(from LCCI Word Processing, June 1984)

50. A word processor, using a records-management program, could be of great benefit to an estate agent.
  a   Briefly describe the three functions – sorting, extracting and reporting – which such a program may contain.
  b   Say how they may be applied to this type of business.
(from LCCI Word Processing, SSC, June 1984)

51. Describe the benefits to be derived from word processing in:
  a   a small legal practice
  b   a large engineering company.
(from LCCI Word Processing Specimen Paper)

52. a   Name and briefly describe four types of work suited to word processors, giving an example of each.
  b   State three kinds of business that could benefit from using a word processor and, for each business, give an example of one particular purpose.
(from LCCI Information Processing, June 1982)

53. Choose the letter **a**, **b**, **c** or **d** which correctly completes or answers the sentence.
    A peripheral is
  a   a particular printing medium (like a daisy wheel)
  b   a paper-feed mechanism
  c   any device linked to a CPU
  d   a computer program detailing the word processing functions.
(from RSA Word Processing Stage I, Specimen Paper)

ACKNOWLEDGEMENTS

The publishers would like to thank the LCCI, RSA and JEB for permission to reproduce the examination questions given in the appendix. The RSA wishes us to point out that the Theory paper has been discontinued from its Word Processing examination.

INDEX